Studies in Economic History

Aims and Scope

This series from Springer provides a platform for works in economic history that truly integrate economics and history. Books on a wide range of related topics are welcomed and encouraged, including those in macro-economic history, financial history, labor history, industrial history, agricultural history, the history of institutions and organizations, spatial economic history, law and economic history, political economic history, historical demography, and environmental history.

Economic history studies have greatly developed over the past several decades through application of economics and econometrics. Particularly in recent years, a variety of new economic theories and sophisticated econometric techniques—including game theory, spatial economics, and generalized method of moment (GMM)—have been introduced for the great benefit of economic historians and the research community.

At the same time, a good economic history study should contribute more than just an application of economics and econometrics to past data. It raises novel research questions, proposes a new view of history, and/or provides rich documentation. This series is intended to integrate data analysis, close examination of archival works, and application of theoretical frameworks to offer new insights and even provide opportunities to rethink theories.

The purview of this new Springer series is truly global, encompassing all nations and areas of the world as well as all eras from ancient times to the present. The editorial board, who are internationally renowned leaders among economic historians, carefully evaluate and judge each manuscript, referring to reports from expert reviewers. The series publishes contributions by university professors and others well established in the academic community, as well as work deemed to be of equivalent merit.

More information about this series at http://www.springer.com/series/13279

Hao Peng

Trade Relations between Qing China and Tokugawa Japan

1685–1859

Springer

Hao Peng
Graduate School of Economics
Osaka City University
Osaka, Japan

ISSN 2364-1797 ISSN 2364-1800 (electronic)
Studies in Economic History
ISBN 978-981-13-7684-9 ISBN 978-981-13-7685-6 (eBook)
https://doi.org/10.1007/978-981-13-7685-6

Translation from the Japanese language edition: *Kinsei Nisshin Tsusho Kankeishi* by Hao Peng,

This Springer imprint is published by the registered company Springer Nature Singapore Pte Ltd.
The registered company address is: 152 Beach Road, #21-01/04 Gateway East, Singapore 189721, Singapore

Preface to the English Edition

It is my great honor to have this opportunity to publish my monograph in English as a volume in the series Studies in Economic History. Its Japanese version is titled *Kinsei Nisshin Tsusho Kankeishi* (the history of the early modern trade relationship between Qing China and Tokugawa Japan) published by The University of Tokyo Press in 2015, and most chapters are based on my doctoral dissertation that was completed in the spring of 2012.

The primary idea on this topic was formed in 2002, when I was a graduate student in the master's degree program of the Graduate School of History, Fudan University. I began to be interested in early modern Japanese history, especially the Sino-Japanese trade relations in that period. Subsequently, I took nearly 10 years to complete the doctoral dissertation, and most parts of the study were conducted during the period I studied at the Graduate School of Humanities and Sociology, The University of Tokyo. Then I had an opportunity to advance my study at the Historiographical Institute for almost 4 years, after receiving the doctoral degree in 2012. Without the guidance and enlightenment of my supervisor Prof. Fujita Satoru, and other professors such as Yoshida Nobuyuki, Yokoyama Yoshinori, Hoya Tōru, Matsui Yōko, and Matsukata Fuyuko, and the help of my colleagues in the Department of Japanese History, especially Mura Kazuaki and Satō Yūsuke, it is hard to imagine that I could have read the Japanese historical documents and carried out the analysis I based on them. So I express the greatest respect to them again, at this time when the English version is being published.

Returning to the content of this book: This is a comprehensive study of the trade system between Qing China and Tokugawa Japan in the early modern period. As seen in the subtitle, the study highlights the period from 1685 to 1859. In 1685, Chinese junks from several ports of the Qing empire arrived in Nagasaki. This was shortly after Qing authorities abolished the Maritime Prohibitions, which had lasted several decades, and the Tokugawa shogunate permitted their trade. This signaled the beginning of legal trade approved by the authorities on both sides, a situation that lasted for more than 170 years. Ultimately, as is well known, the shogunate concluded a series of commercial treaties with several Western countries in 1858. In accordance with those treaties, from the following year the shogunate began transforming the existing trading system in Nagasaki. This was not only a milestone in the history of Japanese modernization but also a significant turning point in the history of Sino-Japanese trade.

As explained in detail in Chap. 1, the junk trade at Nagasaki in this period has long been studied, especially in Japan. Most previous studies mainly focus on the Tokugawa trading regulations and restrictions, and there are also some studies on the management of junks and the activities of Chinese merchants, and the copper import policies of the Qing empire. This book adopts a new approach to the study on this topic: mainly focusing on the interactions of the trading policies of the two sides—the Tokugawa shogunate and the Qing empire—and trying to discuss the kinds of trade institutions created by mutual interactions of various trading policies. On the other hand, the roles of many nongovernmental factors involved in the trade, such as the Chinese merchants and their commercial organizations, and the local merchants of Nagasaki City and their trading associations, also have been focused on and examined in the context of the construction of the trade system. There are a large number of Japanese and Chinese primary historical sources supporting the analysis and discussion, and most of them have seldom been used in previous studies.

All these discussion points were also included in the Japanese version of this book, but I prefer modification rather than a simple translation. That is, firstly, because the Japanese version does not include the explanations concerning basic knowledge of the early modern Nagasaki trade, without which it could be difficult to understand by non-Japanese-speaking readers, especially those outside the field of Japan's history. For that reason, I added a new chapter, Chap. 2 in the English version, which attempts to outline the formation and changes of the transactional institutions in the Nagasaki trade by focusing on the roles and functions of those commercial intermediaries. The first half of it is mainly based on the outcomes of previous studies, and the latter half includes many original discussions in my recent studies.

Moreover, I am also aware that the academic style and narrative method of Japan's historiography is to some extent different from that in some English-speaking countries. That is another reason I think modification was necessary. Given my limited English writing ability, modifying the book directly in English was certainly a great challenge. I am fortunate to have gotten many scholars' kind help. Professors Okazaki Tetsuji, Robert Hellyer, and Fabian Drixler gave me many constructive comments for revision after checking the manuscripts of several parts of this book. Alexander Schweinsberg, Thomas Monaghan, and John D'Amico, Ph.D. students of Yale University, helped me to search for the appropriate English expressions of many specialized Japanese or Chinese terms. I express my deepest gratitude to them. I also thank Kawakami Juno, an editor at Springer Japan, and her colleagues for all their many forms of cooperation and help. Finally, I sincerely hope that the publication of this English version will bring me more opportunities to communicate with historical scholars around the world for my further studies.

Osaka, Japan Hao Peng

Explanatory Notes

1. Translations of Historical Terms

Historical terms that appeared in the original documents and were used in related Chinese or Japanese studies are generally translated into English. The following is a list of the translations of some most significant and often-used terms.

Captains	*Chuanzhu* 船主/ *Chuantou* 船頭
Chief Merchant	*Zongshang* 總商/ *Shangzong* 商總
Chinese Junks /Junks	*Tangchuan /Tōsen* 唐船
Chinese Residence	*Tōjin Yashiki* 唐人屋敷
Compradors	*Urikominin* 売込人
Elders	*Rōjū* 老中
Five-Cities Merchants Group	*Gokasho Shōnin* 五ヶ所商人
Marine Products Office	*Tawaramono Yakusho* 俵物役所
Maritime Prohibitions	*Haijin* 海禁
Nagasaki Trading House	*Nagasaki Kaisho* 長崎会所
National Seclusion	*Sakoku* 鎖国
Official Bureau	*Guanju* 官局
Official Merchant	*Guanshang* 官商
Representative Merchants	*E'shang* 額商
Silk Guild	*Itowappu Nagaka* 糸割符仲間
Shinchi Warehouse	*Shinchi Kurasho* 新地蔵所
Ship-Servicing Neighborhoods	*Yadomachi* 宿町
The Magistrate of Nagasaki	*Nagasaki Bugyō* 長崎奉行
The Regulations of 1715	*Shōtoku Shinrei* 正徳新例
Tribute	*Chaogong* 朝貢
Twelve Families	*Minju* 民局/ *Shi'er-jia* 十二家

A few terms are used as they are in the original documents. For example, *shinpai* 信牌, one of the most significant keywords in this study, is used as it originally was, in order to distinguish it from other trading passes/permits that had similar characteristics and functions in pre-modern East Asia.

2. Abbreviations of Historical Archives and Document Collections

The original documents used in this study are mainly held in three archives. Their abbreviations in this book are given as follows:

FHAC	First Historical Archives of China (中國歷史第一檔案館)
NMHC	Nagasaki Museum of History and Culture (長崎歷史文化博物館)
NPM	National Palace Museum (国立故宮博物院)

Many historical documents, particularly from the Qing empire, can be seen in the collections of published documents. Among them, several of the most frequently used are abbreviated as follows:

GZDQL	*Gongzhongdang Qianlongchao Zouzhe* (Secret Palace Memorials from the Qianlong Period 宮中檔乾隆朝奏摺)
GZDYZ	*Gongzhongdang Yongzhengchao Zouzhe* (Secret Palace Memorials from the Yongzheng Period 宮中檔雍正朝奏摺)
MQD	*Ming Qing Dang'an* (Archives of the Ming and Qing Dynasties 明清檔案)
YZCHW	*Yongzhengchao Hanwen Zhupi Zouzhe Huibian* (Complete Collection of the Chinese Memorials with the Emperor's Comments from the Yongzheng Period 雍正朝漢文硃批奏摺彙編)

3. Dates

In pre-modern history, Chinese and Japanese dates are typically converted to the dates of the Gregorian calendar, except in several direct translations of the historical documents. In references to the original sources in the footnotes, the dates from the Chinese or Japanese calendar are shown first and the corresponding dates from the Gregorian calendar are added in parentheses.

4. Names

Most figures named in this book were Chinese or Japanese. Their names appear in the original order, with the family name first, followed by the given name.

5. Units of Weight

The following units of weight are often seen in related historical documents. They vary by region and time. However, at least in trade-related books and documents, they were relatively stable with regard to the indicated weight. They can be converted as follows:

Silver currency 1 *liang* 両 (Chinese)/tael = approximately 37.3 grams;
1 *kan* 貫/ *kanme* 貫目 = approximately 3.75 kilograms;
1 *kan* 貫/ *kanme* 貫目 = 1,000 *monme* 匁 (Japanese)

Copper 1 *jin* 斤 (Chinese) = approximately 600 grams;
1 *kin* 斤 (Japanese) = approximately 600 grams

Silver currencies are often seen in the related Chinese and Japanese documents. Their values were determined by their weight in the early modern period. The weight of the unit of copper in trade was generally *jin* in Qing China and *kin* in Edo Japan, for which Chinese characters were written the same way, and in trade-related documents the actual weight indicated was also the same.

Contents

About the Author

Hao Peng is an associate professor in the Graduate School of Economics, Osaka City University. He was born and brought up in China. After getting his first master's degree in the Graduate School of History, Fudan University, he went to Japan in the autumn of 2005 and continued to study the history of early modern Japan at the Graduate School of Humanities and Sociology, The University of Tokyo. There, he finished his second master's degree in 2008, and then a doctoral degree in 2012. During the following 4 years, he continued his study at the Historiographical Institute, The University of Tokyo, first as a postdoctoral fellow of the Japan Society for the Promotion of Science and then as a program-specific researcher. He has held his current position since the spring of 2016.

His research book based on his doctoral thesis was published in 2015 by The University of Tokyo Press. The title is *Kinsei Nisshin Tsusho Kankeishi* (the history of the early modern trade relationship between Qing China and Tokugawa Japan). That book earned him the Nikkei Economic Book Culture Award (by the Nikkei Inc. and Japan Center for Economic Research) in 2015. Besides the history of the Nagasaki trade, his study interests cover maritime history, the history of culture exchange, and comparative urbanization.

List of Figures

List of Tables

Chapter 1
Introduction

1.1 East Asia's Early Modernity and the Formation of a Global World

The main purpose of this book is to examine the trading relations between Tokugawa Japan and Qing China in the early modern period by analyzing the formative process and mechanisms of the trading institutions. It is worthy of note that in this period there was neither a commercial treaty, nor any trading agreement, and few direct diplomatic negotiations between the two countries. However, various conflicts of interest between the two countries, including not only between the ruling authorities of the two sides but also between the ruling authorities and the merchants, always existed. Why did these conflicts not escalate to the extent that they affected the maintenance of the trading relationship? This study attempts to find the reasons for this in the trading institutions. This study will use numerous primary sources, most of which have yet to be used in a historical study. Furthermore, based on the outcomes of this examination, this study seeks to expand the discussion of the intra-Asian trading order and the mutual economic and political relations among the countries in the East Asia region. Before examining this in detail, however, it is necessary to briefly outline the historical background of the topic.

As is generally known, in the last years of the fifteenth century and early years of the sixteenth century Western European navigators and explorers achieved the "geographical discovery" and circumnavigation of the globe. These activities developed many significant navigation and commercial routes and thereby connected certain "regional worlds" previously divided by oceans and rarely interacting with one another. In short, it meant the formation of a "global world", especially with the addition of the "New World" to global networks.[1]

[1]The perspective of the "global world" is mainly based on the explanations of Yamakuchi (2006).

H. Peng, *Trade Relations between Qing China and Tokugawa Japan*,
Studies in Economic History, https://doi.org/10.1007/978-981-13-7685-6_1

Consequently, the global movement of goods, people, information, and money occurred with greater frequency, and each country or region responded to these movements either actively or passively. A number of traders and adventures among Western Europeans are thought to have played positive roles in promoting economic globalization. They extended their influnce over other "regional worlds" and eventually advanced beyond the Indian Ocean to Southeast Asia, while promoting the colonization of many countries. They also entered the trade in the East China Sea area.

In East Asia, the Ming China-centered regional political order and economic sphere had already started to collapse from the inside, and in the East China Sea, the trading activities of maritime merchants were challenging the existing framework bound by the "Maritime Prohibitions" (*haijin* 海禁) and "Tribute System" (*chaogong* 朝貢) together (Danjō 2013). Many Chinese official documents and literary novels of that time indicate the presence "Japanese pirates" (*wokou* 倭寇). However, recent studies have argued that those so-called Japanese pirates were, in fact, multiethnic groups consisting of Chinese, Japanese, Korean, and Portuguese natives (Murai 1997). They were not merely pirate groups, and called themselves maritime merchants. They constructed a wide-ranging commercial network by trading on islands off the Chinese coast or those surrounding Kyushu, and responded with force against armed missions sent by Ming authorities.

Under the turbulent regional political situation of the transitional period of the late sixteenth and early seventeenth centuries, the Japanese state came to be dominated by the Tokugawa house. A little later, there occurred a dynastic shift from Ming to Qing in China. After its establishment, the Qing court attempted to reconstruct a China-centered tribute system. After stabilizing its reign over the Chinese area in which the Han people were the main residents in the late seventeenth century, Qing leaders abolished the Maritime Prohibitions and permitted the private merchants under its authority to sail and trade overseas. Moreover, the Qing empire allowed trading with foreigners from those countries without a formal tribute relationship. However, in the eighteenth century, the court gradually turned towards a conservative diplomatic stance. This included forbidding Christianity, with increasing restrictions on immigration and foreign trade. On the other hand, it maintained domestic political stability over the long term.

As discussed in recent years, East Asian countries which avoided colonization in the early modern period such as Qing China, Tokugawa Japan, and Korea during the Li dynasty, faced similar domestic political situations, and adapted similar diplomatic and trading policies (Arano 1988). In short, these countries maintained similar political and economic structures in response to early modern globalization (Kishimoto 1998) (Fig. 1.1).

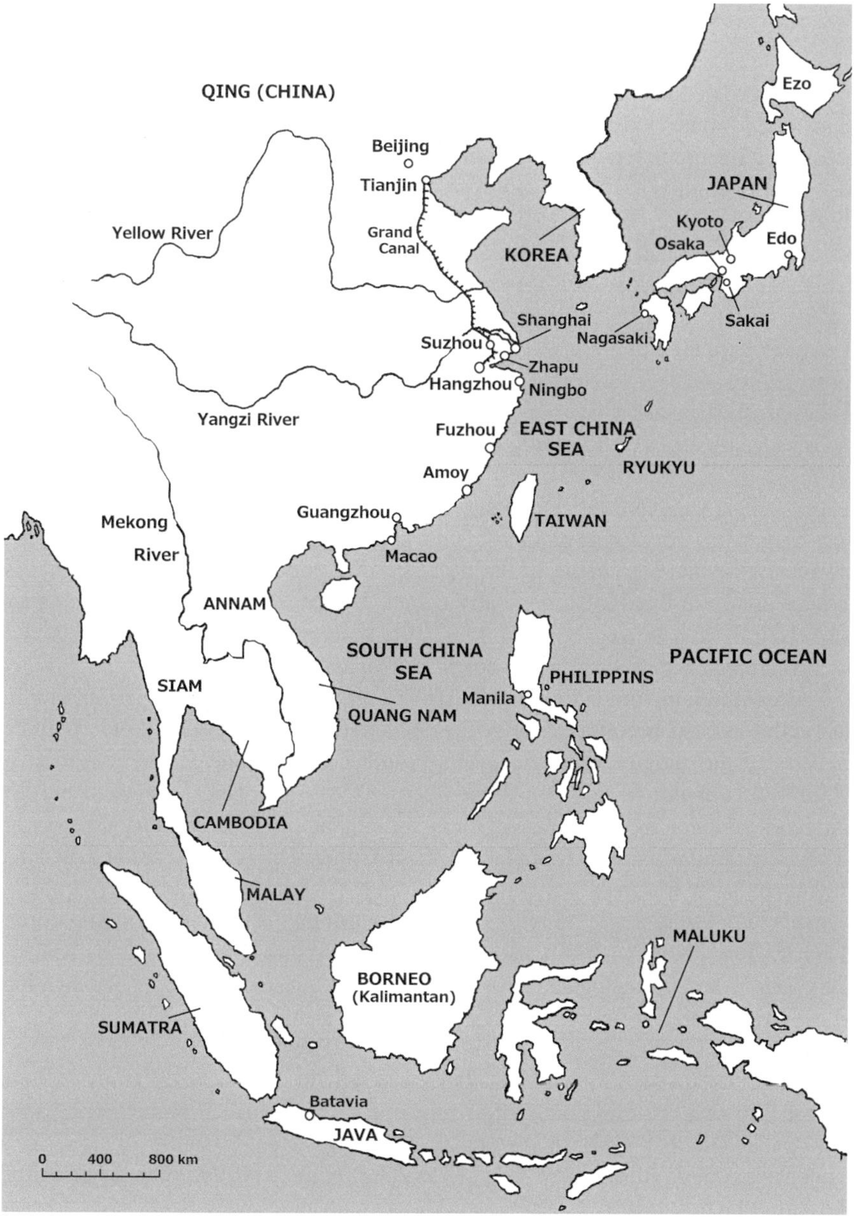

Fig. 1.1 East Asia and Southeast Asia in the middle eighteenth century

1.2 A New Approach to Sino-Japanese Trading Relations

In the seventeenth century, the maritime order represented by the activities of "Japanese pirates" was waning. As pointed out by Arano Yasunori, the seventeenth-century regional situation in East Asia was transformed by two main historical phenomena: the formation of the Tokugawa shogunate's feudal system (*bakuhan-sei-kokka* 幕藩制国家) in Japan and the dynastic shift in China from Ming to Qing. In addition two lesser phenomena also had an impact: the advance of the Dutch and English into East Asia from the south, and the Russians from the north (Arano 1985).

At the beginning of the seventeenth century, the Tokugawa regime attempted but failed to reestablish diplomatic relations with Ming empire (Kamiya 1997). Although the reasons have not yet been clarified, it is possible to conceive that the Ming authorities still regarded the Japanese state as a haven of the so-called Japanese pirates and never relaxed their caution, choosing instead to maintain security. That triggered the shogunate to turn its attention to the construction of a new framework of external relations. This was a long and complicated process, and the most essential step came in the issuance of a series of policies regulating its foreign affairs in the 1630s, generally called "the national seclusion edicts of the Kan'ei Era" (*kan'ei sakokurei* 寛永鎖国令) in current historical textbooks. For foreign ships, trading was limited solely to Nagasaki port.

Around the same time, the shogunate received information that the Ming empire had collapsed and been replaced by the Manchurian Qing dynasty. Some political thinkers of the shogunate regarded this political shift as the "barbarianization of China" (*ka'i hentai* 華夷変態). Remembering the Mongolian invasion in the late thirteenth century, Japanese leaders remained vigilant against the expanding power of the equestrian warriors from the north of China. However, it seemed that the shogunate tried to avoid collisions with such "barbarian authorities" as far as possible. For example, it refused requests for military aid from anti-Qing forces (Ishihara 1945; Komiya 1990), recommended via Satsuma domain that the Ryūkyū Kingdom comply with the Qing's envoy's requests that its people adopt Manchurian hairstyle and costume, and demanded that Satsuma hide its political influence in the Ryūkyūs (Uehara 1981; Kamiya 1990).

Meanwhile, on the Chinese side, after the surrender of the Zheng family's power base in Taiwan, the Qing authorities repealed the Maritime Prohibitions in 1684 with the result that Chinese merchants started to engage openly in trade with Japanese partners. In the same year, 13 trading junks, with two officials of Fujian Province aboard, arrived in Nagasaki. The shogunate allowed these junks to conduct transactions in Nagasaki but also made clear that thereafter no Qing official would be allowed to visit Japan. Following this notification, the two officials left Nagasaki when their trade mission was completed.

The target period of this study is mainly from 1684 when Chinese trade with Japan shogunate became legitimate from the view of the Qing authorities, accompanied by the abolition of the Maritime Prohibitions, to the latter half of the

1850s when the transaction system of the Nagasaki trade began to transform into a Western-style system based on commercial treaties among states. Beginning in the 1680s, both Qing China and Tokugawa Japan officially recognized trade relations with each other and this stable relationship was sustained for more than a century and a half.

Until the 1960s studies on the history of Tokugawa Japan were bound by a framework based on the view of "national seclusion" and primarily focused on how and in what ways the shogunate regulated and restricted foreign trade. The roles of foreign traders and opposing regimes in the creation of trade rules has seldom been acknowledged and discussed.

As will be described in detail below, since the 1970s, historians have challenged the historical perspective of "national seclusion." Against this backdrop recent discussion on the shogunate's view of China and the Netherlands as its "partner states with trade relationships" (*Tsūshō-no-kuni* 通商の国), and Korea and the Ryūkyūs as its "partner states communicating by official correspondence" (*tsūshin-no-kuni* 通信の国), has drawn much attention. Meanwhile, in the field of Chinese history, historians have used the *Daqing Huidian*大清會典 (a basic code of the Qing empire) to develop studies of the tribute system or officially-sanctioned border trade (*hushi* 互市). Many have described the Qing court as having regarded the Japanese state as its *hushi-guo* (互市国), which meant that Japan was merely trading with China and had no political relationship with the Qing empire. These discussions urge us to reconsider the early modern Sino-Japanese relationship by focusing on the mutual influences and interactions in the policies of the two countries' governing authorities.

1.3 Review of Previous Related Studies

The most discussed topic in previous related studies is the management of the Nagasaki trade and its related statistics. Detailed research of early modern Nagasaki's trade can be traced back to the early twentieth century. Yano Jin'ichi's *Nagasakishi-shi: Tsūshō-bōeki-hen, Ajia-shokoku-bu* (history of Nagasaki city: interaction and trade with Asian countries, 1967, first published in 1938) is seen as pioneering research on this topic.[2] Yano's most original contribution concerns the issue of trading benefits. Analyzing the institutional transitions and changes in trading volume over time, Yano revealed an essential characteristic of the Nagasaki trade: Japanese exported copper at a price lower than its cost, making up for the loss and gaining great profits by selling imported goods at high prices in the domestic market and by promoting the export of marine products.

[2] Several articles in Yano's book had been published in the 1920s. Yano explored issues referenced in several previously published narrative history books (Fukuchi 1902; Araki 1903; Kanei 1926).

In accordance with Yano's style of research, studies on the Nagasaki trade became more and more specific and the discussions focused on several issues: the context, background, and significance of the establishment of the transaction methods and trading organizations. For instance, Nakamura Tadashi's *Kinsei Nagasaki Bōekishi no Kenkyū* (studies on the history of early modern Nagasaki trade, 1988), performs detailed quantitative analysis on trading volume in several specific years, and on the other hand attempts to approach the question of management conditions based on many original trade-related documents especially those of the Nagasaki Trading House (*Nagasaki kaisho* 長崎会所) which played a central role in the management of the Nagasaki trade, as Chap. 2 will examine in detail. Another influential study by Ōta Katsuya, *Sakoku-Jidai Nagasaki Bōekishi no Kenkyū* (studies on the history of the Nagasaki trade in the period of National Seclusion, 1992), focuses on the process of the trade policy enactments and the historical background of the institutional transitions. Both studies highlight the series of edicts restricting the Nagasaki trade in 1715 (generally called *shōtoku shinrei* 正徳新例) and regard the issuing of these edicts as the completion of the trading restrictions of the shogunate under the "national seclusion" policies.

As primarily discussed in Yano's book, there are also several studies aiming to reveal the trading policies of the Qing authorities (Kōsaka 1981; Chen 1988; Liu 1999; Jin 2007; Sun 2010). Most of them focus on the significance of the copper imports from Japan for the stability of Qing currency and the ways in which the authorities tried to sustain stable imports. It is known that there are a series of official documents related to these issues, and in recent decades these have increasingly come to attention. Based on these documents, more and more studies have appeared on the management of junks and the activities of Chinese merchants, especially the representative merchants of the two commercial groups which formed in the early eighteenth century and monopolized the junk trade with Japan from the middle years of the same century. Some chapters in Matsuura Akira's *Shindai Kaigai Bōekishi no Kenkyū* (studies on the history of overseas trade during the Qing dynasty, 2002) and *Edo Jidai Tōsen ni yoru Niichū Bunka Kōryū* (Sino-Japanese cultural interaction by Chinese ships during the Edo Period, 2007), and several academic articles by Liu Shiuh-Feng (1986, 1988, 1999) can be seen as representative of research in recent decades.

In addition, the smuggling related to the junk trade also draws many scholars' attention as well and has for a long time accumulated research (Harafuji 1953; Sadamune 1959; Itazawa 1961; Kikuchi 1962; Yamawaki 1964; Nishimura 1973; Shimitsu 1979; Arai 1980; Nakamura 1988). It is reasonable to conclude that trading restrictions and regulations would lead to smuggling, in as far as there were market demands for the trade. Smuggling was an unregulated corollary of the Nagasaki trade, accompanied by the shogunate's strengthening of trading restrictions. Many studies have attempted to shed light on the distribution routes of smuggled goods, the countermeasures enacted to address smuggling, and the punishments meted out by the shogunate. Arano Yasunori (1988) has also opened up a new research approach which attempts to clarify the reasons why the smuggling occurred and which social classes were involved in it by analyzing the social and economic structure of the Edo Period.

1.4 Conclusions from the Recent Discussions on the Trading System

As is well known, compared with surrounding states or areas, many of the empires that emerged in or extended its domination over the area of China held strong military power, political influence and cultural influence, and this allowed them to construct a so-called China-centered world order or hegemony in the East Asian region, or, in other words, the eastern side of the Eurasian continent. Some scholars have revised their view by using concepts like "Chinese world order" or "tribute system" (Fairbank and Teng 1941; Fairbank 1968; Mancall 1968, 1984).

Hamashita Takeshi, who has approached the tribute system from the perspective of economic history, argued that it is not correct to explain the modernization of China as a result of the "Western impact" by which the tribute system was forthrightly shifted to the treaty system. Hamashita stresses that in fact the two systems coexisted until the late nineteenth century. In his theoretical description, from the view of Qing authorities, the trading relationship with foreigners was classified into two types: the tribute trade (*chaogong maoyi*) and the officially-sanctioned border trade (*hushi*), also mentioned to some extent above (Hamashita 1990, 1997).

However, it seems difficult to position some border trade or oversea trade which is not based on a hierarchical relationship—e.g., Guangzhou trade with Europeans or Americans, Kyakhta trade with Russians, as well as Nagasaki trade with Japanese—in the context of the tribute system. Recently, Iwa'i Shigeki has argued that it is necessary to consider border trade or overseas trade outside of the tribute system. He outlined the independent history of the *hushi* model in the following way: in the early years of the Ming dynasty, Chinese authorities adopted an attitude forbidding any trade relations with the foreign merchants of non-tribute countries. Facing a serious smuggling problem and understanding that it was caused partly by strict trading restrictions, the Ming authorities had to permit some private trades in specified ports in the late sixteenth century. After stabilizing their reign over China in the late seventeenth century, the Qing authorities opened port cities for foreign merchants and permitted domestic merchants to trade abroad. In brief, from the point of view of this study it is reasonable to consider the trading and diplomatic system of Qing empire in the eighteenth century as including relations with the Tokugawa regime, in the context of the growth of the *hushi* model instead of merely prolonging the tribute system (Iwai 2004, 2009, 2010a, b).

In the field of Japanese history, beginning in the 1970s historians have reviewed the concept and related theories of "national seclusion", emphasizing Japan's trading and diplomatic relations with other states in East Asia such as China and Korea. Historians noted that using the term "national seclusion" entailed ignoring these relations. Some presented an alternative concept as theoretical reconstructions: the *taikun gaikō taisei* (大君外交体制, diplomacy under the name of *taikun,* which was a title of the shogunate used outside, externally) and *Nihon-kata ka'i-chitsujo* (日本型華夷秩序, "Japan-centered world order" or "Japan-centered civilized–barbaric world order") (Kamiya and Kimura 2002). Meanwhile, another discussion arose focusing on the trading and diplomatic structure of Tokugawa Japan: two "partner states communicating by official correspondence", the Ryūkyūs and Korea, and two "partner states with a trading relationship", China and the Netherlands (Fujita 2005).

Ronald Toby and Arano Yasunori can be seen as the pioneering scholars with respect to discussions of the concept *Nihon-kata ka'i-chitsujo*. Toby mentions that the diplomatic initiative of the shogunate was to withdraw China from the top position in the center of the philosophical international order, in other words, to relativize China (Toby 1984, 1986). Arano expanded the discussion not only to the consciousness but also to the actual situation, and described it thus: the "Japan-centered world order" was established on the premise that the Tokugawa shogunate failed to reconstruct diplomatic relations with Ming China, and the two "world orders", the Chinese-centered and the Japanese-centered, coexisted and competed against each other in early modern East Asia (Arano 1985, 1992). He also argued that apart from Nagasaki there were three other portals—Satsuma, Tsushima, and Matsumae—connecting Tokugawa Japan with the outside world (Arano 1981), and junks trading at Nagasaki were treated by the shogunate as conducting a type of private trade under the administrative control of the shogunate (Arano 2003). Following this elaboration of the idea of "four portals", Robert Hellyer has recently clarified the role of indirect Japanese–Chinese trading via Satsuma–Ryūkyūs and Tsushima–Korea while emphasizing the China market-oriented focus of domain trading policies (Hellyer 2009). Such studies will certainly stimulate historical scholars to further consider the links between early maritime foreign trade and domestic industries.

1.5 Main Discussion Points and Structure of This Book

Even though the quantity of the junk trade at Nagasaki had always been more than that of the Dutch (e.g., on the number of ships, see Fig. 1.2), the degree of attention paid to the Chinese trade and the number of related academic articles is far less than that given to the contemporary Dutch trade.[3] One of the essential reasons seems to be that while abundant historical sources especially documents from the Dutch East India Company (Vereenigde Oostindische Compagnie, in Dutch, generally abbreviated as "VOC") have been available for quite some time, the number of newly discovered Chinese source has been relatively few. In recent years, however, more Qing archival documents have been published or opened for scholarly research, and among them there are many official documents related to the early modern

[3]There is a brief introduction for annual historical studies in every year's Vol. 5 of the journal *Shigaku Zasshi*, which is known as the most important historical journal in Japan. Overviewing the introductions in the most recent decade (2005–2015), the number of academic books or articles on early modern Japanese–Dutch relations reaches roughly 53; on the other hand, those related to Sino-Japanese relations number merely 21.

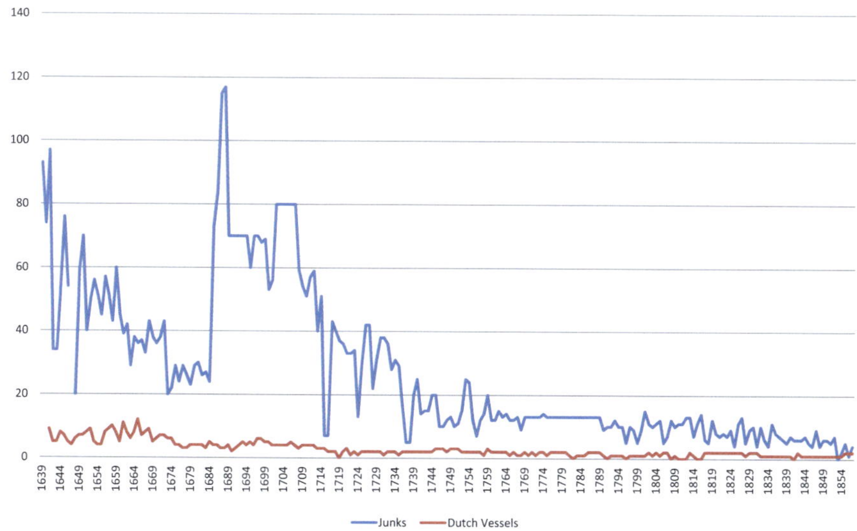

Fig. 1.2 Number of arriving junks and Dutch vessels. *Source* Tanabe Mokei, *The Nagasaki Jitsuroku Taisei* (長崎実録大成, compilation of the documents on Nagasaki, 1760) in the Nagasaki Museum of History and Culture (NMHC); Matsura Tōkei, *Nagasaki Kokin Shuran* (長崎古今集覧, comprehensive records on ancient and modern Nagasaki) in NMHC; Kanei Toshiyuki (ed.) *Nagasaki Ryakushi* (長崎略史, brief history of Nagasaki, Nagasaki: Nagasaki Shiyakusho, 1926). *Note* The years in the figure are those used in the old Japanese calendar

Sino-Japanese trade, especially regarding copper imports. Research of these sources in combination with related Japanese sources will certainly be helpful in leading research on this topic onto a new stage.

On the other hand, although studies of Nagasaki's trade and related topics are abundant, some basic issues in the larger Sino-Japanese trading relationship and their mutual influences or interactions in the construction of trading institutions have been neglected. This discussion seems to have stagnated since Yano's works were published in the 1930s. This research impasse results mainly from the continued discussion of the concept of "national seclusion." Scholars prefer to argue about its underlying policies and why shogunate leaders instituted particular policies, as well as how they restricted and regulated foreign trade. As a result, the roles of Chinese traders and the Qing authorities behind the construction of the trading systems have been almost completely ignored. Fortunately, many newly found firsthand historical sources provide essential clues in discussing these points and certainly will be helpful to promote studying this topic from a new approach.

The achievements of previous studies can be summarized as follows: first, trading by Chinese junks was maintained throughout early modern times, but on the whole, it tended to shrink gradually from the late seventeenth century (see Fig. 1.2). Second, the Qing empire and the Tokugawa regime had no diplomatic relations and did not engage in direct negotiation over trading issues. Third, in order to prevent the outflow of precious metals like silver or copper, the shogunate issued a series of trading restrictions. Fourth, on the Chinese side, the Qing authorities took a proactive attitude towards the import of copper used for casting coins.

Naturally, a question arises: how was the trading relationship maintained with such stability and for such a long time despite an obvious conflict of interest existing between the two regimes regarding the demands for Japanese copper by Qing China and the limitation of copper exports by the Tokugawa shogunate? It is difficult to imagine that such a problem could be resolved with no reasonable trading institutions. Therefore, revealing whether they did exist, and if so, what they were, can be considered an issue essential to deepening our understanding of the characteristics and structures of both sides of the trading relationship.

This study treats this issue as its central topic. There are several key points with which the following chapters will deal.

As mentioned above, previous studies have examined the trading policies adopted by the shogunate in detail. It is noteworthy that under Japanese trading institutions, all trade was to have been carried out via the mediation of the Nagasaki Trading House (*Nagasaki Kaisho* 長崎会所). In other words, the Trading House played the role of trading intermediary connecting the domestic market with the global economy. Chapter 2 aims to outline the trading framework of the Nagasaki trade which functioned on the basis of the Nagasaki Trading House's central position within it.

As noted above, smuggling occurred frequently and shaped the trading restrictions of the shogunate. Issuing *shinpai* (信牌) as trading passes or permits to Chinese merchants was an essential anti-smuggling measure, and moreover it was also a way for the shogunate to control the scale of the junk trade. Chapter 3 reveals the mechanisms and functions of these Tokugawa policies by analyzing the related original sources, while Chapter 4 explores the attitudes of Qing authorities toward the *shinpai* system. As a matter of fact, not only Chinese merchants accepted the use of the *shinpai*, but Qing authorities also ultimately approved its use after 2 years of consideration. More interestingly, some firsthand and recently discovered official Chinese documents indicate that the Qing authorities also viewed the system positively and strove to use the *shinpai* in the possession of Chinese merchants to maximize copper imports from Japan.

The *shinpai* policies were not able to resolve all the problems stemming from illegal trading and transactions as long as there continued to be trading restrictions. Those junks without the *shinpai* had to seek opportunities to engage in smuggling on the Japanese coastline; on the other hand, many Chinese crews tried to hide smaller, expensive goods such as ginseng in their clothes or baggage, furtively bringing them into their settlement in Nagasaki, and selling them secretly to Japanese buyers. In other words, this so-called illegal activity can be seen as an unregulated side of the junk trade. In practice, strengthening the enforcement and punishment of these Chinese "criminals" was always accompanied by a risk of damaging the benefits brought by Chinese traders and thereby deteriorating Japanese–Chinese commercial relations. Chapter 5 will discuss how the shogunate balanced its enforcement against "illegal trading" by maintaining "authorized" trading.

Meanwhile, in addition to the "illegal transactions", there was another factor that brought instability to these trade relations: the personal and dispersed trading styles of junk traders. In the case of the Dutch trade, until the last years of the eighteenth century the trading partner of the Japanese was the VOC, a trading company that ran trade with Japan in a unified way. The Dutch side generally observed the Tokugawa's trade policies once the consent of the company was obtained. Therefore, it was not necessary to apply the *shinpai* system to the Dutch trade. Regarding Chinese trade, however, despite the introduction of the *shinpai* system, disputes among merchants frequently occurred over possession of the *shinpai*. Additionally, the volume of trade had been shrinking on the whole and thereby limiting trading opportunities. These issues led to a need to integrate the management of the Chinese traders. As a result, in the middle of the eighteenth century, in separate actions, two trading groups—the Official Bureau and the Twelve Families—were organized. Chapters 6 and 7 will deal with these issues based on many firsthand official documents related to the policy determinations of the Qing authorities.

After their formation, the two trading groups cooperated with each other and gradually monopolized the junk trade with Nagasaki. Qing authorities approved this trading monopoly after being convinced that it was the most rational way to ensure the stable supply of Japanese copper. Despite having no approval of the monopoly from the Tokugawa regime, the two groups practically became the only trading partners on behalf of the junks. This study breaks new ground by analyzing the management structures and mechanisms within the junk trade with Nagasaki. Chapter 8 will challenge these issues by detailing the content of various related official documents and attempt to outline them by drawing several conceptual diagrams.

The last important point, which will be mainly discussed in Chap. 9, is related to the emergence of a new trading style based on commercial contracts. After the formation of the two trading groups among the Chinese merchants, the junk trade in practice merged into the transactions between the two groups on one side and the Nagasaki Trading House on other. As the representative of private merchants, both had a common agenda: how to revitalize the trade. Facing the rigid trading framework based on the Tokugawa regime's restrictions and regulations, they tried to import or export some seldom-traded goods. For example, in the late eighteenth century, various kinds of silver and gold currencies were imported into Japan via junks. Because Japan had been a country well known for exporting such precious metals, it is easy to imagine that these Chinese merchants were unsure as to whether this new transaction would become profitable. Hence, the Nagasaki Trading House agreed to draw up a contractual agreement to ensure the purchase of imported metals under pre-arranged transaction conditions. As shown in the detailed explanations in Chap. 9, this trading model was not seen in the history of trade prior to the middle of the eighteenth century. Thus the silver currency import trade created a new trading relationship in the Nagasaki trade, and its emergence is deeply connected to the organization of the Chinese trading groups.

Chapter 2
Commercial Intermediaries in the Nagasaki Trade

2.1 A New Approach to the Study of the Nagasaki Trade

In early modern Japan, there were four portals to the outer world: Nagasaki, the port frequented by Chinese and Dutch (the Dutch East India Company, in the seventeenth and eighteenth centuries) merchants; Satsuma, with access to the Ryūkyūs; Tsushima, whose Sō clan (宗家) mediated trade and diplomacy with Korea; and Matsumae, which dominated Ezo (蝦夷) through indirect control over its indigenous Ainu population.[1] Among the four portals, Nagasaki was the only one directly controlled by the Tokugawa shogun. Furthermore, from the early 1640s to the late 1850s, it was the sole port in which the Tokugawa permitted foreign merchants to trade in Japan, and the import and export of goods through Nagasaki had the largest effect on the domestic market as well.

It has been well known since at least the 1930s (Yano 1967, first published in 1938) that the Nagasaki trade was strictly controlled and limited in many ways by the shogunate. First, trading with many countries like Spain and Portugal was prohibited in the early seventeenth century, leaving only the Chinese merchants and the Dutch East India Company (VOC) as its trading partners.[2] Second, in the late seventeenth century the shogunate began to restrict the annual trading volume and

---

[1] The term and notion "four portals" (*yottsu no kuchi* 四つの口) was introduced by Arano Yasunori in his discussion criticizing the historical view of "national seclusion" (mainly in Arano 1981).

[2] The Tokugawa shogunate did not issue any edict to restrict the trading partners merely to the Chinese and the VOC in this period and instead seemed to welcome trading ships from other regions, especially many southeast Asian states such as Siam and Cambodia. However, the truth is that merchants from southeast Asia did not have enough commercial ability to compete with the junks and the VOC in the intra-regional trade of East Asia. In the last years of the eighteenth century and early nineteenth century, when the Russian embassies visited Japan and negotiated with the Tokugawa shogunate for opening a new trade relationship, the shogunate refused and explained that they must obey the "Ancestors' Law" (*sohō*, 祖法)—the trade relationship merely limited to China and the Netherlands. Recent studies discuss the creation of the Tokugawa "Idea of the Ancestors' Law." For details of this discussion, see Fujita (2005).

H. Peng, *Trade Relations between Qing China and Tokugawa Japan*,
Studies in Economic History, https://doi.org/10.1007/978-981-13-7685-6_2

the number of foreign trading ships. In addition, foreign merchants were isolated from Japanese society: the VOC were restricted to the island of Dejima and Chinese merchants to the Chinese Residence (*tōjin yashiki* 唐人屋敷). Fourth, the Nagasaki Trading House (*Nagasaki kaisho* 長崎会所) established with the Tokugawa's direction at the end of the seventeenth century, dealt with all trade through the port, and the shogunate appointed city elders (*machi-toshiyori* 町年寄) to manage the Trading House.

The shogunate forbade foreign traders from conducting transactions directly with private Japanese merchants after the formation of the Trading House. Nonetheless the Nagasaki trade could not have functioned without commercial intermediaries. Despite this, previous studies mainly focus on the shogunate's trading regulations and seldom pay attention to the commercial factors such as trading brokers or agents. In order to allow scholars to better understand how Nagasaki fulfilled its function as a regional and global port, this chapter will focus on the various commercial intermediaries in the Nagasaki trade and discuss how they brokered foreign trade in Nagasaki.

This study has identified the Nagasaki Trading House as the largest commercial intermediary of the Nagasaki trade since its formation, and will discuss how it mediated the trade between foreign maritime merchants and domestic merchants. Furthermore, this study also focuses on the roles of other merchants or agents such as compradors (*urikomi-nin* 売込人) and Ship-Servicing Neighborhoods which helped the Trading House to fulfil its role as a commercial intermediary.

2.2 The Opening and Expansion of Nagasaki as a Trading Port

This section will briefly review the early history of Nagasaki port city. It is generally accepted that Nagasaki was opened as a trading port in 1570. Until then, it was an undeveloped land in the territory of Ōmura Sumitada (大村純忠). Ōmura is well known in Japanese history as a famous Christian lord who welcomed trade with Western European merchants, especially the Portuguese, who appeared in the Japanese archipelago in the late sixteenth century and rapidly expanded their trade through missionary work. In the warring states era, many lords similar to Ōmura took a positive attitude towards overseas trade, not only by Western Europeans but also by their established trading partners, the Chinese merchants.

Throughout this era, Ōmura was unable to avoid military conflicts with neighboring lords such as the Ryūzoji (竜造寺, Saga 佐賀), Matsura (松浦, Hirado 平戸), and Fukabōri (深堀, adjacent to Nagasaki). Relying on the power of the Portuguese can be considered Ōmura's strategic choice for domain defense. Against this backdrop, Ōmura declared himself a Christian and donated the Nagasaki port to the Jesuits in 1580. He offered almost all his powers, such as imposing land taxes and administrative authority, to the Jesuits, keeping only the right to impose commercial taxes (An'no 1992). As a result, Nagasaki soon developed into the most important Portuguese base in the Japanese archipelago.

After its opening as a trading port city, a number of domestic merchants gathered here from other places, especially from adjacent areas such as Hirado, Shimahara (島原), Yokoseura (横瀬浦), and commercial cities in the Kyushu region such as Hakata (博多) (see Fig. 2.1). Many of them chose to settle and engage in the management of inns. They not only offered accommodations to foreign traders or domestic merchants, but also acted as commercial intermediaries.

In the late 1580s, Toyotomi Hideyoshi expanded his dominance over the Kyushu region and placed Nagasaki under his direct control. At the same time, the anti-Christianity policy was enacted and was to last for decades. Inheriting the unified administration, the Tokugawa shogun strengthened the anti-Christianity

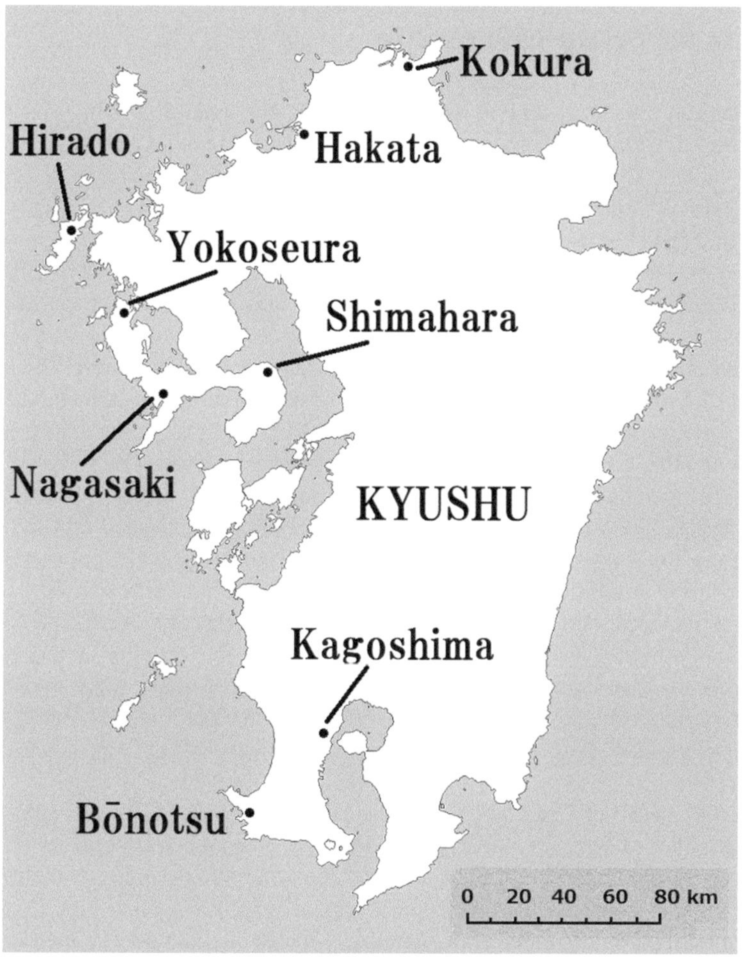

Fig. 2.1 Nagasaki and other port cities in Kyushu

policy: expelling the missionaries, forcing Japanese Christians to disavow their faith, and limiting the trade activities of Portuguese merchants. The shogunate further instructed the Nagasaki magistrate to isolate and accommodate all Portuguese in Japan at that time. Under the direction of the magistrate, local merchants built an artificial island called Dejima in 1634. This has been seen as a symbol of the "national seclusion." A few years later, relations with Portugal deteriorated and finally all Portuguese were expelled from Japan; instead, the VOC's factory, located in Hirado, was ordered to move onto Dejima. In conjunction with this, the shogunate designated Nagasaki as the sole legitimate port for the junk trade.

2.3 Various Commercial Intermediaries in the Seventeenth Century

Even though trade was limited to only one port, Nagasaki, the living and trading activities of Chinese merchants were still relatively free for the first 30 years. Initially, there were few restrictions on their transactions, except for those regarded to the sale of Chinese silks.

It is well known that Chinese silk was one of the most significant Chinese exports, and in the sixteenth century huge amounts of silver from the Americas and the Japanese archipelago flowed into China in exchange for silk. Raw silk was also in great demand in the Japanese market and therefore not only the Chinese but also Western Europeans, including the Portuguese and Dutch, carried Chinese silks into Japan. In the early seventeenth century, a method for silk transactions came into use, by which silk would be bought by the Japanese merchants in bulk. In response, a Silk Guild (*itowappu nakama* 糸割符仲間) consisting of merchants from several commercial regions—initially Sakai, Kyoto and Nagasaki (Edo and Osaka were added later)—was established and received a grant from the shogunate to monopolistically purchase imported Chinese silks. To be more precise, the Silk Guild could purchase all imported Chinese silks in bulk and at a set price after they had been first offered to the shogunate, and then the merchants affiliated with the guild would distribute the benefits of this type of monopolistic transaction according to the allocation of share. This system was applied to the trade with Chinese junks in 1631 and the VOC in 1641, and then was abolished in 1655 due to the soaring price (Nakamura 1988, Chap. 3; Ōta 1992, Chap. 2).

In the case of transactions of goods other than Chinese silk, these above-mentioned inns for junks played the role of commercial brokers. Chinese merchants would not be allowed to carry out their transactions without going through an authorized junks-inn. When a junk arrived in Nagasaki port, its captain would be asked by the officials of Nagasaki which junks-inn they wanted to lodge at. These inns delivered various trade-related services besides accommodation, with the services of the transaction intermediary being without a doubt the most

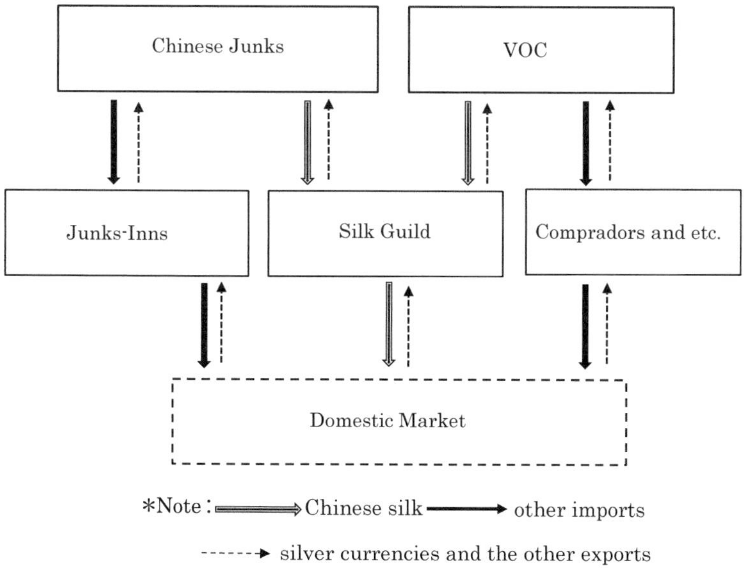

Fig. 2.2 Trading framework for the period 1635–1655

essential. Needless to say, these innkeepers would obtain commission fees in turn. In general, domestic Japanese merchants would pay the fees after the transaction negotiations had begun (An'no 1967) (Fig. 2.2).

From the late sixteenth century to the middle of the seventeenth century, a number of Chinese merchants sailed to Nagasaki for trade. Some of them chose to live and earn their living by managing junks-inns. It appears that they won the trust of and kept permanent commercial relations with the Chinese traders.

Merchants living in a port city like Nagasaki saw brokerage commission fees as their most essential source of income. When such intermediary services were monopolized by only a few innkeepers, especially Chinese immigrants, local dissatisfaction and the demand for a fair distribution of profit gradually increased.

In response, in 1666 the magistrate of Nagasaki applied a new regulation to the junk trade. Under this regulation, all neighborhoods (*machi* 町; which numbered 80 at that time) except for Dejima and the two brothel districts—*maruyama-machi* (丸山町) and *yoriai-machi* (寄合町)—would take turns being in charge of trade-related services for junks. Each time, two neighborhoods operated as a unit (the one assuming the main responsibility was called *yadomachi* 宿町; the other one playing the role of assistant neighborhood was called *tsukimachi* 附町) to deliver these kinds of services for junks. They were permitted to broker the merchandise carried on board that junk. In general, the junk's captain resided in the home of the head of the neighborhood association (*otona* 乙名) and other merchants and crew resided in the homes of residents in the same neighborhood; in return they were permitted to broker the merchandise carried on board that junk (Yamawaki 1964, pp. 276–280; Nakamura 1988, pp. 270–276).

This plan, which aimed to equalize the opportunities for the residents of Nagasaki to earn a profit from the trade, was carried out to some extent, but various market economy factors complicated it. Many innkeepers desired to continue providing services for junk traders as they had done previously; like their regular clients, many junk merchants also wished to hold on to the existing commercial partnerships. On the other hand, not every neighborhood was good at trade-related services. Under such circumstances, many innkeepers negotiated with neighborhoods to subcontract the services. According to the contracts, they would undertake some trade-related services in place of the designated Ship-Servicing Neighborhoods, or serve as assistants to them. They could take commission fees from the domestic merchants, but in return, according to the contracts, they were to share them with those Ship-Servicing Neighborhoods at a fixed rate, which generally was one-third. These kinds of junks-inns or innkeepers were generally called *koyado* (小宿) (An'no 1967; Nakamura 1988, pp. 270–276).

After the abolition of the Silk Guild in 1655, soaring prices of imported goods become a serious problem once again because foreign traders seldom found domestic products attractive except for some precious metals, that is, silver, gold, and copper. For the shogunate, the price increase also meant more precious metals would flow out of the country. In response, the shogunate decided to reintroduce the mechanisms of the Silk Guild system to control trade.

In 1672, a merchant association called *gokasho shōnin* (五ヶ所商人 Five-Cities Merchants Group) formed at the direction of the shogunate. The *gokasho* meant five commercial districts respectively centered on large cities—Sakai, Kyoto, Nagasaki, Edo, and Osaka—and the *shōnin* is the Japanese term for "merchants." Its agency in Nagasaki was called the *shihō-kaisho* (市法会所) (Fig. 2.3).

The Five-Cities Merchants Group bought the imports from foreign traders in bulk at uniformed-agreed prices; the target goods were not only Chinese silk but all imported goods. The prices were determined unilaterally by its Nagasaki agency.

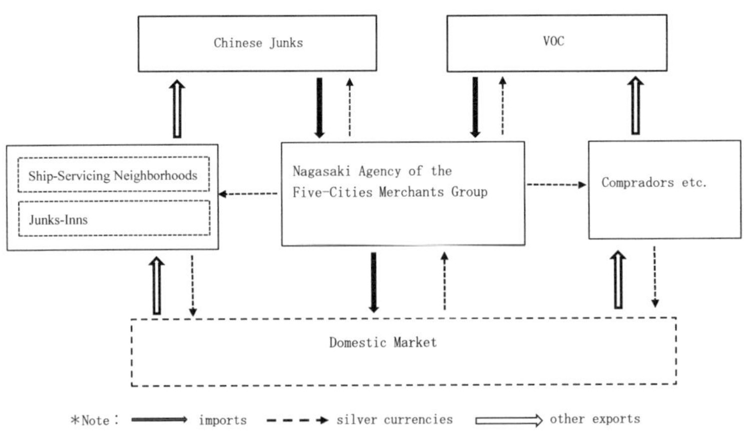

Fig. 2.3 Trading framework for the period 1672–1685

If the foreign traders were not satisfied with the prices, their only choice was to give up the trade (Yamawaki 1964, pp. 36–46; Nakamura 1988, pp. 277–284; Ōta 1992, Chap. 4).

2.4 Concentration of Trading Intermediaries in Nagasaki

In 1684, the Qing empire conquered Taiwan, which had been dominated by the Zheng Family (*Zheng Chenggong* 鄭成功, also known as *Koxinga* or *Coxinga*, and his successors) for decades, and they shortly thereafter withdrew the ban on overseas trade that had been maintained for several decades.[3] The merchants under the domination of the Qing empire were again permitted to engage in overseas trade, and thereafter the number of junks coming to Nagasaki increased sharply. As seen in Fig. 2.4, the number reached 85 (includes the junks whose trades were not permitted), which was three times more than that in previous years. It increased further in the following years, and nearly 200 junks arrived in Nagasaki in 1688. Because there were few valuable exports other than silver and copper in this period, it can be assumed that there was a huge outflow of silver and copper from Japan to China. On the other hand, shogunate policymakers had already grasped the concept of bullionism, which meant that they regarded precious metals as the most important forms of national wealth.

In response, in 1685 the shogunate adjusted the existing trade system in certain ways: fixing the annual amount of trading by the junks, abolishing bulk purchases by the Five-Cities Merchants Group, and reviving the Silk Guild. It is understandable that fixing the annual amount of trading aimed to control the outflow of silver and copper.[4] In order to make it practical, three years later the shogunate set the annual number of junks to 70, and revised the number several times according to changes of situation.[5] This is why the number of junks fell to around 70 in the last years of the seventeenth century, which can be seen in Fig. 2.4.

As to why the shogunate believed the abolishment of bulk purchase by the Five-Cities Merchants was necessary, the answer is not obvious, due to a scarcity of relevant sources. Given the situation at that time, it can be inferred that there were two reasons. Firstly, it was highly likely that the Nagasaki Agency of the Five-Cities

[3]In order to isolate Zheng's forces, Qing authorities issued Maritime Prohibition edicts many times after 1655, strictly forbidding the Chinese people from sailing abroad and forcing coastal residents to move inland.

[4]See records dated on the 1st and 13th day of the ninth month of Genroku 14 (October 2 and 14, 1701) in *Tōtsūji Kaisho Nichiruku* (Working Dairies of Chinese Interpreters 唐通事会所日録) in the Nagasaki Museum of History and Culture (NMHC). They have been published with the same title (Historiographical Institute, The University of Tokyo (ed) *Tōtsūji Kaisho Nichiruku*. Tokyo: The University of the Tokyo Press, 1955–1968).

[5]The number was fixed at 80 in 1698, 59 in 1708, 30 in 1715, 40 in 1717, 30 in 1720, 25 in 1736, 20 in 1740, 15 in 1749, 13 in 1765, and 10 in 1791. See Yamawaki (1964), pp. 317–322.

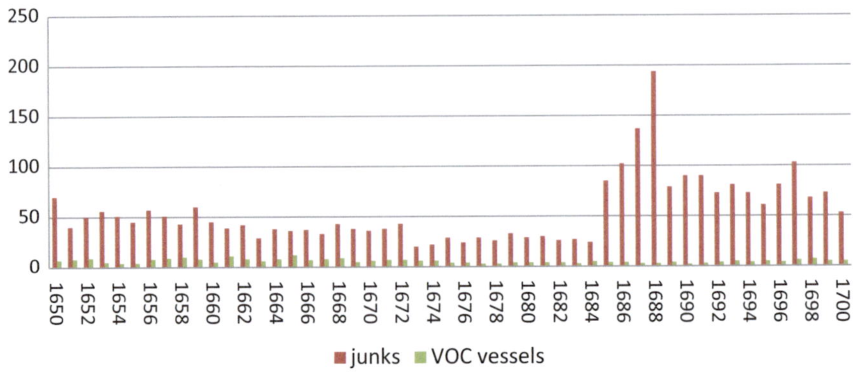

Fig. 2.4 Number of junks and VOC vessels arriving in Nagasaki 1650–1700. *Source* same as Fig. 1.2. *Note* the dates are a little different to those in Fig.1.2, because they include the number of the junks for which trade was refused. The years in the figure are those used in the old Japanese calendar

Merchants Group had insufficient capital and human resources, especially expert staff such as appraisers (*mekiki* 目利) and accountants (*kanjō-yaku* 勘定役), to deal with the sharp increase in the scale of trading. Therefore, shifting bulk purchases from all imports to just Chinese silk, the most valuable import, can be considered a realistic and temporary measure to deal with the increased amount of trade. Secondly, nearly several times as many overseas products were imported into Japan with the increasing number of junks, and accordingly it was highly likely that the market prices of these imports would drop considerably as well; it thereby became less essential for the shogunate to sustain the bulk-purchase system, the function of which had been mainly to control the prices of imports.

As mentioned above, not only the annual amount of imports but also the annual number of trading junks was limited by the shogunate. When the fixed number was reached, the trade of later-arriving junks would be prohibited. Certainly, sailing back without carrying out a transaction would lead to huge economic losses for those Chinese merchants. As a result, many of them turned to smuggling, which gradually developed into a serious problem.

Against this backdrop, the shogunate adopted several anti-smuggling policies. For instance, local merchants built the Chinese Residence (*tōjin yashiki* 唐人屋敷) in 1688, and all visiting Chinese were ordered to move into it early the next year under the direction of the magistrate. The Chinese Residence (more than 30,000 m^2) was more than twice as large as Dejima (approximately 15,395 m^2) and able to accommodate nearly one thousand people (Figs. 2.5 and 2.6).[6] Several officials selected from among chief officials of the neighborhoods, were in charge

[6] As isolation facilities, the Chinese Residence and Dejima were similar in function and management. Regarding the reasons for their establishment, however, they were obviously different: Dejima was established in response to Anti-Christianity policies, and the Chinese Residence was established to directly restrict trade as a countermeasure to junks' smuggling.

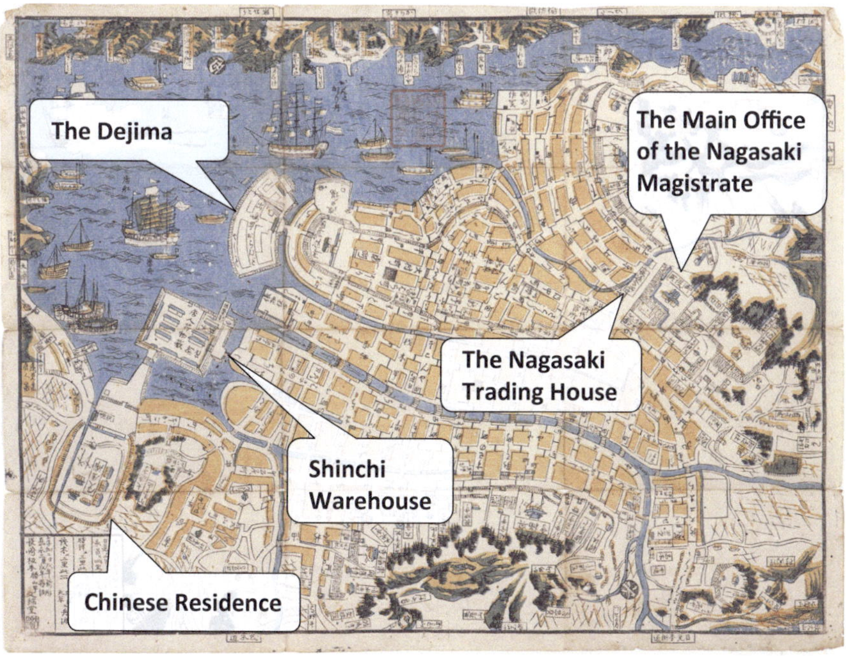

Fig. 2.5 An old map of Nagasaki City (*Nagasaki Saiken-Zu* 長崎細見図, detailed map of Nagasaki). 1851 reprint of the 1802 version. Courtesy of the Nagasaki Museum of History and Culture

of the management of this facility, and more than 20 men were employed and dispatched by the office of the magistrate to be responsible for its security. The Chinese interpreters were also stationed in turn and their duties included not only translation but also undertaking negotiations for trade and other trade-related activities.[7]

10 years later, a centralized warehouse for junks trading was constructed as well. Unlike in Dejima, there was no space to store cargo in the Chinese Residence. Even after moving into the settlement, Chinese merchants still had to use warehouses scattered throughout several places in the city just as before. In 1698, a large fire burnt more than half the warehouses in which junks' cargos were stored, causing a serious lack of sufficient storage space for cargo. With the approval of the shogunate, 39 local merchants who managed warehouses built an artificial island near the Chinese Residence as a new centralized warehouse in that same year.

[7]For more details about the Chinese Residence, see Yamamoto (1983).

Fig. 2.6 *Nagasaki-Kō no Zu* (The port of Nagasaki 長崎港之図, 1792, by Okayama Ōkyō). Courtesy of the Nagasaki Museum of History and Culture

It was called *shinchi-kurasho* (新地蔵所), literally meaning "the warehouse on a new land", and was quite large (approximately 13,795 m^2), similar in size to Dejima. The project cost more than 600 *kanme,* about one-third of which, 200 *kanme,* was loaned by the shogunate.[8]

Around the same time, the Nagasaki Trading House was established as well. Certainly, it was similar to the bulk-purchase system by the Five-Cities Merchants Group in some aspects, such as its role as a trading broker and its methods of purchasing imported goods; however, its establishment was by no means the revival of the old system. The differences of their positions in the trading framework will be clarified in the following sections.

[8]The related dates are seen in the *Tōsen Kurachi Kaiki no Oboe* (唐船蔵地開基之覚, memorandum on the opening of Chinese junks' warehouse) in the Historiographical Institute, The University of Tokyo, and *Shinchi Tsukitate Hottan Narabini Tōjin Kuranushi Haitōgin Chōshō Kakitsuke* (新地蔵立発端并頭人蔵主配当銀調書書付, investigation on the beginning of the Shinchi Warehouse and profit distributions of its managers and owners) in NMHC.

2.5 The Trading Framework for Imported Goods

Before any formal transactions, the shogunate would begin with its own purchase. This followed a tradition in foreign trade since the Hei'an Era (794–1185): the royal court dispatched a commissioner to the port to purchase the valuable goods first before opening the trade to ordinary merchants. In the Edo Period, this sort of transaction was similar to a tribute ceremony in the hall of the magistrate's office (see Fig. 2.7). Valuable imports such as high-quality silk fabrics, Chinese books, porcelains, and elephant tusks were exhibited there. Some of them seemed to be items ordered by the shogunate, and others might have been selected by the staff of the Trading House, or by the Chinese merchants themselves.

In addition, the Nagasaki Trading House also sold certain special goods to specific clients. Tsushima Domain (its territory was mainly Tsushima Island, situated in the Korea Strait) was one of them. The lord of Tsushima received from the Tokugawa shogunate the privilege of obtaining certain special goods, such as water buffalo horns (mainly used as a crucial material in the manufacture of Korean bows), for a fixed price. These important items were in turn traded to Korea.

Most imports traded by Chinese junks and the VOC's ships were purchased by the Trading House in bulk. As the first step, appraisers affiliated with the Trading House would enter the Shinchi Warehouse and draw up price lists after checking the quality of the items. The prices written in the lists might be tweaked via a conference of the executives of the Trading House. After that, the captains and

Fig. 2.7 Goods exhibition in the office of the Nagasaki magistrate. In: *Zai Nagasaki Nisshin Bōeki Emaki* (在長崎日清貿易絵巻, Illustrated Scroll of the Nagasaki Japanese-Chinese trade). Courtesy of the Matsura Historical Museum

accountants of the junks would gather at the Trading House and be asked whether they would accept the prices. According to the lists compiled in surviving books, it appears that the prices could be adjusted slightly after negotiation between the two sides. The determination of the prices also resulted in these imports being sold to the Trading House in bulk (Figs. 2.8 and 2.9).

Subsequently, this merchandise would be sold to a domestic merchant association, the Five-Cities Merchants (see Fig. 2.10). It was via these merchants that

Fig. 2.8 Price negotiation in the Nagasaki Trading House. In: *Zai Nagasaki Nisshin Bōeki Emaki* (see Fig. 2.7)

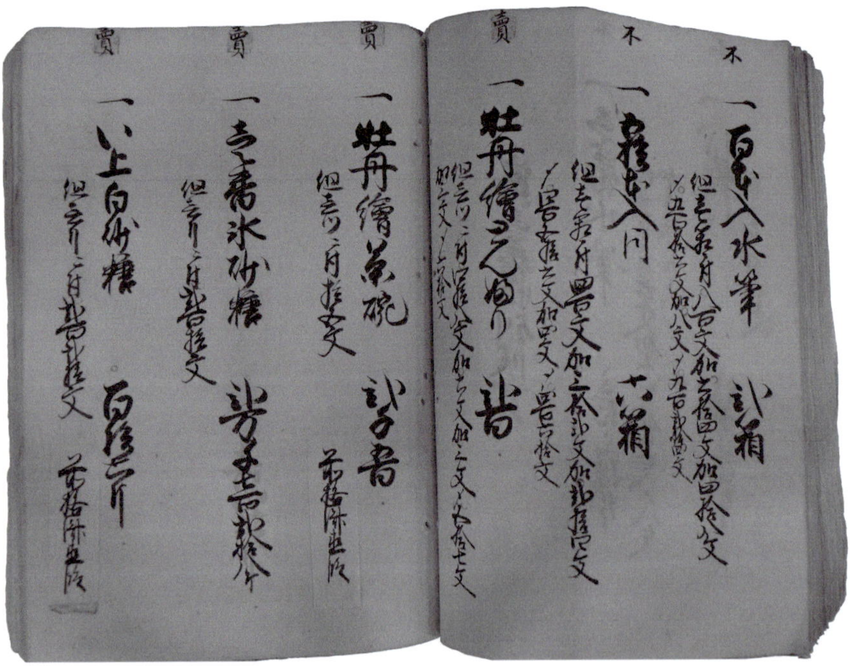

Fig. 2.9 A page in the accounting book *Moto'uri Negumichō* (本売直組帳, The Accounting Book for Price Negotiation of the Principle Trade), created in Tenpō 1 = 1830. Courtesy of the Nagasaki Museum of History and Culture

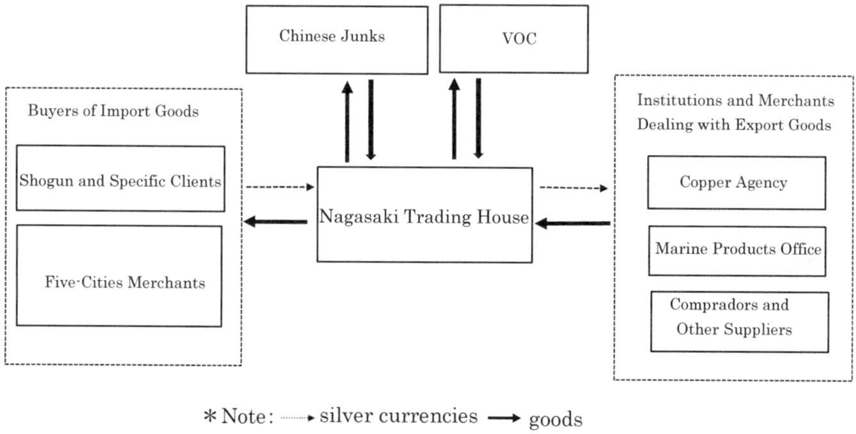

Fig. 2.10 Trading framework of the Nagasaki trade

imports found their way to the domestic market, especially the markets of Osaka and Kyoto. They or their agents were allowed to enter the warehouse and see the samples of all categories of imports. Unlike the price negotiations, a bidding contest would be held: merchants who offered to buy at the highest price would obtain the goods (Yamawaki 1964, pp. 302–305).

The Five-Cities Merchants can be seen as a kind of commercial association authorized by the shogunate. Every member could obtain imports directly in principle, and more generally, the money itself from the transaction's profits. However, it was not a completely closed commercial organization. If a merchant attempted to enter this field, he had some choices: for example, contracting with or employing an agent who was a member of the Five-Cities Merchants, or purchasing the qualification from that commercial community.[9] To be more specific, one of the most respected merchants in Edo Japan, the Mitsui family (三井家), always purchased Chinese silk or silk fabrics from specific Kyoto wholesalers dealing with overseas goods, and it also employed a merchant in Nagasaki named Nakano Yōsuke (中野用助), who was a member of the Five-Cities Merchants, giving him the money to directly obtain the imports they sought (Morioka 1963; Yamawaki 1964, pp. 260–266).

As for price determination, it is obvious that authority lay with the Trading House. It benefited by suppressing the purchase price, then using bidding as a direct way to maximize its profits. Incidentally, in the first 15 years after its formation imports could be sold by foreign traders to the Japanese merchants through the bidding process. However, the shogunate leaders gradually became aware that

[9]*Nagasaki Kaisho Gosatsu Mono* (five volumes of records on the Nagasaki Trading House), NMHC. They can be seen in Nagasaki Kenshi Hensan I'inkai (ed) *Nagasaki Kenshi Shiryō Hen* (history of Nagasaki prefecture: source materials) vol. 4. Tokyo: Yoshikawa kobunkan, 1966, pp. 1–243.

the bidding had resulted in the soaring prices of imports; thus, a large amount of copper flowed overseas. In 1715, the shogunate decided to shift the method of price determination from bidding to negotiation (Yano 1967, p. 372; Ōta 1992, Chap. 9). From then on, the pricing system stabilized: the Trading House bought imports from the foreign traders via price negotiation and then sold them to domestic merchants through a bidding process.

2.6 The Trading Framework for Exported Goods

Regarding exports, copper steadily replaced silver and gold as the most significant export commodity for Japan in its trade with Chinese merchants and the VOC from the middle of the seventeenth century (see Fig. 2.10). The easily-worked copper ores were delivered to Osaka and refined at fixed workshops (*dōfukiya* 銅吹屋) under the direction of the Copper Agency (*dōza* 銅座) established in Osaka in 1701 by the shogunate. The Copper Agency maintained a close commercial collaboration with the Nagasaki Trading House.[10] A certain amount of refined copper was delivered to Nagasaki and sold to foreign merchants via the Trading House; the rest entered the domestic market.

The second most significant export that left via in the Chinese trade was a class of luxury marine products (collectively called *tawaramono* 俵物). This included dried abalone, dried sea cucumber, and, to some extent, shark fin, as evidenced in Nagasaki's accounting books. From 1744 to 1785, contract merchants (*ukeoi-shōnin* 請負商人) had been responsible for purchasing these marine products from all over the country. In 1785, the Marine Products Office (*tawaramono yakusho* 俵物役所), a specialized agency affiliated with the Nagasaki Trading House, was formed at the instruction of the shogunate to handle this task rather than through the contract merchants (Ogawa 1973, Chap. 1). As mentioned in the next section, certain other exported items were handled by compradors (*urikominin* 売込人).

With respect to Dutch trade, recent studies have provided some information about how the compradors interacted with the VOC (Matsui 2013, 2015). Before 1641, the VOC had its factory on the island of Hirado (see Fig. 2.1). Many compradors enjoyed a stable trading relationship with the VOC. In 1641, the VOC was forced to move its factory from Hirado to Nagasaki. There were some merchants in Nagasaki who obtained the authority from the shogunate to take order from the Dutch merchants of VOC and sell domestic products to them. They kept commercial association with the VOC. Those compradors were called *compra nakama* (コンプラ仲間), or *urikominin* in Japanese sources, acting as commercial brokers for the Dutch merchants.

[10]The Copper Agency of Osaka was twice abolished and reestablished.: First abolished in 1712, it was reestablished in 1738; in 1750 it was once again abolished, only to be resurrected in 1766.

Compared to the studies on its counterpart in Dutch trade, little is known about the compradors of the junk trade. Hence, it is worth shedding light on the commercial activities of the compradors for the Chinese junks in detail.

2.7 *Urikominin* for the Junks Trade

Since its formation, the Nagasaki Trading House began acting as a commercial intermediary instead of the Ship-Servicing Neighborhoods and the junks-inns. However, the Trading House did not deal directly in all exports by itself. The compradors called *urikominin* helped the Trading House purchase products for export from various places.

There is a surviving notebook which lists the prices of certain exports and the affiliated transaction taxes in 1814.[11] As seen in the illustration, in the upper section, there is a list of merchandise such as sumac gallnut (*gobaishi* 五倍子), poria cocos (*wari bukuryō* 割茯苓), camphor (*shōnō* 樟脳), ginseng produced in Satsuma (*sassyū shōninjin* 薩州小人参), and mushrooms (*shi'itake* 椎茸). Under each item there are two lines: on the right is the fixed selling price for the junks merchants and on the left is the rate of the related tax that those Japanese seller merchants should pay to the Trading House. In the lower section, the names of the compradors can be seen. The compradors who dealt with the sumac gallnut were *wayakuya* (和薬屋) and *shoshikiya* (諸色屋) (Fig. 2.11).

Based on the dates in this book, Table 2.1 indicates the merchants' names and information for the items. There were two types of merchants in charge: the comprador and the contractor (*ukeoinin* 請負人). Still, no evidence can explain the differences between the two clearly. Nevertheless, the purchasing of domestic marine products offers some clues. These *ukeoinin* here may be similar to the contractors of marine products, who had been in this position in 1744–1785, before the formation of the Marine Products Office. It seemed that *ukeoinin* were merchants who had direct contracts with the Trading House. They purchased certain goods from the sites of production and then delivered them to the Trading House for a set price. On the other hand, the compradors were simply merchants who received qualifications to deal in certain kinds of goods with Chinese merchants. The quantity of each good that the comprador was permitted to deal in, was decided primarily by the demand of the Chinese merchants.

There is another interesting source in the Nagasaki Museum of History and Culture (NMHC).[12] This regards a dispute over a transaction involving sumac

[11] *Tōkatawatari Shoshiki Nedan Narabini Myogagin Toritate Motoshime Kakitsuke* (唐方渡諸色直段并冥加銀取立候元極書付, decision papers in terms of the prices of various supplying goods for Chinese trade and the commercial taxes) in the Manuscript Library of the Kyushu University Library.

[12] *Tōkata Urikomi Gobaishi no Gi ni tsuki Shoshikiya tomo Negaide sōrō Shidai Wayakuya Kaemon ai Tadashi Torishirabe Moshi sōrō Kakitsuke* (唐方売込五棓子之儀ニ付諸色屋共願出

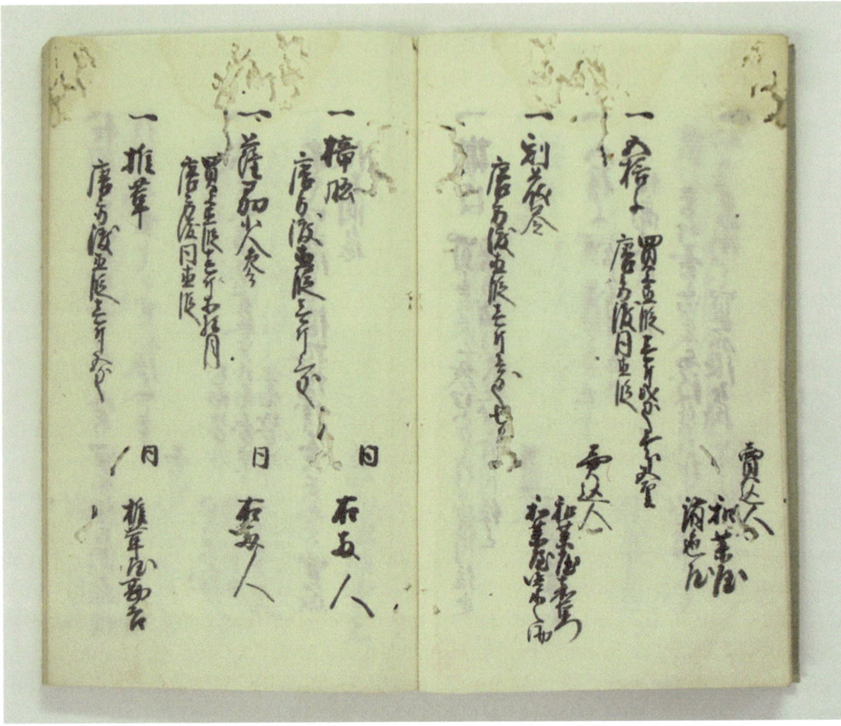

Fig. 2.11 Pages 6 and 7 in the book *Tōkatawatari Shoshiki Nedan Narabini Myōgagin Toritate Motoshime Kakitsuke* (see Note 11). Courtesy of Manuscript Library of the Kyushu University Library

gallnut. Sumac gallnut is a nut that can be used not only as medicine but also as a kind of dye. The dispute described in this document happened in 1814 between two compradors: a Japanese-medicine merchant (*wayakuya*) and a general-goods dealer (*shoshikiya*). The former dealt in Japanese medicine and the latter in various goods. This source offers the information that the medicine merchant was permitted by the Nagasaki magistrate to sell sumac gallnut to Chinese merchants for use as medicine, and the general-goods dealers were permitted to sell sumac gallnut for use as a dye. However, in 1814, the medicine merchant received permission to monopolize the trade of sumac gallnut with Chinese merchants. At that point, the general-goods dealers delivered a petition to the magistrate to protest this decision.

According to the petition, they had been ordered by the magistrate to be the dedicated general-goods compradors (*shoshiki urikominin* 諸色売込人) when the Chinese Residence was established and had been supplying various goods that

---

□□□, 和薬屋嘉右衛門相糺取調子申上候書付 The documents on the complaints of *shoshikiya* over the sale of sumac gallnut for junks and the investigation papers of the *wayakuya kaemon*) in NMHC.

Table 2.1 The compradors and contractors for junks trade, 1814

Goods	Name/comprador (*urikominin*) or contractor (*ukeoinin*)
Dried squid and others	Not fixed
High-quality dried squid	Hiratoya Shinemon, Ougiya Shinbei/compradors
Cockscomb laver	Sameya Shigekichi, Oyamaya Shinshirou, Tawaramonoya Hirahei, Yamaguchi Sanrouji/contractors
Dried shellfish	Tawaramonoya Mojiemon, Kochi Kichirouhei/compradors
Dried bonito	Katsuoya Denbei/comprador
Otter fur	Not available
Sumac gallnut	Shimizuya Hirashichi/contractor
Sumac gallnut	Wakusuriya, Shoshikiya/compradors
Poria cocos	Wayakuya Kaemon, Wayakuya? (an undecipherable charactor)nosuke/ compradors
Satsuma ginseng	Same as above/compradors
Camphor	Same as above/contractors
Satsuma camphor	Satsuma residence in Nagasaki/special agent
Mushrooms	Shiitakeya Kankichi/not available
Agar	Kantenya, Shoshikiya, Yasaisakanaya/contractors
Kimono fabric	Gofukuya Taihei/not available
Lacquers; others	Komamonoya Uhei, Chuhei, Bunsuke, Shingoro/not available

Source Tokata Watari Shoshiki Nedan Narabi Myōgakin Toritate soro Motokime Kakitsuke (see Note 11)

the Chinese traders had ordered from that time. They were in charge of selling daily necessities to the Chinese Residence. The prices of these goods were officially fixed, but since the market price of the goods had actually increased recently, their profits suffered. As a way to make up for these losses, they had received sanction to sell agar (*kanten* 寒天) and sumac gallnut to Chinese merchants as trade goods. Unfortunately, the source does not reveal the result of this dispute.

2.8 Various Trade-Related Services and Accounting Systems

As mentioned above, the Ship-Servicing Neighborhoods and the subcontracted inns acted as the main service provider for the junks trade for a long time in the seventeenth century. The function of providing accommodation and the role as transaction mediator were replaced by the Chinese Residence and the Nagasaki Trading House, respectively, after their formation at the end of the seventeenth century. However, those neighborhoods were still in charge of other trade-related services: delivering necessary commodities for Chinese daily life in Nagasaki,

Table 2.2 Transactions in the Chinese residence based on the magistrate's instruction, 1708

Items/number of sellers	Limitation of business hours and number permitted each time of business	Transaction style
Luxury marine products/2	No limitation	Preorder
Copper products, lacquer craft, sundry goods/25	10:00–14:00, day before departure/N/A	Stall
Imari porcelain/8	No limitation	Stall
Sticks/15	No limitation/3	Preorder
Clothing related/12	No limitation/2 or 3	Preorder
Vegetables/10	Every other day/5	Stall
Dried sea cucumber, dried squid, shark's fin, dried bonito/5	Daily/2	Stall
Fresh fish/12	Every other day/6	Stall
Sauces, salt, vinegar/12	Daily/3	Stall
Paper, flour, noodles/9	Daily/2	Stall
Knives, slips/2	Daily	Stall
Rental of floor mats and folding screens/3	No limitation	Stall
Medicines/3	No limitation	Stall
Charcoal, nets (N/A)/1	No limitation	Stall

Source Peng 2016; date from *Totsūji Kaisho Nichiruku* (see Note 4) Vol. 4, pp. 300–306
Note Date shown are from the old Japanese calendar

keeping and guarding the junks, organizing labor and arranging for sampans on which to load cargo, and so forth. Although all charges were without doubt ultimately paid by the Chinese merchants, the on-duty neighborhoods received money for them from the Trading House.

Concerning the daily necessities of the visiting Chinese, the magistrate of Nagasaki appointed some specific merchants to deal in the most-often consumed vegetables and fish, soon after the establishment of the Chinese Residence. They received wooden passes, marked with the brand of the chief official (*otona* 乙名) in charge of managing the Chinese Residence, entered the gate and opened stalls at the square between the main gate (*daimon* 大門) and the inside gate (*ninomon* 二ノ門), according to dates and times fixed by the magistrate. In 1708, the magistrates strengthened its control over those merchants supplying goods for Chinese merchants (Peng 2016). As seen in Table 2.2, there were various other merchants besides those selling vegetables and fish. The term *urikominin* does not appear in the original sources of this time. Judging by their functions, most of them can be seen as the predecessors of the compradors, examined in the section above (Fig. 2.12).

In terms of the accounts of these transactions, in the case of a stall, the Chinese purchased merchandise by using either the special copper coins cast in Nagasaki or bills for exchanging silver currency (*ginsatsu* 銀札), both of which were issued by the Nagasaki Trading House at stated periods and worth a certain amount (Koga 1934). In the case of pre-ordered goods, after ensuring the ordered goods were delivered to the Chinese who ordered them, the Japanese officials of the Chinese Residence would issue a receipt certificate to the seller merchant; then, after

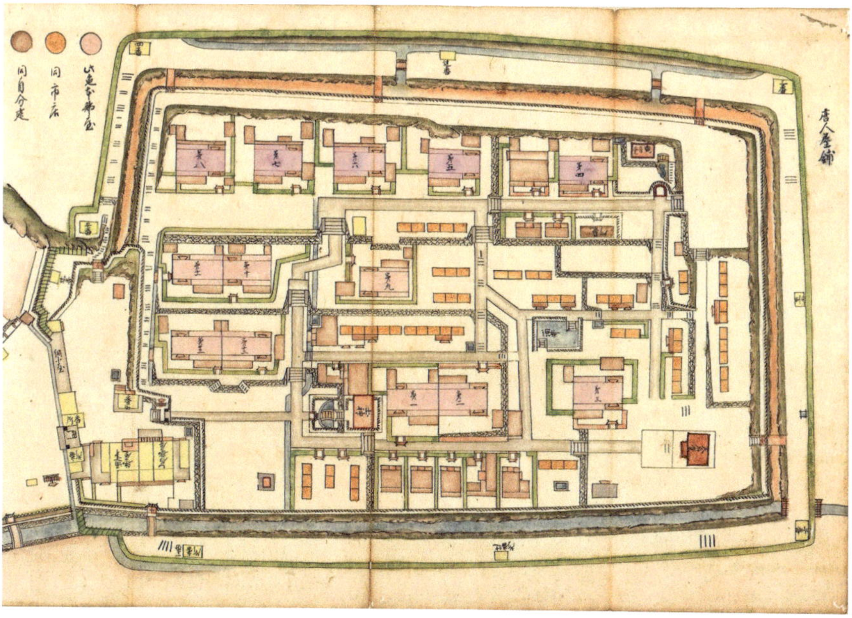

Fig. 2.12 Chinese residence in *Nagasaki Shoyakusho Tatemono Ezu* (長崎諸役所建物絵図 Pictures of Public Office Buildings in Nagasaki). Courtesy of Historiographical Institute, The University of Tokyo

showing the certificate, the merchant could receive his money from the Ship-Servicing Neighborhood.[13]

Some trade-related services, especially cargo handling, needed a certain number of laborers. Providing these laborers was also one of the main tasks of the Ship-Servicing Neighborhoods. The cargo-handling work was undertaken by day laborers (*hiyatoi* 日雇 or *hiyō* 日用). They were organized into many working teams and generally in each team there were 40 men with a leader (*hiyadoi-gashira* 日雇頭). Sometimes the Ship-Servicing Neighborhoods might contract with the team leaders to recruit the day laborers instead of directly employing them (Wakamatsu 1997). These day laborers were permitted to get some commodities as subsidies in addition to their fixed salaries. For example, they could collect and process the sugar that spilled to the ground when being carried (Ya'o 1998). These day laborers also seemed to find other jobs at trade-related facilities such as the Trading House, the Marine Products Office, and sometimes with the domestic merchants (Figs. 2.13, 2.14 and 2.15).[14]

---

[13]*Tōtsūji Kaisho Nichiruku* (Note 4) Vol. 4, pp. 300–306.

[14]Various types of day laborers can be seen in the criminal cases recorded in *Hanka-chō* (犯科帳, precedent case collection) in NMHC, which has been published (Morinaga Taneo, ed. *Hanka-chō: Nagasaki Bugyōsho Hanketsu Kiroku*. Nagasaki: Hankachō Kankokai, 1958–1961).

Fig. 2.13 Unloading a junk in *Tōkan-Zu* (唐館図, Illustrated Scroll of the Chinese Residence). Courtesy of the Nagasaki Museum of History and Culture

Fig. 2.14 Goods transportation by sampans in *Tōkan-Zu* (see Fig. 2.13)

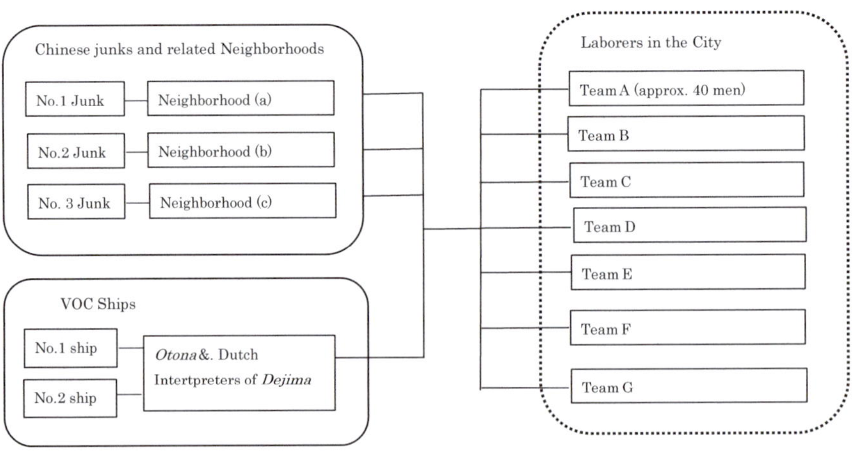

Fig. 2.15 Organization of cargo-handling day laborers

Carrying cargos between the junks and the Shinchi Warehouse was another essential job which needed not only physical energy but also skill in rowing a boat. In general, the weight of the cargo was too heavy to go directly to the shore and had to be transferred separately into sampans (*nikogibune* 荷漕船). This was a normal solution, seen at other ports during the same time. The Ship-Servicing Neighborhoods were also tasked with organizing sampans and employing rowers. Based on some related sources, however, the detailed work of recruiting and employment seemed not to be undertaken by the officials of the neighborhoods themselves but entrusted to sampans-arrangement agencies (*nikogibune sahainin* 荷漕船差配人). These agencies contracted with the holders of sampans, and, through them, recruited rowers.[15]

Cargo storage was another crucial trade-related service. As explained above, the Shinchi Warehouse was built near the Chinese Residence. The magistrate of Nagasaki initially selected six men from the 39 holders (*kuranushi* 蔵主) to serve as chief managers (*tōnin* 頭人) of the warehouse; this number was afterwards reduced to three. These managers employed six assistants and several guardsmen as full-time staff. Their salaries were paid from the warehouse charges of the Chinese merchants. Additionally, the neighborhood officials assisted in the security of the warehouse.[16]

Although all the service charges related to the junks trade were ultimately paid by the Chinese merchants, almost all the payments were mediated by the Nagasaki Trading House. As mentioned above, the Chinese were permitted to buy some foods or daily necessities directly from stalls at the square between the main gate and the inside gate of the Chinese Residence. Even in this sort of direct transaction, however, all the monies used in this case were issued by the Trading House at stated periods and for a certain amount, and they took the form of bills for exchanging silver currency or special copper coins cast as explained above.

Briefly speaking, the intermediate transaction by the Trading House at Nagasaki was a sort of barter trade. The Trading House purchased all imports in bulk no matter from which side, the junks or the VOC's vessels, and utilized *kan* (貫) and *monnme* (匁), the units of silver currency used in Edo Japan, to display the prices of those imports in their accounting books. Nevertheless, the means of practical payment were not the silver currencies themselves but the commodities for export and the trade-related services. There were five items in the accounting books concerning the payments: copper, luxury marine products, other minor export goods, various official charges, and various services charges. The prices of most

---

[15]There was a case in 1795 indicating an employment relation between a sampan-arrangement agency and a holder of a sampan in *Hankachō* Vol. 5, p. 129.

[16]Generally, every neighborhood had a duty to provide security-related work. Every night, 10 neighborhood officials called *kumigashira* (組頭), which was the position immediately beneath the *otona*, the chief neighborhood officials, attended the night watch of the Shinchi Warehouse. This detail can be seen in a book titled *Ryōmachi Otona Kumigashira Nichikōshi Tsutomekata Hikae* (両町乙名組頭日行使勤方書控, a binding book of the reserve documents on the work directory of *totona*, *kumigashira*, *nichikōshi* in the Two Neighborhoods) in NMHC.

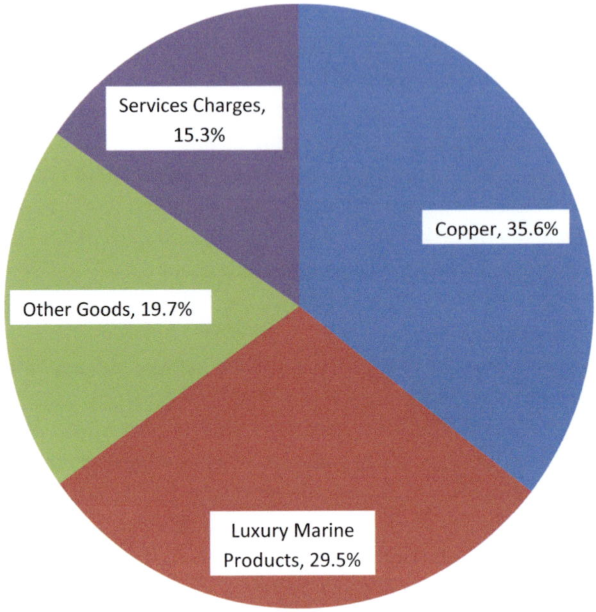

Fig. 2.16 Exports, services, charges for paying for the imports by junks

exports were already determined and changed little over a long period. The last two items listed above were called *sho-jōrei* (諸定例) and *sho-tsukaisute* (諸遣捨) in Japanese, respectively; in interpreting these terms, *sho* literally means "various" and *jōrei* indicates fees or charges that should be taken in accordance with regulations; *tsukaisude* meant consumption. The charges of all the trade-related services mentioned above obviously came from the *sho-tsukaisute*, at least in principle.

The following parts of this section will focus on the structure of the payment for imports by using two charts based on the dates in the *Nagasaki Kaisho Gosatsu Mono* (see Note 9), which was a handbook of various trading regulations and methods. The dates reflect the trading conditions from the late eighteenth century to the mid-nineteenth century. As shown in Fig. 2.16, about 84.6% of the payments were paid for the exports, including copper, luxury marine products, and other goods, and the expenses related to various service charges accounted for about 15.3% of the total.

Figure 2.17 lists the items involved in the service charges. Among them, more than half were administrative fees including one called "official grant" (*yakuryō* 役料), and the cost of "gifts" (*inmotsu* 音物 and *hasakugin* 八朔銀), which were paid to the magistrate, the city elders, and other city officials including the Chinese interpreters, as a bonus for their duties of managing and mediating transactions or delivering various trade-related services. Most of the remainder can be regarded as service charges. Some items such as cargo handling and warehouse use have been explained earlier.

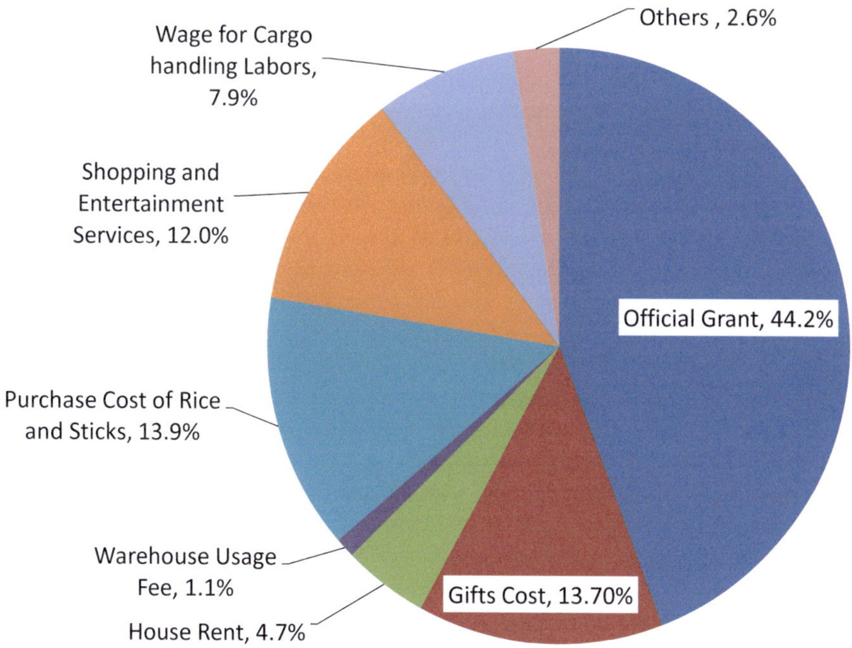

Fig. 2.17 Miscellaneous expenses

Concerning the as-yet unidentified items, some brief explanations are required. Firstly, in terms of rice, the specified merchant took charge of the supply. For example, Yoshino-ya (芳野屋), a rice merchant in Kyoto, had undertaken to provide the rice supply, and Ze'niya Ribē (銭屋利兵衛) and Take'uchi Washichi (竹内和七) were assigned to rice polishing in the middle of the eighteenth century.[17] Secondly, this "shopping" mainly reflects the fact that the Chinese purchased those goods they needed for sustenance; and "entertainment services" mainly meant they paid for sex workers. Lastly, other charges included are for such things as junks storage or the cost of copper packing.

2.9 The Tokugawa Management of Trade Centered Around the Nagasaki Trading House

There had been various merchants, agents, and associations playing the role of trading intermediaries or trade-related services intermediaries in the seventeenth-century Nagasaki trade. The Tokugawa restricted the overseas trade step by step in

[17] *Nagasaki Kaisho Gosatsu Mono* (Note 9), Vol.2.

order to prohibit the outflow of precious metals, by controlling direct transactions with the foreign traders. At the end of the century, the Nagasaki Trading House was formed and became the sole commercial agent conducting the trade directly with foreign merchants. It is obvious that there was a trend to concentrate those trading intermediaries.

While the Nagasaki Trading House was established under the direction of the shogunate and always accepted its guidance and supervision, it was managed in practice by the officials and merchants in the community of Nagasaki City and thereby represented the interests of local society to some extent. Hence, it can be considered a semi-governmental commercial organization. This is also reflected in the distribution of the trading profits. In the first 15 years or more since its formation, the Trading House had to pay all the surplus profits as a kind of commercial tax (*unjōkin* 運上金) to the shogunate, after keeping a certain amount to distribute to local communities. That was reversed in 1715 as part of policy rearrangements (the *shōtoku-shinrei* 正徳新例)—fixing the commercial tax to a certain amount and permitting the Trading House to deal with the rest (Yamawaki 1964, pp. 280–283). This policy shift provided a strong motivation for the Trading House to promote trade proactively, in a context in which the shogunate had to downsize the scale of the overseas trade in view of the outflow of various precious metals.

To some extent, the whole port city of Nagasaki played a role as a commercial mediator between the Japanese domestic market and the global economy, and almost every resident was more or less involved in trade-related work. Besides receiving their shares from the trading profits, most residents could earn other income that originated from trading. For instance, some obtained salaries as employees of the Trading House, and some earned fees by delivering trade-related services as explained above. It is notable that all payments were provided by the Trading House, and in this sense the Trading House had a role as an accounting center as well, including for trading and municipal administration. This is why the Dutch merchants called it the *geldkamer* (counting house).

Another characteristic of the management of the Trading House was its collection system for exports. Yano pointed out in his 1938 study that copper was exported to the Chinese merchants and the VOC at a price much lower than its price in the domestic market. Recent studies on the copper trade of Tokugawa Japan have focused on and re-emphasized this point (Shimata 2006; Nagase-Reimer 2015). The Trading House was associated with the Copper Agency at Osaka to ensure the supply of copper processed for trade and also to enable the Trading House to purchase copper at a relatively affordable price. This sort of collection system was later adapted to the supply and purchase of other articles. For example, luxury marine products became more and more significant exports in the eighteenth century as copper production decreased. In order to increase the supply for exports, the shogunate issued edicts to encourage increasing production and on the other hand to limit their domestic consumption. It is obvious that the management of the Trading House would have been more difficult without the full support of the shogunate.

As discussed above, the Nagasaki Trading House can be seen as the central accounting body of the Tokugawa trading management system. It needed commercial partners, however, in order for the shogunate's strict control of foreign trade to function. Many other commercial intermediaries such as the Five-Cities Merchants Group as well as the compradors assisted in completing the role and functions of combining the maritime trade with the domestic market. In this sense, the functioning of the Tokugawa trading management system was based on the Trading House, whilst also having a multi-layered construction.

Chapter 3
The Mechanism and Functions of the *Shinpai* Trading Permit System

3.1 Introduction to Study of the *Shinpai* for the Junks Trade

The magistrate of Nagasaki, under the direction of the shogunate, began to issue *shinpai* (信牌), a kind of trading pass or permit, to the junk merchants in 1715 and declared that junk trader without the *shinpai* could not be permitted to trade in Japan. The Tokugawa Regime used the *shinpai* for the junk trade until the late 1850s.

The study of the *shinpai* and the related policies drew scholarly attention as early as the 1930s. Yano Jin'ichi (矢野仁一) addressed the trading control system based on the *shinpai* by analyzing the text of the regulations of 1715 (*shōtoku-shinrei*, 正徳新例), while he also discussed the process of the dispute in China over the use of the *shinpai* that emerged right after the issuance of the *shinpai* in Japan (Yano 1967:330–335, 382–387, and 535–547, first published in 1938). The dispute (which will from here onwards be expressed by the term "*shinpai* dispute") concerned whether or not the Qing authorities should allow Chinese merchants to receive the *shinpai* as a license for entry into the Nagasaki trade. Following Yano's research studies, Saeki Tomi (佐伯富), Yamawaki Teijiro (山脇悌二郎) and Kikuchi Yoshimi (菊地義美) in the 1950s and 1960s revealed further important details of the related policies (Saeki 1986; Yamawaki 1960, Chap. 2, and 1964; Kikuchi 1964).

Since the 1970s, the study of the administration based on *shinpai*, as well as the use of *shinpai* by Chinese merchants, have earned further specific academic attention. For example, Ōba Osamu (大庭脩) analyzed the relationship of Chinese merchants by focusing on the changes in the holders' names registered on these *shinpai* (Ōba 1984). As more Chinese sources have been published recently, Matsuura Akira (松浦章) and Iwa'i Shigeki (岩井茂樹) promoted separate research studies on the aforementioned *shinpai* dispute in Qing China. Matsuura made clear that the *shinpai* dispute was finally brought to an end by the decision of the Emperor Kangxi in 1717, while Iwa'i pointed out that the real reason for Qing's

H. Peng, *Trade Relations between Qing China and Tokugawa Japan*,
Studies in Economic History, https://doi.org/10.1007/978-981-13-7685-6_3

concern about the Japanese *shinpai* policy in this dispute was not the anger of Qing officials about the fact that the name of the Japanese ruling era was written on the *shinpai*, but rather the fear of the Qing authorities of an emerging trade monopoly by a handful of Chinese merchants exclusively holding the *shinpai* issued by the Nagasaki magistrate (Matsuura 1988; Iwai 2007).

Yet, despite the numerous studies on the *shinpai*, it is still not clear how they functioned as a method of trade management in practice, and how the Qing authorities utilized them through Chinese merchants in order to sustain copper imports from Japan. It is essential to discuss how the *shinpai* worked as well as the roles of all the involved actors. Therefore, by having recourse to rarely used Chinese and Japanese sources, this chapter aims to clarify the mechanism of the trade-control system based on the *shinpai*. Examining the countermeasures of the Qing authorities against this system will be the main topic of the following chapter.

3.2 Various Trading Passes in the Pre-Modern Maritime World

The precise nature of the *shinpai* can be considered a basic issue of this study. In order to better understand it, this section will introduce some trading passes similar to the *shinpai* in their functioning as certificates issued by the political administration.

The pass used as a certificate in maritime trade is better known in early modern maritime history, and the *cartaz* issued by the Portuguese in the maritime area of Asia can be seen as the most famous example in early modern maritime world history. The merchant who promised to obey the rules of and paid the fee to the Portuguese colonial government would obtain the *cartaz*, and the *cartaz* system was a way for the Portuguese to show and maintain their maritime hegemony (Lius 2001). In fact, this system seemed to be a model for the overseas expansion of other Western powers such as the Dutch and the English. Contrary to the *cartaz*, the passes utilized by other West European countries in the early modern period have seldom been noticed by scholars. For instance, we find by reading the diaries kept by the heads of the Dutch factory in Japan[1] that the VOC issued some trading passes/permits, called *pas* in Dutch, to the Chinese merchants who wished to call on and trade at some ports on the island of Taiwan occupied by the VOC.

In the East Asian world, the pass certificate and the trading pass have a long history. In the case of China, there was an official certificate called *gongyan* (公験), which began to be used at the latest in the Tang dynasty (618–907) more than a thousand years earlier. If someone attempted to make a journey, it was necessary for him to apply for approval from the local government first, and he would obtain

[1]Many records related to *pas* can be seen in *Diaries Kept By the Heads of the Dutch Factory*, Vol. XII. The book was edited by Historiographical Institute, The University of Tokyo, and published by The University of Tokyo Press in 2015.

a piece of paper, the *gongyan*, after receiving that permission (Komai 1957 and Naka 2015).

As its general image, China in the Tang dynasty was an open society with multiple cultures, and numerous foreigners including diplomatic officials, merchants, monks, and so forth traveled to China during that time. Therefore, the *gongyan* was widely used not only by the Chinese but also by those foreign travelers and traders. Furthermore, it seems that some other states, especially those around China, attempted to introduce a similar system in their emigration and immigration control. One of them was Japan. In ancient history, many people expected to visit China, and they knew that the *gongyan* was necessary for their journeys. This is why there is still extant some pieces of original *gongyan* in the Tokyo National Museum. They are all related to the pilgrimage to Tang China of a Buddhist monk named Enchin (円珍). One of them was issued before his departure from Japan by the *Dazaifu* (大宰府), an administrative agency located in Kyushu and in charge of diplomacy and foreign trade. For Enchin, the *gongyan* would be an identification and certificate of his purpose for visiting China. The other *gongyan* of Enchin were granted by the local administrations of China after his arrival in the country.

In the Song dynasty (960–1279), *gongyan* still played the role of a kind of passport in domestic traffic, and there also appeared a trading pass used in the control of overseas trade, called *gongping* (公凭) (Mori 1948, pp. 20–21). In the history of China, the Song dynasty is known as a high-growth period in the commerce and money economy, and Song authorities strongly supported the overseas trade of private merchants for obtaining commercial taxes and thereby maintaining the troops with the ability to defend against threats from the northern political powers such as Liao (遼) or Western Xia (西夏). Hence, it is better to say issuing *gongping* was a way to avoid the merchant's evasion of tax and to secure the country's income through taxation.

It seemed the *gongping* system was utilized as well by the Yuan empire (1271–1368), which overthrew the Song and established a conquering dynasty in China. However, its use was not continued by the new Chinese dynasty, the Ming (1368–1644). After expelling the Mongols from China, the Ming attempted to rebuild the "China-centered world order" and therefore demanded the tribute of foreign states, especially those around or near China. They permitted the Chinese merchants to trade with those foreign merchants accompanied by the tribute envoys at specified ports in China but strictly prohibited any Chinese from overseas activity. Hence, it became less necessary to issue the passport to ordinary people under the Maritime Prohibitions. However, checking the qualification of the tribute missions became a new agenda for the regime, and as a solution, the Ming authorities issued official certificates called *kanhe* (勘合), which are often called "tallies" in related studies, to the tribute states, and the envoy without a "tally" would not be allowed to enter Ming China. In fact, for many countries the real purpose of sending an envoy to China is thought to have been for trade purposes rather than to seek any political support (Hashimoto 2010).

The Ming's Maritime Prohibitions prohibited private trade, and naturally the smuggling problem became serious. In 1567, the first year of *Longqing*, the Ming authorities had to relax the Maritime Prohibitions and allow the merchants under its domination to engage in overseas trade from a specified port called *Yuegang* (月港), a port of the district centered on Zhangzhou City (漳州) in the south of Fujian province. Nevertheless, the government decided to impose taxes on the maritime trade and use them for military expenses. As a certificate of trade permission and tax payment, the government issued the merchants the trading pass called *wenyin* (文引), which in function was similar to *gongping* during the Song dynasty (Kobata 1967; Fu 1956; Sakuma 1992).

In the early years of the seventeenth century, there existed some trading pass systems other than *wenyin* the of Ming China, such as the *shuinjō* (朱印状) in early modern Japan and *paizhao* (牌照) in the Zheng's maritime realm (Iwa'o 1985; Zhang 1968). The *paizhao* of the Zheng regime was similar to the *wenyin* of the Ming and the *cartaz* of Portugal in function. Paying money was the basic means of obtaining the pass. However, there is no evidence to indicate that the Tokugawa regime merely granted the *shuinjō* to those who paid money for it. It can be seen as a way for the shogunate to pursue a new regional trading order in the East Asian maritime world.

3.3 The Formulation of the Regulations in 1715

Chapter 1 outlines the historical background of the resumption of the Sino-Japanese trade relationship, including the political situation of the two countries and the conditions of the trade. A turning point came when the Qing authorities repealed the Maritime Prohibitions in 1684 and began to permit the private merchants to sail and trade abroad, which caused a trading boom among merchants (see Fig. 1.2 or Fig. 2.4), especially those living in the southeast coastal region. Furthermore, the Qing empire adopted a positive attitude towards the promotion of trade, since more and more copper would be imported to China, which would then be used for casting coins. Consequently, the annual number of junks to Nagasaki suddenly increased to 85 (including the junks for which trade was refused; see Fig. 2.4) in 1685, which was about triple the average level of the previous year.

Not surprisingly, the sudden increase of junks from China led to a degree of chaos in terms of the insufficiency of accommodation, the lack of staff providing services for the trade, and other matters. A more serious problem was the large outflow of precious metals, especially silver and copper. Facing these problems, the shogunate had to consider limiting the scale of the trade. First, it fixed a maximum annual amount (*sadametaka* 定高) for trade in 1685, and at the same time ordered the junks to sail back without unloading their goods once the approved annual total amount had been reached. Three years later, the shogunate fixed the number of the trading junks as well.

Consequently, junks arriving earlier had an advantage over late-comers. Needless to say, no one was glad to sail back without conducting trade. Yet, on the Chinese side until the middle of the eighteenth century, there had been neither a united overseas trade organization like the VOC nor an official overseas trade institution controlled by the Qing authorities that could have arranged schedules for junks according to the maximum annual number approved by the Tokugawa regime. Therefore, junks coming to Nagasaki could not avoid surpassing the permitted annual number due to the lack of necessary information. Since sailing back without trade led to a huge loss each time, many of these merchants chose to conduct smuggling in coastal areas adjacent to Nagasaki.

In this situation, it became necessary for the Japanese authorities to introduce an effective system to let Chinese merchants know in advance whether their trade would be approved before they set sail for Nagasaki. In the early 1710s, Arai Hakuseki (新井白石), one of the most famous Confucian scholars in Edo history, had serious attention to the large outflow of silver and copper to other countries. Concerned about the trade disorder at Nagasaki due to increasing smuggling activities, among other things, he suggested certain reforms to the shogunate. The shogunate accepted and amended his suggestions after consulting with the magistrates of Nagasaki, and issued a series of edicts in 1715 to regulate and scale down the trade both with the Chinese merchants and with the VOC. This was done in the 5th year of the Shōtoku (正徳) era, therefore the regulations of 1715 are generally called the *Shōtoku Shinrei* (正徳新例). These edicts were drawn up in 1714, and a mission from Edo brought them to Nagasaki and declared them effective at the beginning of the year 1715.

The regulations of 1715 are generally regarded by scholars as a landmark in the restriction of the Nagasaki trade (Nakamura 1989, p. 358). The regulations reduced the fixed amount of trade and the fixed amount of copper exports for both the Chinese and Dutch trade, and one of the most significant items in these regulations was the introduction of trade control based on the *shinpai* (Fig. 3.1).

3.4 Basic Issues concerning the Trade Control of the *Shinpai*

In 1715, the messengers of the shogunate forwarded these new regulations to the magistrates of Nagasaki. One of the regulations was a so-called Regulation of the Chinese that was to be announced to all Chinese in Nagasaki.[2] Another was an instruction about the *shinpai* that had to be forwarded to Chinese interpreters[3] (*tōtsūji*唐通事).[4] According to the latter regulation, there were eight items that had

[2] *Tsūjitomo Tōjin no Yakujō Sōan* (通事共唐人の約条草案) in the Nagasaki Museum of History and Culture (HMHC).

[3] Most of the Chinese interpreters were descendants of Han Chinese people who had lived on the southeast coast of Ming China and fled to Japan in order to avoid being involved in the civil wars in the early and middle seventeenth century, late Ming and early Qing times.

[4] *Tsūjitomo yori Tōjin e Aiwatasubeki Wappu no Jō* (通事共より唐人江可相渡割符之条) in NMHC.

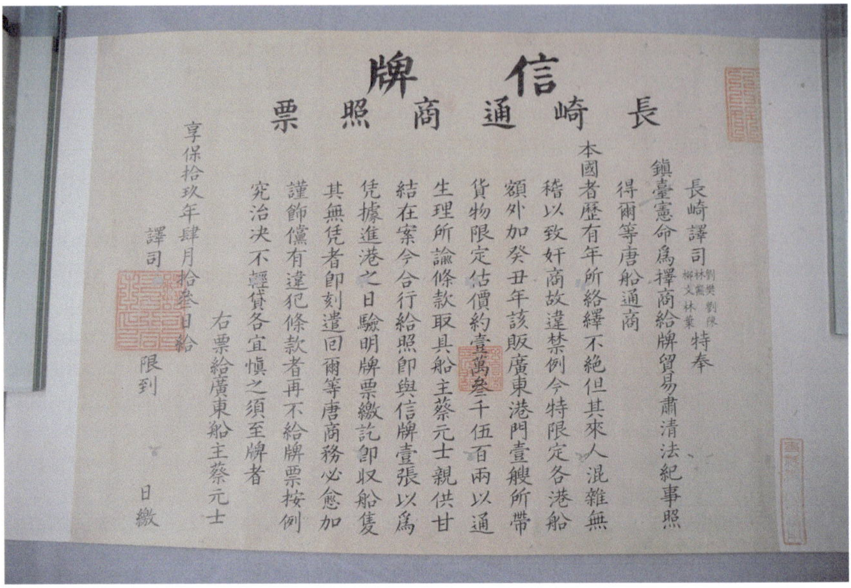

Fig. 3.1 *Shinpai* issued in 1734. Courtesy of Historiographical Institute, The University of Tokyo

to be registered on a *shinpai*: (1) year of arrival, (2) port of departure, (3) annual number of junks fixed according to the departure ports, (4) the total cargo amount of the junk, (5) name of the *shinpai* holder, (6) reason for requiring the *shinpai* to be returned after being used, (7) a summary of the regulations, and (8) the era and date of issue. Besides these, a red seal had to be affixed on the *shinpai*.[5]

Why were these items so significant for the shogunate? The regulations of 1715 fixed the number of junks that were allowed to trade at 30 annually and also fixed the total cargo of all these junks to 6,000 *kan* (貫 indicated by silver currency). In order to enssure the effectiveness of these regulations, it was necessary to fix the cargo amount of each junk. On the other hand, the size of the junks from China varied according to their departure ports. Junks coming from southeast Asia (*okubune* 奥船) were of a larger type, while those coming from southeast China (*nakaokubune* 中奥船) were middle size, and those coming from the Yangtze Delta (*kuchibune* 口船) were relatively small. Thus, it became necessary to fix the cargo amount for each junk according to the departure port and also to register this on the *shinpai*.

Next, why was it necessary to include "port of departure" and "annual number of the junks fixed according to their departure ports"? The reason is because the import

[5]*Wakan Kibun* 和漢寄文 (Mutual Translation Japanese to Chinese of Documents, WKKB) in Ōba (1986, p. 110). *Wakan Kibun* is a collection of formal documents including the applications submitted by Chinese merchants to the Nagasaki Magistrate's office and the ordinances of the Nagasaki Magistrate etc. It was compiled in approximately 1726 by Kanzan Matsumiya (松宮観山), who served at the Nagasaki Magistrate's office in the Kyōhō 享保 Era (1716–1735). The original source can be seen in NMHC.

of special local products from foreign ports to Japan was based on the quantity and categories of Japanese domestic needs.

As mentioned above, the principle of the system was that each Chinese merchant who agreed to follow the regulations of 1715 could receive a *shinpai*. Previously, there had been far more than just 30 junks arriving in Nagasaki every year, so not surprisingly the number of merchants who decided to agree to the new regulations was also over 30. Consequently, it became necessary to divide *shinpai* among the merchants according to the years of arrival. In April 1715, 47 Chinese merchants in Nagasaki agreed to this new system, and the magistrate's office provided 26 of them with *shinpai* for the year 1715, and 21 of them with *shinpai* for the following year.[6]

Since a *shinpai* was also a sort of certificate by the shogunate, items such as "name of the *shinpai* holder", "the era and date of issue", "summary of the regulations", as well as "the reason for requiring the *shinpai* be returned after being used" all had to be written on the *shinpai*.

From *Wakan Kibun* (和漢寄文),[7] it is known that Mukai Gensei (向井元成), a local Confucian official in Nagasaki, and Sakaki Soken (彭城素軒), a senior Chinese interpreter, were ordered to draft a sample of the *shinpai*.[8] The sample had to include all the items from (1) to (8) discussed above. In the opening sentence of the sample *shinpai*, one can also see where the names of several Chinese interpreters should be written.

This draft of the *shinpai* is the same in content as in the actual ones. Several original *shinpai* have been preserved in the Nagasaki Museum of History and Culture, as well as in the Historiographical Institute in The University of Tokyo. Nevertheless, there is a remarkable difference between the two; that is to say, one can see three seals affixed on the real *shinpai*, while those are missing in the draft. Although the characters in the seals are difficult to read, some hints can be found in *Shinpaikata Kiroku* (信牌方記録).[9] One of them was a type of half seal affixed on the upper left of the *shinpai*, while the other half was affixed on another paper document which would be stored in the magistrate's office as a counterfoil to the *shinpai* in order to check the *shinpai* after the junk had arrived (Figs. 3.2 and 3.3). The characters of this seal are *yong yi wei hao* (永以爲好), which means "be friendly forever". The second seal is put on "the total cargo amount of the junk" with the characters *jie xin yong yuan* (結信永遠), meaning "be creditable forever". The third one is put on the right-most side of the *shinpai*, engraved with *yisi huitong zhi yin* (譯司會同之印), meaning "the joint seal of these Chinese interpreters".

Many *shinpai* counterfoils were collected and bound as a book that was called *wappu tomechō* (割符留帳). Some counterfoil books can be seen at the Nagasaki Museum of History and Culture (NMHC), as referred to in Ōba's aforementioned

[6]*Shinpaikata Kiroku* (信牌方記録 Records of the Shinpai-Secretaries, SPKK) in NMHC, edited by Osamu Ōba and published in 1986.

[7]See Note 5.

[8]WKKB, p. 110.

[9]SPKK, p. 13.

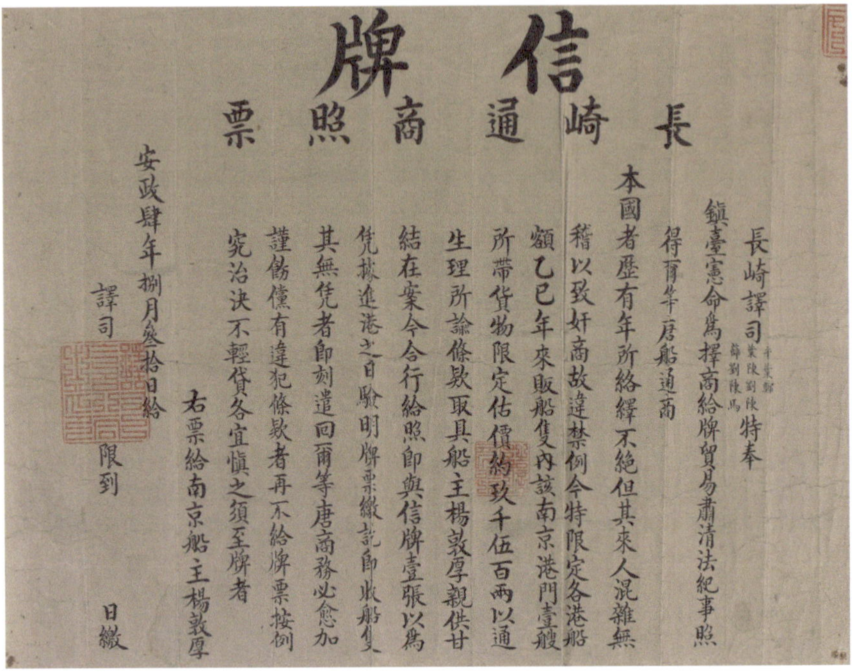
信牌

長崎通商照票

長崎譯司 特奉

鎮臺憲命爲擇商給牌貿易肅清法紀事照

得向年唐船通商

本國者歷有年所絡繹不絕但其來人混雜無

稽以致奸商故違禁例今特限定各港船

額乙巳年來販船隻內該南京港門壹艘

所帶貨物限定估價約玖千伍百兩以通

生理所諭條款取具船主楊敦厚親供甘

結在案今合行給照即與信牌壹張以爲

凭據進港之日驗明牌票繳訖即收船隻

其無凭者即刻遣回爾等唐商務必愈加

謹飭儻有違犯條欵者再不給牌票按例

究治決不輕貸各宜愼之須至牌者

右票給南京船主楊敦厚

安政肆年捌月叁拾日給

譯司 限到 日繳

Fig. 3.2 *Shinpai* issued in 1857. Courtesy of Nagasaki Museum of History and Culture

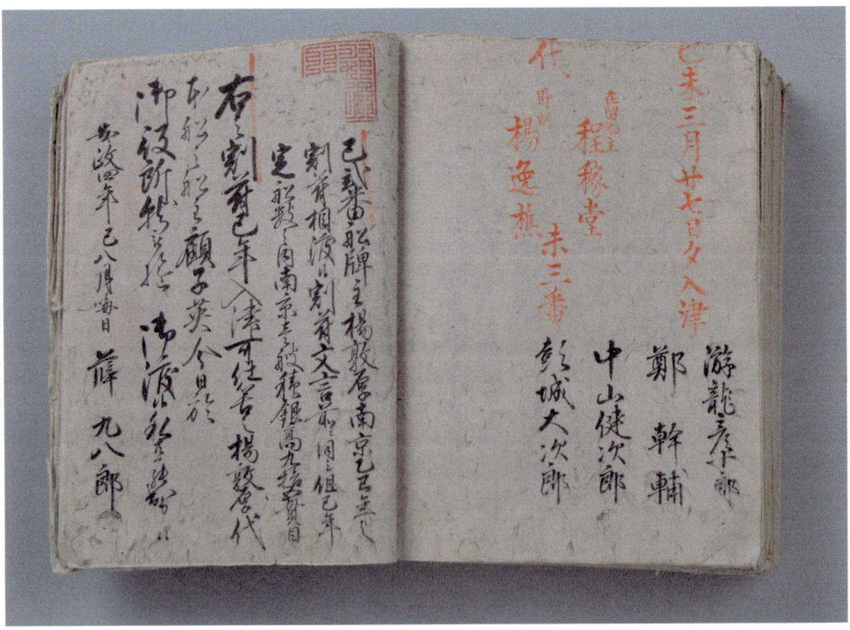

Fig. 3.3 *Shinpai* (Fig. 3.2) counterfoil bound in the *wappu tomechō*. Courtesy of Nagasaki Museum of History and Culture

illustration. In these counterfoil books, the following items are written in black: (1) name of the registered *shinpai* holder, (2) name of the receiver who went to Nagasaki in person and who actually received the *shinpai* from the magistrate's office, (3) a summary of the receiving of the *shinpai*, (4) names and seals of the Chinese interpreters who were present as witnesses at the formality of the receiving of the *shinpai*. What is most significant in the *shinpai* counterfoil book is the red half-seal that was used to check the validity of the *shinpai* when the junk had arrived.

3.5 The Tokugawa Response to the *Shinpai* Dispute

A dispute over whether to allow private Chinese merchants to receive and use the *shinpai* issued by the Tokugawa regime occurred among Qing authorities in 1715, just after the Tokugawa's *shinpai* policy went into effect in the same year (for details, see Chap. 4). The dispute lasted for almost 2 years, and 42 *shinpai* issued in the spring of that year were confiscated by the Qing authorities. This caused a survival crisis for the new system and became a challenge for the politicians of the shogunate as to whether they could maintain their newly introduced trading control system.

As seen in Fig. 3.4, 20 junks arrived in this year. However, 13 of them were not allowed to trade since they had no *shinpai*, and just 7 junks with *shinpai* were permitted to trade. Among these 7 junks, 4 departed from the ports in south China —Taiwan, Guangzhou, and Amoy—and because these ports were far from where

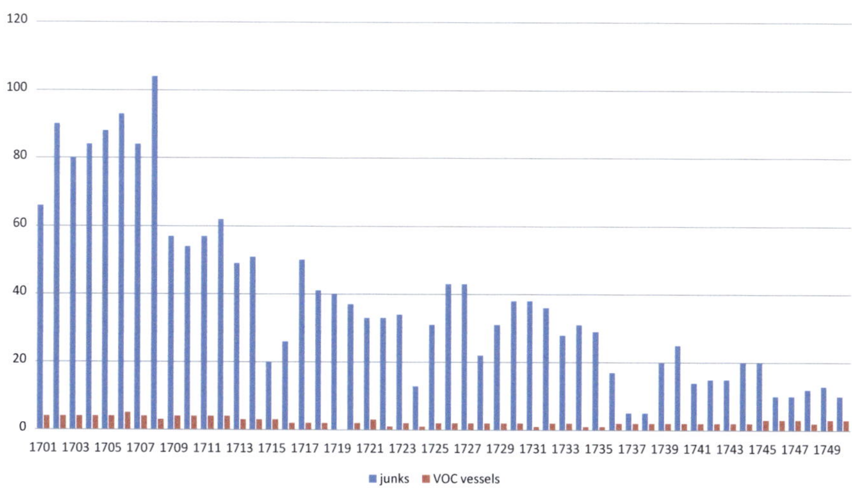

Fig. 3.4 Number of junks and VOC vessels arriving in Nagasaki 1701–1749. *Source* See Fig. 1.2. *Note* the dates are a little different to those in Fig. 1.2, because they include the number of the junks for which trade was refused. The years in the figure are those used in the old Japanese calendar

the incident occurred, Jiangsu and Zhejiang provinces, and on their return trips, they did not stay long in the ports of Zhejiang province such as Ningbo, they were fortunate not to be involved in the incident and kept the *shinpai* in their hands. After entering Nagasaki port, their transactions were completed and the *shinpai* were also renewed without hindrance. The three other junks were from ports in southeast Asia —Quang Nam, Siam, and Batavia (see Fig. 1.1)—and the captains had sailed to Nagasaki at regular intervals in previous years. Therefore their arrival in this year had been forecast by the Nagasaki officials. As previously planned, they also received the *shinpai* from the magistrate after the transactions.

In the following year, the number of trading junks was merely 7 and the others failed to trade for not having *shinpai*. Actually, most of them were merchants who received the *shinpai* in 1715 but could not bring them for having been involved in the "*shinpai* dispute." Under the direction of the Qing authorities, more than 10 junks without *shinpai* arrived in Nagasaki and asked the magistrate for permission to trade after explaining why they could not bring their *shinpai* back. However, the *shogunate* took a strict attitude and demanded that the magistrate firmly refuse their requests for trade. Consequently, those junks had to leave Nagasaki, and as mentioned in Chap. 5 in detail, it is highly possible that some of them chose to conduct smuggling in other coastal areas.

The influence of the "*shinpai* dispute" seemed to continue, and there were no indications that the Qing authorities would change their negative attitudes towards the Japanese *shinpai* policy and return to the merchants the *shinpai* that they had confiscated. However, the sharp drop in the number of trading junks and the trade amount caused several negative impacts on the Tokugawa economy. Firstly, the amount of imports was not able to meet the demands of the domestic market and accordingly there would be a high possibility that the prices of imports would soar and, furthermore, might affect the prices of other merchandise in the domestic market in a chain reaction; secondly, plenty of goods for export would be in stock for a long time, meaning a huge deficit not only for the Nagasaki Trading House but also for the shogunate. Hence, dealing with the annual number of the trading junks became a significant issue for the shogunate from the viewpoint of the stability of the domestic economy and the shogunate's finances.

Against this background, the shogunate determined to shift the annual number of junks from 30 to 40 as a temporary measure and to issue more regular *shinpai* to the Chinese merchants. In early 1717, the magistrate's office issued another 10 *shinpai* on which the arrival year was "Kyōhō 2" (1717). Except for the captains, there were many more than 10 merchants—all of the captains were *shinpai* holders—in the junks staying in Nagasaki at that time. The magistrate instructed the officials in charge of the Chinese Residence and the Chinese interpreters to deliver a list of names of the appropriate persons to receive the *shinpai*, and the selection criterion was referred to as "personality." In this case, the merchants with the evaluation of "good personality" can be considered as those exemplarily complying with the Japanese regulations or taking a relatively cooperative attitude towards the Tokugawa trading restrictions.

In the summer of this year, the information that the Qing authorities returned the *shinpai* to the former holders and allowed the merchants to use the *shinpai* for trade was transmitted to Nagasaki. Soon afterwards, the junks in possession of *shinpai* permitting the holders to come and trade in the year of 1715 or 1716 arrived in Nagasaki port one after another. By the end of the year, the number of trading junks was beyond the fixed number and had reached 43. The magistrate renewed those *shinpai* in accordance with the prescribed regulations. Moreover, as they did so one year earlier, nine merchants including some who were not in Nagasaki at that time received *shinpai*. Since they were regarded as men with "good personality", they were selected with the same criteria as before to be the receivers of the newly issued regular *shinpai*.

After adding these new *shinpai* and adjusting the arrival years written on the newly issued ones and the renewed ones after deliberate calculation, it became possible for the shogunate to ensure the fixed annual number of junks. As seen in Fig. 3.4, the numbers of arriving junks in 1718 and 1719 was at or very near 40, the fixed number, and cases in which junks appeared without *shinpai* also became rare. Following this achievement, the shogunate reset the annual number of junks from 40 back to 30. In other words, the shogunate had succeeded in overcoming the crisis of the *shinpai* system by utilizing the system's own unique mechanism.

3.6 The *Shinpai* Secretary and Related Work

As mentioned above, one of the drafters of the sample *shinpai* was Mukai Gensei. Before 1715, Gensei had been a professor (*saishu* 祭酒) at the Nagasaki Confucius Temple (*Nagasaki Seidō* 長崎聖堂),[10] while he had also been appointed as an inspector of imported books (*shomotsu aratameyaku* 書物改役)[11] by the shogunate. His work was to censor books imported by junks in order to prevent Christian books from being smuggled into Japan. The head of the Mukai family served as the inspector of imported books and also as a professor of the Nagasaki Confucius Temple for generations until the very last days of the Tokugawa period. Many sources about the *shinpai* can be seen in the archives of the Nagasaki Confucius Temple (*seidō-bunko* 聖堂文庫).[12]

From a memo on Gensei's application, it can be seen that in April 1715 Ōka Kiyosuke (大岡清相), the magistrate of Nagasaki (1711–1717), ordered Gensei to draw up *shinpai* according to the approved annual number of junks and the

[10]The Nagasaki Confucius Temple was founded in 1647 by Gensho Mukai 向井元升, a medic-Confucian scholar in Nagasaki, and it was used as a school to teach Confucianism and also to hold ceremonies for Confucianism. From 1680, the heads of the Mukai family were in charge of this temple for generations.

[11]About the duties of the heads of the Mukai family as inspectors of imported books, see Matsukata (2008).

[12]This set of archives is stored in the NMHC.

proportion of these junks based on their departure ports.[13] Two Chinese interpreters, Gotō Jirō (呉藤次郎) and Sakai Hachiemon (彭城八右衛門), were appointed as Gensei's assistants (*shinpai shokiyaku* 信牌書記役), while their duties as interpreters were terminated. Nonetheless, both of them were reappointed as interpreters two and three years later, respectively.[14] Magistrate Ōka ordered that Chinese interpreters should not interfere in work related to *shinpai*[15]; therefore, one can venture to say that the reappointment of the two Chinese interpreters signified the end of their duties as assistants to Gensei.

In the following year, the aforementioned "*shinpai* dispute" broke out. The number of junks arriving in Nagasaki decreased significantly, and many of them did not even hold *shinpai*. In this situation, Ishikawa Masasato (石河政郷), the new magistrate of Nagasaki (1715–1726), consulted with Gensei about the fixed number and proportion of junks, who became an advisor to the magistrate on *shinpai*-related issues. Gensei gradually came to be considered a *shinpai*-secretary (*shinpaikata* 信牌方) in charge of work connected with *shinpai*, although he in fact was not willing to undertake this hard, demanding job.[16]

The content of the *shinpai*-secretary's work can be seen in the same aforementioned source. Gensei in two of his application reports to the deputy administrator (*daikan* 代官) of Nagasaki in 1726 describes his works related to the *shinpai* in detail. He had to draw up drafts including "name of the *shinpai* holder", the "name of the departing port", and "year of arrival", and also had to affix a red seal onto the *shinpai*. Besides, he also had to deal with problems such as deciding the port from which a junk should depart, the year the junk should arrive in Nagasaki, readjusting the departure ports according to the approved maximum total trade amount, and the fixed annual number of junks when receiving the order from the magistrate to change the departure port of a junk, rearranging the years of arrival of the junks along with their departure ports in case of other temporary changes.

These tasks were so difficult to handle that Gensei did not want his young son to succeed to the position as the *shinpai*-secretary. However, his appeal was ultimately not accepted. The reason might have been that there was no other man better suited for the work. As is widely known, Edo Japan was a society with a hereditary system, and this case was not exceptional. The head of the Mukai clan had to be in charge of the work connected with the *shinpai* for generations, until trade control based on the *shinpai* was abolished in the 1850s.

---

[13]SPKK, p. 13. "Kōjō no Oboe" (口上之覚 A Memo on the Talks), in *Seidō Bunko* (SB) of NMHC, 660–732.

[14]*Yakushi Tofu* (訳司統譜 Genealogies of Interpreters), in *Nagasaki Kenshi: Shiryohen* 4, Tokyo: Yoshikawa Kobunkan, 1966, p. 677. *Yakushi Tofu* has been edited by Egawa Kunpei 潁川君平, a descendent of a Chinese interpreter, and published in 1897. This book shows us a genealogical tree of the Chinese interpreters at Nagasaki.

[15]"Kōjō o no Oboe". Ibid.

[16]Ibid., NMHC-SB, 660-732.

From another application report to the deputy administrator submitted in 1811 by Mukai Genchū (向井元仲), the family head at this time, it can be seen that the personnel organization of the so-called *shinpai*-secretariat, consisting of one chief secretary and two or three assistant secretaries barely changed thereafter, with one exception.[17] Namely, the assistant secretaries were no longer appointed from among the Chinese interpreters but from among the assistants of the inspector of imported books. The assistant secretaries had to undertake almost the same work as the chief secretary, as can be seen in a record of the way they worked.[18]

There were many issues that could not be completed without the decision of the magistrate of Nagasaki. For example, it was necessary for the *shinpai*-secretaries to keep close contact with the steward (*yonin* 用人) of the magistrate's family, who was ordered to convey information about the trade to the magistrate. In the archive of the Mukai family, one can find an order by the magistrate to the *shinpai*-secretaries from which the working connection between the *shinpai*-secretaries and the steward can be seen.[19] When a Chinese merchant decided to apply for a *shinpai* or intended to change certain items in it, the *shinpai*-secretaries had to inform the steward about the reason for the appeal. When a junk arrived, the *shinpai*-secretaries had to go to the magistrate's office to check the seal of the *shinpai*, and then they would submit a report to the steward. After checking the cargo of the junk, the *shinpai*-secretaries would inform the steward about whether the actual cargo amount was the same as the one registered on the *shinpai*.

In fact, there were many applications issued by Chinese merchants for changing the *shinpai* holder's name or the departure port. When such applications were approved by the magistrate, the *shinpai*-secretaries had to conduct the necessary rearrangements according to the previously approved proportion of junks based on the arrival year and their departure ports. However the *shinpai*-secretaries had no authority to make final decisions. Instead, they had to send an inquiry letter (*ukagaigaki* 伺書) to the magistrate concerning whether their arrangement proposal was appropriate. One can find such inquiry letters in the archives of the Mukai family.[20]

[17]"Negai Tatematsuru Kōjōsho" (奉願口上書, A Memo on the Oral Application), NMHC-SB 660-731.

[18]"Tsutomekatasho no Oboe" (勤方書之覚, Memos on the Work), NMHC-SB 370-418.

[19]An official memorandum without a title, NMHC-SB 660-729.

[20]"Shinpaiwari Ukagaigaki" 信牌割窺書 (Inquiry Letter for the Judgement of the Nagasaki Magistrate Regarding to the *Shinpai* Issuance), SB 660-733. "Genchū Nikki" 元仲日記 (Diaries of Genchū), in Yabuta Yutaka and Wakaki Taiichi (eds.) (2010) *Nagasaki Saishu Nikki* (長崎祭酒日記 Diaries of the priest of Nagasaki Confucius Temple). Osaka: Kansai University Press. This book collects the dairies of the Mukai family stored in *Seidō Bunko*.

3.7 Procedures of Issuing, Checking, and Renewing *Shinpai*

Based on the records of the magistrate's office in Nagasaki,[21] when receiving the information of a junk's arrival, the magistrate would dispatch the Chinese interpreters to the harbor. They would ask the captain of the junk about their departure port and also about whether they were holding a *shinpai*. Thereafter, the magistrate would dispatch inspectors (*kenshi* 検使) to take the *shinpai* back, and then would inform the *shinpai*-secretaries to come to the magistrate's office to check the *shinpai*. After looking it over, the magistrate would order his steward to hand the *shinpai* to the *shinpai*-secretaries, who then would check the *shinpai* again in the counterfoil book.

When the date of a departing junk was decided, the *shinpai*-secretaries generally would present an inquiry letter to the magistrate about the draft of the *shinpai* for that junk. After receiving the permission of the magistrate, they would draw up a real *shinpai*. One day before departure, they presented these *shinpai* based on the number of departing junks to the magistrate's office. On the departure day, the Chinese merchants would be summoned to the magistrate's office. The Chinese interpreters would read the names of the merchants in the presence of the magistrate, answer the questions by the magistrate, and pronounce that these merchants could receive the *shinpai* because the trade had been completed smoothly and that they should obey the laws of Japan. Thereupon the *shinpai*-secretaries would take over the *shinpai* from the magistrate office and affix the seals so that they overlapped the *shinpai* and the counterfoils. Then the steward of the magistrate would receive the *shinpai* and forward them to the merchants. The merchants then read the received *shinpai* and promised they would obey their terms. Finally, the Chinese interpreters affixed their seals on the counterfoils, and these *shinpai* counterfoils would then be bound as a book.

Given the above-described issuance process, it is reasonable to see the *shinpai* as official documents with the authorization of the Tokugawa regime. In fact, however, even though the primary plan was an attempt to issue a sort of official certificate (*kugen* 公験) to Chinese merchants, the shogunate finally decided to treat them merely as private documents (*shiken* 私験)—the Chinese interpreters issued them to the Chinese merchants as certificates demonstrating these merchants had promised to obey the Japanese regulations. This attitude change was mainly based on the suggestion of the magistrate Ōka Kiyosuke. Ōka insisted that the dignity of

[21]Nagasaki Prefectural Nagasaki Library (ed.) (2005) *Bunrui Zassai: Nagasaki Bugyosho* 分類雑載:長崎奉行所 (Compilation of Various Documents related the Nagasaki Magistrate Office). Nagasaki: Nagasaki Prefectural Nagasaki Library. pp. 129–171. *Bunrui Zassai* is one of the most important municipal documents that has been preserved in the Nagasaki magistrate's office and was a kind of companion of the city's official *nengyōji* (年行事). From its contents, it can be assumed that these materials were edited as a book after 1828, but there is no obvious information about the time and author of the compilation.

the shogunate might be compromised in the case that those Chinese merchants did not comply with the *shinpai*-related regulations (Kikuchi 1964; Ōta 1992, Chaps. 8 and 9). Moreover, there might have been another reason, that is, the shogunate leaders had considered that by treating the *shinpai* as a private certificate it might soften the possible resistance of the Qing authorities to the related policies. At any rate, regardless of what the shogunate declared primarily, in practice it was not these Chinese interpreters but the magistrate as the representative of the shogunate who had the responsibility to issue the *shinpai* to the Chinese merchants. The purpose was to help these trade regulations and restrictions to be put into effect smoothly.

Chapter 4
Qing China's Response to the *Shinpai* Trading Permit System in the Eighteenth Century

4.1 Copper Administration in the Middle Years of the Qing Dynasty

After the establishment of the Tokugawa *shinpai* system, discussed in the preceding chapter, the Qing empire had to face the problem of how to respond to it. Based mainly on previous studies , this section will first give a brief outline of the copper supply system in China, which in the Qing dynasty was called the Copper Administration (*tongzheng* 銅政).

Copper coin was one of the most significant currencies in the Qing Chinese monetary system and was used for various purposes, such as (1) to exchange merchandise that would meet the daily needs of common people, (2) to pay the salaries of soldiers, and (3) to pay for the construction expenses of the imperial administration, among other users. Therefore it was crucial for the Qing authorities to cast enough copper coins to meet these needs.

There were numerous coinage services in the Qing empire, all controlled in principle by the central or local administrations. One can distinguish two types: central services and provincial services. Needless to say, copper was the main source for copper coins. In the Qing dynasty, copper used for coinage was mainly supplied from Yunnan province and Japan. In the middle of the Qing dynasty, especially before the Qianlong Era (1735–1796), Japanese copper had been considered superior to that from Yunnan due to its better refinement and a more convenient transport system. This is why Qing authorities attempted to import ample amounts of Japanese copper every year.

The Japanese copper import system changed several times. At the beginning, local custom houses (*shuiguan* 税関) were ordered to purchase and supply copper to coinage services. Later, wealthy merchants belonging to the Imperial Household Department (*neiwufu* 内務府) became engaged in copper supply too. Since the copper supply was not sufficient to meet the needs of coinage services, Qing authorities decided to reform the system in 1716. They set a total annual amount for

H. Peng, *Trade Relations between Qing China and Tokugawa Japan*,
Studies in Economic History, https://doi.org/10.1007/978-981-13-7685-6_4

copper import and distributed this amount to eight provinces (Jiangsu, Anhui, Jiangxi, Zhejiang, Fujian, Guangdong, Hunan, and Hubei), divided equally, and ordered these provinces to take responsibility for importing Japanese copper and completing the fixed supply quota. Each of the local administration in these provinces appointed one local official to take charge of the import of copper for a certain period of time, and after the official's term expired they could assign another person to the job. This official would withdraw silver currencies from the provincial depository as funds to pay for the importation of copper and go to Suzhou (蘇州), the city where most of the merchants engaged in the Nagasaki trade usually lived, and recruit merchants there who wished to take on the work. After their return from Nagasaki, the official checked the quality and quantity of the imported copper and supplied it to the central coinage services. Until 1737, there had been some changes

Fig. 4.1 Provinces of the Qing Empire

in terms of which provinces and how many provinces should share responsibility for copper imports, but the basics of this provincial quota system did not change (Fig. 4.1).

4.2 The Dispute Over the Adoption of Japanese Trading Passes (1715–1717)

As mentioned in Chap. 3, the "*shinpai* dispute" broke out in China immediately after the Tokugawa shogunate launced the trading control policy based on the *shinpai*.

In April 1715, 47 merchants, who were also the captains of junks staying inNagasaki at the time, agreed to obey the regulations of 1715 and received *shinpai* from the magistrate of Nagasaki. At the same time, however, six merchants who were also captains of their junks could not receive such *shinpai* and consequently lost their qualification for trading. Thus, Chinese merchants who were engaged in trading at Nagasaki fell into two groups: those who could obtain such *shinpai* (the so-called *shinpai* holders) and those who could not (those who were rejected). This separation soon led to the "*shinpai* dispute."

From April to August of the same year, these merchants returned to China one after the other. Zhuang Yuansu (荘元枢) and some other rejected merchants brought a charge to the local administration office against those who had received such *shinpai*, which they preferred to call the "Japanese passes" (*wozhao* 倭照), for their betrayal and monopolization of the trade at Nagasaki. It must be noted that according to an ancient view held in China, using the calendar of another country (*zhengsuo*正朔) meant "wishing to follow the reign of that country"—at least in principle. Since the name of the Japanese era was registered on the *shinpai*, accepting such a "Japanese pass" was considered accepting the rule of the Japanese regime. Secondly, they were also obviously afraid that the trade with Nagasaki would be monopolized by a handful of merchants who had close relations with the Tokugawa regime, since only those who had received such trading passes from the shogunate were qualified to trade at Nagasaki according to Japanese regulations. The Qing authorities ordered the Maritime Customs House (*haiguan* 海關) of Zhejiang province to confiscate the *shinpai* held by Hu Yunke (胡雲客) and the other 42 merchants staying in Suzhou at the time.

This news was immediately conveyed to Nagasaki by the next junk arriving from China. At that time, only seven junks were staying in Nagasaki. The merchants who heard of this news first organized a boycott against receiving the *shinpai*. However, Guo Hengtong (郭亨統), who was born in Guangdong and was the captain of a junk coming from Quang Nam,[1] agreed to trade according to the

[1] *Quang Nan* (廣南), which was pronounced as *kōnan* in Japan, *guangnan* in Chinese, referred to the southern part of Vietnam.

shogunate's regulation including the control of trade based on the *shinpai*. Worried that the trade in Nagasaki would be monopolized by Guo himself, the other merchants gave up their boycott and decided to accept the *shinpai* one after the other, while Guo was praised as a hero by the shogunate for his contribution to maintaining the system (Ōba 1984, pp. 461–463).[2]

On the other hand, the shogunate not only refused to permit trading with merchants who did not have a *shinpai*, but also with those who had previously received such *shinpai* but those *shinpai* had been confiscated by the Qing authorities. Nonetheless, the shogunate emphasized that a *shinpai* was only a certification for checking the junks, and that its holder could be transferred to another person on the grounds that the new *shinpai* holder would agree to bring the special products of the designated departure port in the same quantity as was fixed on the *shinpai*. In other words, it was coded within the *shinpai* system that it could not be monopolized by a handful of merchants.

Back on the Chinese side, Qing officials also fell into two groups. Some insisted that Chinese merchants should not accept the *shinpai* from Japan, while others decided that the ruling authorities should not feel concerned about whether Chinese merchants would receive such passes or not. The debates lasted for about two years, until finally the decision of the Kangxi emperor put an end to the dispute by allowing Chinese merchants to receive *shinpai*. As a result, those *shinpai* that had been confiscated by the Qing authorities were returned to the merchants who had held them previously.

4.3 The Utilization of the *Shinpai* in the Later Years (1717–1722) of the Kangxi Era

The Emperor Kangxi's positive decision can be seen in an imperial edict,[3] as Matsuura has pointed out (Matsuura 1988). Meanwhile, Iwa'i has given attention to the abstract of the report by Xu Yuanmeng (徐元夢), the provincial governor (*xunfu*, 巡撫) of Zhejiang province, which was cited in the edict (Iwa'i 2007). This report shows Xu's proposal regarding how to treat the trading passes. The following translation helps to understand the Qing's countermeasures against the *shinpai* system to be discussed below.

[2]As mentioned in Ōba's article, Guo and his family were engaged in the trade at Nagasaki for a long time. In addition, Guo also accepted orders from the shogunate to import horses from China secretly, and was given three *shinpai* as a reward.

[3]*Shinpaikata Kiroku* (see Chap. 3 Note 6) pp. 25–26. A similar source can be seen in the *Kangxi Qijuzhu* (康熙起居注)Vol. 3, Beijing: Zhonghua Book Company, p. 2373. In the Qing dynasty, the *Qijuzhu* official 起居注官 had the duty of recording the sayings and activities of the emperor's daily life. These records are called *Qijuzhu*. One can also see some information about the political affairs in the imperial court in the Kangxi Era besides the records of the Emperor Kangxi's daily life.

> Considering the approved number of junks and the approved number of cargos by the Japanese, why not order the merchants to conduct the trade based on the regulations of the Japanese? There is only one problem: those who hold the "trading pass" (*shinpai*) can go back and forth frequently, but the goods of those who do not hold a "trading pass" cannot be sold. Should they not be treated equally, as they all pay duties to the imperial administration? The authorities ought to order the chief official of the Maritime Customs House to summon and assemble the merchants, and inform them clearly that the "trading passes" should be utilized flexibly. For example, several merchants may load their goods in the same ship, or several merchants may utilize one pass in turns. The authorities ought to order Hu Yunke, Zhuang Yuansu and some other merchants to consult with each other about the modes of using the "trading passes" in good faith.

In the report, Xu suggested that merchants who intended to participate in the trade at Nagasaki and to pay duties to the Qing authorities should be treated fairly. He submitted a proposal draft saying that there were two methods to avoid confrontation between those who held such Japanese trading passes and those who did not. One was that several merchants should load one junk with their goods on an equal basis and should use one trading pass to trade at Nagasaki. The other method was that Chinese merchants should go to Nagasaki and take turns to trade there using one pass. According to Xu, it should be left to the decision of the merchants in the two groups which of these methods should be adopted.

From the last part of the imperial edict, it can be seen that the Emperor Kangxi accepted Xu's proposal after having discussed it with the Grand Secretariat (*neige* 内閣). As a result, the Chinese merchants came to cooperate with each other by leasing or transferring their *shinpai* under the guidance of the Qing authorities (Ōba 1984, p. 458). In fact, the actual use of these *shinpai* was not always done in the way proposed by Xu. Yet this measure, which could be called the open-use policy of the *shinpai*, made it possible for more merchants—also including those who could not receive a *shinpai* from Japan directly—to participate in the trade at Nagasaki.

4.4 The Common Utilization of the *Shinpai* in the Yongzheng Era (1722–1735)

As mentioned above, certain provinces designated by the Qing empire were ordered to import Japanese copper. The governors-general (*zongdu*, 總督) as well as the provincial governors of these provinces were in charge of giving reports to the central authorities about the state of the copper imports. Some of these reports include significant information for understanding how these provincial administrations took advantage of the trading pass system to import Japanese copper.

In the 1730 report by Yin Jishan (尹継善), the provincial governor of Jiangsu province, it can be seen that certain local officials who were ordered by the provincial administration to take charge of the copper import had to go to Suzhou in person, where the merchants engaged in the import of copper usually stayed.

They then recruited merchants to import copper from Japan for the Qing authorities.[4]

How did these officials in charge of the copper import take advantage of the trading pass system? On the one hand, they made contracts concerning the copper supply with merchants who were holding *shinpai*. However, there was another way that can be seen in the 1732 report by Hao Yulin (郝玉麟), the governor-general of Fujian province, and Zhao Guolin (趙国麟), the provincial governor of Fujian province:[5]

> As usual, the circuit intendants (道) or prefectural magistrate (知府) are dispatched to Suzhou to purchase the copper imported from Japan in advance, then supply this copper to Beijing. For such occasions, they purchase the trading passes first, then select the merchants and pay them the funds, and after that hasten them to stock the goods and to depart from the port.

In the report, Hao and Zhao suggested that the officials in charge of the copper supply should first purchase *shinpai* and then select the merchants. Previous studies made clear that the *shinpai* became a kind of good that could be exchanged in the market for a certain price (Saeki 1986a, Matsuura 2000). Thus there seems to have been two ways that the Qing authorities used the *shinpai*. One was to directly employ merchants who were holding such *shinpai*, and the other was first to purchase such *shinpai* from their holders and then to select other merchants who would then use them for the trade at Nagasaki.

4.5 The Appearance of Official Trading Passes

After hearing the news of the "*shinpai* dispute", the Tokugawa shogunate ordered an increase in the approved annual number of junks to 40 and also increased the approved annual total amount of trade with the junks to 8000 *kan* (貫) in order to solve the problem caused by overstocking of export goods after the number of junks decreased during the "*shinpai* dispute." After the stabilization of the trade order, however, the shogunate in 1719 ordered a decrease in the permitted number of junks back down to 30, as was fixed in the regulations of 1715. Therefore Chinese merchants could not import sufficient copper that could have met the quota demanded by the Chinese officials. Consequently, these officials could not meet the quota demanded by the central authorities either. This led to the loss of

[4] "Yin Jishan's Report on the 3rd day of the sixth month, Yongzheng 8 (July 17, 1730)" in *Yongzhengchao Hanwen Zhupizouzhe Huibian* (雍正朝漢文硃批奏摺彙編 complete collection of the Chinese memorials with the emperor's comments of the Yongzheng period, YZCHW) Vol.18, Nanjing: Jiangsu Ancient Publishing House, 1989–1991, pp. 830–831.

[5] "Hao Yulin's Report on the 21st day of the tenth month, Yongzheng 10 (December 8, 1732)", YZCHW, Vol. 22, p. 482.

government funds, because the provincial administrations used tax revenues to pay those merchants for the copper imports in advance.

Regarding the delay of the copper imports as a serious problem, the Emperor Yongzheng (雍正) ordered an increase in the supply of copper mined and processed in Yunnan, and also a decrease in the amount of imported Japanese copper. The emperor also instructed the governors-general and provincial governors to investigate the responsibilities of the officials who were in charge of copper imports but could not meet the demanded quota. Subsequently, Zhao Guangmo (趙光謨), the former vice prefectural magistrate (*tongzhi* 同知) of Suzhou-fu, and Cai Yongqing (蔡永清), the former prefectural magistrate (*zhifu* 知府) of Suzhou-fu, among others, were punished and ordered to compensate for the authorities' loss.

In November of 1727, Chen Shixia (陳時夏), the provincial governor of Jiangsu province, presented a report to the emperor about the investigation as well as a proposal concerning the so-called Zhao case.[6] In the report, Chen said that he summoned the merchants involved in the case and examined them severely. These merchants explained that they had a large stock of export goods in return for the copper in Japan, and agreed to Chen that they would use these goods to import copper from Japan and pay for the authorities' loss within a year. Chen forced these merchants to draw up account books showing their mortgaged properties. Interestingly, the *shinpai* that these merchants were holding were also confiscated by the government as a part of their private property. In the following year, these *shinpai* registered in the account books of mortgaged properties became so-called official trading passes (*guanzhao* 官照). To Chen's proposal, the Emperor Yongzheng made just one simple comment: "this way is appropriate."[7]

4.6 The Utilization of Official Trading Passes

As can be seen from the report by Zhang Tanlin (張坦麟), the former acting governor of Jiangsu province, these merchants had supplied only about 300,000 *kin* (斤) of copper to the Qing authorities by the following August, being 2700,000 *kin* of copper in arrears.[8] Yin Jishan, the new governor of Jiangsu province, described the failure of Chen's proposal to the emperor in the following way:[9]

> In 1727, Chen Shixia, the former provincial governor of Jiangsu province, presented a report to the authorities, and in that report he suggested investigating the responsibilities

[6]"Chen Shixia's Report on the 25th day of the ninth month, Yongzheng 5 (November 8, 1727)", YZCHW Vol.10, pp. 720–721.

[7]Ibid., p. 720.

[8]"Zhang Tanlin's Report on the 3rd day of the seventh month, Yongzheng 6 (August 8, 1728)", YZCHW Vol.12, p. 819.

[9]"Yin Jishan's Report on the 9th day of the eleventh month, Yongzheng 6 (Deccember 9, 1728)", YZCHW Vol.13, p. 887.

> and the debts of the merchants involved in the Zhao Guangmo case, and extending the term of debt repayment for one year. The so-called investigation, however, has not been put into practice, and he allowed the merchants to declare the amount of properties owned by themselves at more than the actual amount. Chen has not confiscated all the properties declared by those merchants as hypothecated goods. He just stocked the trading passes confiscated from those merchants in the official treasury and has not taken measures for utilizing them. Many merchants are carrying their goods to remote places and conducting trade secretly. Although the deadline for debt repayment is due this year, the amount repaid by those merchants has not reached one-tenth of the approved amount of the repayment.

In this section it can be seen that the passes that Chen confiscated from the merchants were simply stored in the official treasury without at all being utilized, while, on the other hand, the merchants could not fulfill their duties on time. In the next part of the report, Yin made the following proposal:

> I think it was expected that the duties would be fulfilled if the deadline of the repayment was extended. However, the fact is that the longer the deadline is extended, the longer the term for repayment becomes. There seems to be no end to the debt problem without a modification. Now I am estimating precisely and investigating thoroughly the properties and debts of those merchants one by one, and planning to arrest the merchants escaping to far places and to confiscate all the goods being sold secretly. There is also a problem relating to the utilization of the passes stocked in the treasury. According to the regulations of the Japanese, the pass could not be renewed in case it were one year later [than the term of validity], and would become useless if further delayed. Now I am trying to recruit some merchants and to lease or sell the passes to them, while interrogating them as to whether they have hidden properties, and to uncover them as payment.

As seen in this part of Yin's report, Yin was quite aware of that the *shinpai* had a term for utilization, and he wished to continue importing Japanese copper by leasing or selling these *shinpai* to new merchants. To this plan, the Emperor Yongzheng commented that Yin would get a mandate after he presented a detailed report to the Grand Secretariat. Regrettably, neither the continued report by Yin nor the emperor's mandate has so far been found.

Nevertheless, the way in which the Qing authorities used the "official passes" can be seen in the 1738 report by the Ministry of Revenue (*hubu* 戸部) to the Grand Secretariat.[10] In this report it was suggested that the passes that had been confiscated by the Qing authorities from merchants who were involved in the Zhao Guangmo and Cai Yongqing cases should first be sold off, and if no one was willing to buy them, then they should be leased to merchants who wished to participate in the trade at Nagasaki and would agree to provide the Qing authorities with Japanese copper as a lease fee. Yin's proposal to use "official passes" was ultimately adopted by Qing authorities, and the Qing authorities were instructed to sell or lease "official passes" to other merchants and receive copper as the lease fee in return.[11]

---

[10]"The Report of the Ministry of Revenue on the 6th day of the twelfth month, Qianlong 3 (January15, 1739)", First Historical Archives of China (FHAC): 02-01-04-13050-010.

[11]"Chen Dashou's Report Without Date", FHAC: 02-01-04-14541-001.

4.7 The Reform Plans regarding the Copper Imports in the Early Qianlong Era

In 1732, locusts caused great damage in western Japan, and like other regions, Nagasaki also suffered from a serious famine. Ōmori Tokinaga (大森時長), the magistrate of Nagasaki, without the permission of the shogunate, diverted funds that were stipulated to purchase copper for export from the refineries in Osaka to buy rice to ease the famine (Suzuki 2007, pp. 106–107). Consequently, copper could not have been carried from Osaka to Nagasaki on time, and junks had to wait for the copper beyond the designated term of staying there. As a countermeasure, the shogunate ordered a decrease in the number of junks. Additionally, in this period, the output of copper in Japan was declining year by year to the extent that the shogunate came to take a negative attitude towards copper exports.

In this situation, the Qing authorities had to reform the system of copper imports. At first, two reform plans were presented. The first one, submitted in May 1735 by Lu Zuo (盧焯), the provincial governor of Fujian province, was to stop dispatching local officials to Suzhou and, instead, appoint a full-time official there to take charge of the Japanese copper imports.[12] One and a half months later, Li Wei (李衛), the governor-general of Zhili province, presented another plan suggesting that the chief of the Maritime Customs House be ordered to take charge of the Japanese copper imports.[13] The reason for this was that the official of the Maritime Customs House was familiar with the merchants engaged in overseas trade as well as the *shinpai*. To these plans, however, the emperor did not give a clear reply.

In the same year, 1735t, the Emperor Yongzheng died and thereupon his son succeeded to the imperial throne, becoming the Emperor Qianlong. In April of the following year, Gu Cong (顧琮), the provincial governor of Jiangsu province, presented a new reform plan, which can be seen as a middle path between the plans by Lu and Li.[14] It suggested appointing a full-time official at the Maritime Customs House to take charge of the Japanese copper imports. According to the report by Zhang Qu (張渠), the provincial administration commissioner (*buzhengshi* 佈政使) of Jiangsu province, Gu's plan was adopted by the central authorities.[15]

This reform project also had an effect on the utilization of the Japanese *shinpai*. In November, Ji Zengyun (嵇曾筠), the governor-general of Zhejiang province, and Shao Ji (邵基), the provincial governor of Jiangsu province, submitted a report with

[12]"Lu Zuo's Report on the 20th day of the leap fourth month, Yongzheng 13 (June 10, 1735)", YZCHW, Vol.28, p. 271.

[13]"Li Wei's Report on 4th day of the sixth month, Yongzheng 13 (July 23, 1735)", YZCHW, Vol. 28, p. 522.

[14]"Gu Cong's Report on the 25th day of the second month, Qianlong 1 (April 5, 1736)", FHAC: 04-01-35-1226-030.

[15]"Zhang Qu's Report on the 24th day of the fifth month, Qianlong 1 (July 2, 1736)", FHAC: 04-01-35-1227-001.

their joint signature to the emperor, suggesting a reform of copper imports.[16] Their report contains a paragraph related to the utilization of the trading passes, which can be summarized in the following four points: (1) all the trading passes, both official and private, should be stored in the financial warehouses of Zhejiang and Jiangsu provinces and handled by local officials; (2) the local administrations should lease these trading passes to rich merchants for a rental fee; (3) the profits from the leasing of these passes should be shared between the authorities and private pass holders; (4) the use of temporary trading passes should be banned.

As seen in this source, the "Japanese trading passes" in China were actually divided into official and private ones. The official ones were those stored and owned by the authorities, as mentioned above. The private ones were undoubtedly those that were held by private merchants who had previously received them from Nagasaki or bought them from other merchants. The plan by Ji and Shao suggested that all these "trading passes" should be managed by the Qing authorities without changing their ownership.

There are two points here that need further explanation. One is the question of why it was a matter of concern for Chinese officials whether the chosen merchants were rich. The reason for this is that poor merchants were considered to have no capacity to pay for the authorities' losses in case they could not fulfill the demanded quota for the copper import. The other question pertains to the temporary *shinpai*. The temporary *shinpai* differed from regular ones in two ways. Firstly, a temporary *shinpai* could be used only once in principle, while the regular one could be renewed at Nagasaki. Ōba illustrates that the shogunate issued temporary *shinpai* to merchants who promised to invite technical experts or to bring rare animals to Japan (Ōba 1984, p. 464). Secondly, the permitted amount of copper for purchase was also different. As seen in the report by Ji and Shao, the holders of such temporary *shinpai* could be permitted by the Tokugawa shogunate to import 10,000 *kin* (斤) or 20,000 *kin* copper from Japan. On the other hand, a regular *shinpai* generally referred to the amount of about 76,000 *kin* copper.

In the report by Nasutu (那蘇図) in 1739, the governor-general of Liangjiang,[17] there is also an official letter (*ziwen* 咨文) by Ji to the Ministry of Revenue.[18] As seen in this source, Ji suggested that the "trading passes" should be leased at the rate of "one official and three private", according to the actual possession rate of the "trading passes."[19] However, this plan was never put into practice. In 1738, Yin Jishan, who was promoted to the governor-general of Yungui,[20] proposed that all the copper used in central coinage services should be shifted to Yunnan copper

[16]"The Report by Ji Zengyun and Shao Ji on the 13th day of the tenth month, Qianlong 1 (November 15, 1736)", FHAC: 04-01-35-1227-005.

[17]両江, a district made up of three provinces: Jiangsu, Anhui, and Jiangxi.

[18]"Nasutu's Report on the 17th day of the thrid month, Qianlong 4 (April 24, 1739)", FHAC: 02-01-04-13202-013.

[19]There were 83 *shinpai* in the possession of merchants and 27 stored in the financial warehouse.

[20]雲貴, a district made up of two provinces: Yunnan and Guizhou.

from that year, because the output of Yunnan copper had been greatly increasing. The proposal was accepted by the central authorities.[21] Meanwhile, the Qing authorities declared that Chinese merchants could import copper from Japan freely from that year, and the plan by Ji and Shao was thus abandoned.

4.8 The Utilization of Official Trading Passes by the Official Merchants

Since 1738, the supply of raw copper for central coinage services had begun to shift to Yunnan copper, while Japanese copper seemed to have become less significant for the Qing authorities than before. Nonetheless, Japanese copper continued to be imported for the use of provincial coinage services. In this year, 1738, the Qing authorities appointed an official merchant called Fan Yubin (范毓馪), who belonged to the Imperial Household Department, to participate in the Nagasaki trade. Fan seldom personally went to Nagasaki but just dispatched subordinate merchants there. The merchants group, run by the official merchant Fan, was called the Official Bureau (*guanju* 官局). Some years later, a trade organization of private merchants called "the Twelve Families" (*shierjia* 十二家) was established with the permission of the Qing authorities. It monopolized the trade with Japan until the late 1850s, except for the commerce conducted by the Official Bureau (see Chap. 6).

The participation of official merchants had an effect on the utilization of the "trading passes". In an official letter by Kong Chuanhuan (孔傳煥) to Nasutu, the acting provincial administration commissioner of Jiangsu province, and Zhang Ruozhen (張若震), the provincial administration commissioner of Zhejiang province,[22] Kong and Zhang proposed a plan for how to meet the demands of the Official Bureau. Their plan was that the authorities should lease the official trading passes to the merchants in the Official Bureau first, and then to permit these merchants to lease private trading passes. Why was it considered necessary that official trading passes should be leased first? Firstly, it was because the rate of "one official and three private" came to be considered unnecessary after the abandonment of the Ji–Shao plan; secondly, because most of the private merchants were already holding trading passes, thus they did not need to lease official trading passes any longer; and thirdly, because official trading passes would become useless if they were not leased during the designated time written on the pass. This being the case, why was it considered necessary for the Qing authorities to permit official merchants to lease passes from private merchants? It was because official trading passes might not have been sufficient for meeting the needs of official merchants.

[21] "The Report of the Ministry of Revenue on the 6th day of the twelfth month, Qianlong 3". See note 10.

[22] "Nasutu's Report on the 17th day of the third month, Qianlong 4". See note 18.

This proposal was presented to the Ministry of Revenue by Nasutu. Unfortunately, the result of the ministry's decision is unknown. Nevertheless, the statement about the utilization of official trading passes can be seen in the report of the Suzhou office, which had been cited in the report by Chen Dashou (陳大受), the governor of Jiangsu province.[23] As seen in this report, Fan Qingzhu (范清注), the son of Fan Yubin, went to Suzhou in 1739 and leased five official trading passes. The merchants in the Official Bureau went to Nagasaki with these *shinpai* and their trade was allowed by the office of Nagasaki magistrate, while the *shinpai* were also renewed without hindrance. After these merchants returned, they handed the new *shinpai* to the Qing authorities. From this report it becomes clear that the official trading passes were first leased by official merchants and then renewed in Nagasaki. However, owing to the lack of related sources it is unknown whether or not this way of using *shinpai* was later changed.

4.9 The Upgraded System and Its Role in Stabilizing the Trade Order

The so-called Great Navigation Age, from the fifteenth century to the first half of the seventeenth century, may be regarded as the first wave of globalization. The advance of Western powers into East Asia caused great impacts on the countries in this area, and sooner or later they adopted similar counter-policies, which can be called Maritime Prohibitions, as Arano Yasunori (荒野泰典) has pointed out (Arano 1988). One of the most critical aspects of these Maritime Prohibitions refers to the systems of controlling overseas trade. In Japan, the shogunate in 1715 issued a list of regulations and introduced the trading control system based on the *shinpai* for the trade at Nagasaki. The *shinpai* system can be seen as the most significant means by which the shogunate controlled the trade with Chinese junks in early modern times.

As mentioned in the introduction of Chap. 3, scholars have previously focused on the *shinpai* by analyzing the contexts of the regulations of 1715, and have studied the reasons and processes of the so-called *shinpai* dispute. Based on these previous research studies, Chap. 3 described briefly the historical background and process by which the shogunate established such a *shinpai* system. Besides attempting to offer some fresh insights by drawing upon rarely used Japanese and Chinese sources, the study has clarified that the *shinpai* was not just a kind of certificate to be used to check a junk's "legitimacy" for trade, but also a useful method to control the number of junks and the quantity of their cargos. This chapter has then examined the countermeasures undertaken by the Qing authorities to utilize the *shinpai*, which they preferred to call "Japanese trading passes."

[23]"Chen Dashou's Report, undated". See note 11.

Although there was no official relationship, even no direct route of communication between the Qing court and the Tokugawa shogunate, the trade at Nagasaki with Chinese junks was regarded as legitimate by both sides, benefited both administrations, and was maintained until the middle of the nineteenth century. The *shinpai* system was one of the trade restrictions unilaterally introduced by the shogunate in the early eighteenth century. However, there was a flexible rule in this system, that is, a *shinpai* could be used by anyone regardless of the registered *shinpai* holder. This rule created the possibility that the *shinpai* could be used by the Qing authorities as well. Although there was a dispute over the *shinpai* system soon after its establishment, the Qing authorities, via a deliberative discussion, decided to permit its use, and moreover, adopted flexible ways to use these "trading passes" without confronting the Tokugawa regulations. In this way, the *shinpai* could be utilized by both sides, and thus an upgraded trade system based on *shinpai* became the institutional basis of maintaining the Sino-Japanese trade relationship in early modern times.

Chapter 5
The Underside of the Junk Trade: Maritime Smuggling and Urban Trafficking

5.1 Illegal Trade: A Reaction to the Tokugawa Trading Restrictions

It is reasonable to conclude that as long as there were market demands for the trade, restrictions and regulations upon it would lead to smuggling. Similar to the so-called Japanese pirates problem in the sixteenth century, smuggling by junks inevitably developed alongside the introduction of trading restrictions imposed by Tokugawa regime. In order to prevent large outflows of silver overseas as a result of sharp increases in the number of trading junks, as mentioned in Chap. 2, the shogunate began to fix the annual trading amount (6,000 *kanme* in 1685) and then the number of annual trading junks (70 in 1688, with many later changes) in the late seventeenth century. Under these regulations, for instance, in 1689, once the 70th junk had arrived, the authorities forbade any more junks to trade in Japan. This certainly meant a huge financial loss for junk merchants, and many turned to smuggling in coastal areas other than Nagasaki port to avoid these losses.

In 1715, the shogunate slashed the number of trading junks to 30, which caused an explosion of smuggling by junks in the following years. The smuggling not only damaged the Tokugawa regime economically, but also disrupted the trading order under the Tokugawa administration. In response, the shogunate instructed lords with domains near Nagasaki to crack down on smuggling in their territorial waters. Accompanied by the enforcement of the trading control based on *shinpai* (trading pass/trading permit), as examined in Chap. 3 in detail, it appears that the authorities managed to control junks' smuggling on the sea to a large extent after domain naval forces implemented a series of strict anti-smuggling operations.

H. Peng, *Trade Relations between Qing China and Tokugawa Japan*,
Studies in Economic History, https://doi.org/10.1007/978-981-13-7685-6_5

Such illegal transactions also frequently occurred in the urban area of Nagasaki city. In response, the shogunate was determined to build a settlement facility for the visiting Chinese. The settlement, called the Chinese Residence (*tōjin yashiki* 唐人屋敷), was built in 1688 and all the Chinese arriving by junk were forced to live there from the spring of the following year. As a regulation, imports for trading would be unloaded from the junks and carried directly into the specified warehouse, and except for articles for daily use during their stay in Nagasaki, any other cargo was strictly forbidden in the Chinese Residence. However, reading "the Judgement Records" (*hanka-chō* 犯科帳) of the office of the Nagasaki magistrate (see Chap. 2, Note 14), violations of these rules seem to have occurred frequently.

Smuggling is also considered an essential part of the Nagasaki trade, and accordingly attracts a great deal of attention by scholars. There are several comprehensive studies that aim to portray smuggling history (Itazawa 1961; Kikuchi 1962; Yamawaki 1965), and more studies attempt to shed light on some specific aspects or subjects, such as the distribution of smuggled goods in domestic markets (Nakamura 1988), countermeasures enacted to address smuggling (Nishimura 1973; Shimitsu 1979), and punishments that were meted out by the shogunate (Harafuji 1955).

In the 1980s, Arano Yasunori opened up a new research approach by focusing on communities within Nagasaki and taking merchants' distress and the explosion of unemployment to be the leading causes of smuggling (1988). Following this approach, in recent years, academic articles focusing on the lives of common Japanese have increased in number (So'eda 2008; Hashimoto 2009).

Moreover, it can be seen that two other related subjects have been given attention recently: discussion of the shogunate's anti-smuggling initiatives and those of related domains (Ya'o 2002; Yamamoto 2004, 2005; Matsuo 2010, Chap. 9), and Chinese "illicit activities", especially those that occurred in or around the Chinese Residence (Minoru 2002, 2007; Matsuo 2010, Chap. 7; Fukase 2008).

Yet, a significant discussion point has been neglected completely. As indicated in Chap. 1, it is easy to imagine that strengthening the enforcement and punishment of Chinese smugglers or relative "criminals" was always accompanied by a risk of damaging the benefits of Chinese trade and thereby causing the Japanese–Chinese commercial relationship based on trade in Nagasaki to deteriorate. With this in mind, it is important to note how the shogunate balanced the strength of its crackdown against illegal trade and the maintenance of the authorized trade.

This chapter aims to discuss this point by broad use and comprehensive analysis of various primary historical sources related to several actors involved, including the shogunate leaders, the magistrates of Nagasaki, and those domains involved in the practice of expelling smugglers. There are some domains' official documents and private diaries of the officials of those domains that record the process of expelling smuggling junks in the 1710s and 1720s, and on the other side there are many duplicates of official letters from the shogunate.[1] Some books written or edited by the officials in Nagasaki also provide important information on the subject.[2]

5.2 The Shogunate's Anti-Smuggling Policies Around 1715

It can be assumed that smuggling by junks occurred after the enforcement of the restrictions on trading volume in 1685. However, there are few related sources until the years around 1715. As a commonly-held view, the regulations of 1715 are generally regarded as the accomplishment of the restriction system in the Nagasaki trade.[3] The number of junks with permission to trade in Nagasaki was fixed at 30 every year, which was less than half of what it had been previously. As a result, many Chinese merchants lost their trade qualifications, and accordingly it can be thought of as a natural consequence that smuggling by junks dramatically increased in number and scale in the following years.

As a matter of fact, in the process of developing the regulations of 1715, the shogunate was to some extent aware of the consequences of these regulations, including the sudden increase in smuggling, and accordingly they had begun to seriously consider countermeasures. The shogunate issued a decree to the lords with domains in western Japan in May 1714, and meanwhile to the magistrates of

[1]The first one is an official document of the Hagi clan called *Tōsenkoto Okakitsuke* 唐船事御書付 (the documents on the Chinese junks, TSK), which is 5 volumes long and can be seen in the Morike Collection of Yamaguchi Prefectural Archives. The second is an official document of the Kokura clan, edited in a book titled *Tōsen-Hyoryū-Ki* 唐船漂流記 (the records on the drifting junks, TSHRK), which is in the possession of the Ogasawara Collection in the Museum of the History of Miyakomachi, Fukuoka. The third is the private diary of the Yoshida clan, *Yoshida Kadenruku: Fukuoka-han* 吉田家伝録: 福岡藩 (biographies of the Yoshida families, YSDK), who served as one of the chief retainers (*karo* 家老) of the Fukuoka domain for generations. Their original sources are in the possession of the Institute of Research in Kyushu Cultural History, Kyushu University, which was published in 1989 by the Daizaifu Tenmangu. There are another two related sources in the same institute. One is a book titled *Tōsen-Hyoryū-Ki* (the records on the drifting junks). Its title is same as that of the Kokura domain's document, explained above, but they are completely different in content and in authorship; the other is a book titled *Tōsen-Uchiharai-Ki* 唐船打払記 (the records on the expelling of junks, TSUH), which was written by Kato Narihiro, a retainer of the Fukuoka domain, who was in charge of the action against smuggling junks.

[2]*Wakan Kibun* 和漢寄文 (WKKB, Chap. 3, Note 6). *Nagasaki Jitsuruku Taisei* 長崎実録大成 (compilation of the documents on Nagasaki, NGJR). The original version was compiled in 1760 by the local office of Nagasaki, Tanabe Mokei. It was published in 1973 (Nagasaki: Nagasaki Bunkensha).

[3]As the authority on the study of the Nagasaki trade, Nakamura argued that it represented the completion of the trading restrictions of the shogunate under the so-called national seclusion policies (Nakamura 1989, p. 358).

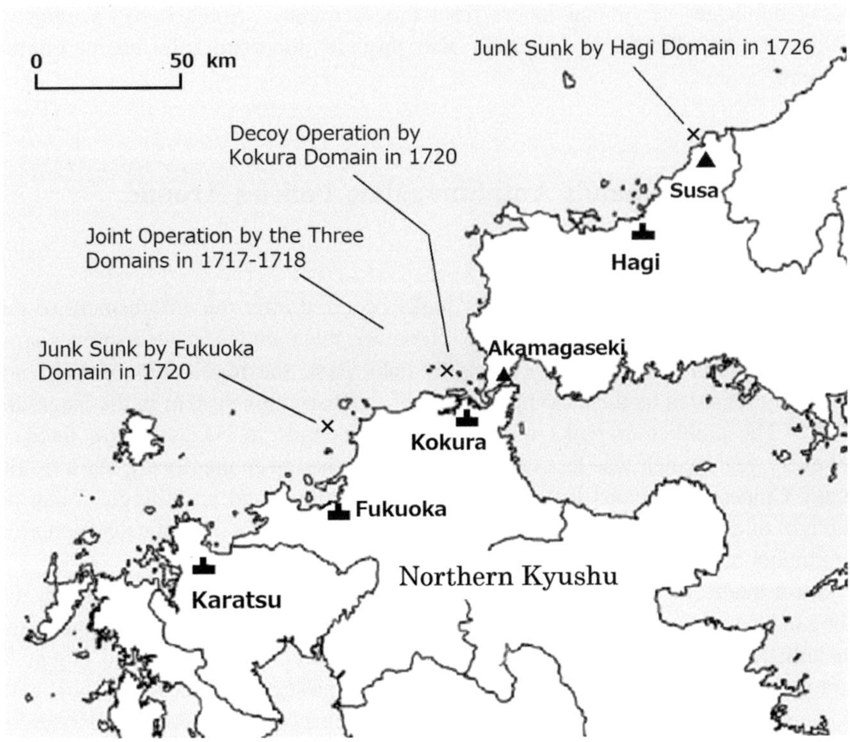

Fig. 5.1 Maritime area of junks smuggling in the period 1710s–1730s (map)

Nagasaki (there were three magistrates during 1713–1715 and the number became two after 1715) in the following month (Matsuo 2010, Chap. 7). It complained that recently there were some junks engaging in smuggling and some sailors of junks who would land on shore to cut down and collect bamboo and wood, without the permission of the Japanese authorities; some of them even stole fish from local residents; this behavior was illegal, violent and definitively an act of piracy; since then, officials in charge of marine security would board those junks and arrest or even kill the sailors. After the enforcement of the regulations of 1715, dozens of junks arrived at Nagasaki without holding *shinpai*, and after being denied the right to trade, many of them left Nagasaki and sailed to the northern Kyushu area, especially the seas near the Kanmon Strait (between Honshu and Kyushu), which was known as an essential shipping route for Japanese commercial ships. The coastguards of some domains reported the junks' smuggling activities, including Kokura (小倉), Fukuoka (福岡), Hagi (萩), and Chōfu (長府, a subsidiary domain of Hagi) (Fig. 5.1).

The shogunate urged the magistrates of Nagasaki and local lords to pay attention to smuggling by junks and to strengthen patrols on the sea.[4] There was a large possibility, as Liu Shiuh-feng noted, that the junks that appeared in the northern Kyushu maritime area in 1715 and 1716 were Chinese junks whose transactions in Nagasaki were refused because they did not hold a *shinpai* (Liu 1997).

In the spring of 1717, junks once again collectively appeared in the maritime areas around northern Kyushu; there were reported to be 15 in March. The domain administration dispatched Confucian scholars (*Jūsha* 儒者) who were able to read and write Chinese to communicate with the junks' merchants in writing. Communicating in this way, the Chinese merchants argued that their junks came adrift due to adverse winds and that they were preparing to depart after a brief stop. However, it soon came to light that they were in fact engaged in smuggling. Receiving such reports from these related domains, shogunate quickly issued a decree expelling smuggling junks by force.[5] The main points can be summarized as follows: the domains should crack down on smuggling junks and expel them by brandishing their firearms; the coastguards should fire in case they meet resistance; they were permitted to sink resisting junks if necessary. These points can be considered the basic principles of the shogunate's smuggler-expelling policies.

Similar principles can be seen in the policies on coastal defense that were introduced more than a half-century earlier. In the middle of the seventeenth century, the shogunate strengthened the anti-Christianity policy and consequently abolished its relationship with Portugal. For defense against a possible attack from the Portuguese, the shogunate issued a series of countermeasures against Portuguese vessels. For instance, in 1654, the magistrate received a decree from the shogunate: sink the vessel when illegal acts were committed, and failing to pursue the vessel would not be punished if it fled (Matsuo 2010, Chap. 4). In other words, the ultimate aim of the policy was to force the Portuguese vessel to leave; if it resisted, it would be necessary to conduct a heavy attack.

5.3 The Strengthening of the Policy to Expel Smugglers in 1718

The shogunate dispatched Wadanabe Nagatomo (渡辺永倫), a superintendent official (*metsuke* 目付) to northern Kyushu to arrange the smuggler-expelling policies of the related domains. Under his supervision, in February 1716 the soldiers of three domains—Kokura, Fukuoka, and Hagi—launched a joint operation

---

[4] *Tsūkō Ichiran* 通航一覧 (a collection of the sources on foreign exchange) Tokyo: Kokusho Kankokai 1913, Vol. 4, pp. 364–367.

[5] The copies of the decree can be seen in several official documents of the related domains. Some scholars, such as Yao and Matsuo have focused on the decree and given brief introductions on the subject (Ya'o 2002; Matsuo 2010, Chap. 9).

for cracking down on the smuggling junks (Yamamoto 2004). In order to make this more effective, the shogunate instructed that they were permitted to shoot the men in the smuggling junks, to injure or even kill them.[6] Consequently, the crackdown operation escalated and a few junk crews were reported to be shot dead.

After being attacked, many junks suffered huge damage and had to flee in haste from this maritime area. In May, one of them came adrift at Hirado, an island midway between northern Kyushu and Nagasaki. The surviving Chinese crew members, including the captain Li Huayu (李華宇), were sent to Nagasaki and imprisoned. The Chinese merchants living and trading in Nagasaki asked the magistrate for them to be pardoned. Li and some others were finally released and returned to China on other junks several months later. Meanwhile, the shogunate issued the following notice to all visiting Chinese in Nagasaki.

> When the Chinese junk sails adrift by adverse wind, wherever in Japan, the local patrol boats will sail there [to help them] and take care [of the drifted junk and its crews] very well. If the fittings or some other parts are damaged, [the officials in local administration] will supply new ones. [After being repaired] the junk will be allowed to go back. However, anchoring without permission is a serious violation of the law. Even though the Chinese should have known this since a long time ago, it has been seen in recent years that some Chinese junks anchored at places like Nagato (長門 Hagi Domain), Buzen (豊前 Kokura Domain) and Chikuzen (筑前 Fukuoka Domain), and have stayed there for several days. In spite of the fact that local offices demanded them to leave, they not only refused to obey but also committed excesses. Moreover, they seized the chance to conduct smuggling when patrol ships were absent. Such behavior is strictly illegal and unpardonable. Hence, the lords of domains in those areas have received orders [from the shogunate] to drive such junks out and to dispatch soldiers to sink them. Since this spring, several more junks have anchored. The coast guards took their boats, approached, and shot the junks lightly with guns. As the junks escaped immediately, [the soldiers] stopped attacking them and let them get away.[7]

The first part of the notice aims to show that the Tokugawa regime always treated junks involved in maritime accidents carefully and with kindness. The topic then shifts to the smuggling problem: the approaching and anchoring on any sea-coast in Japan without special cause such as a maritime accident would be treated as a violation of Tokugawa law; with no exception, smuggling could not be permitted. Next, the notice points out the smuggling issues that took place in the maritime areas of northern Kyushu and southern Honshu. The latter half of the notice explained how the problem of smuggling by the junks was dealt with, and it can be seen that the shogunate attempted to send a clear message to the Chinese merchants that any smuggler would face a strict crackdown.

---

[6]The article dated the fourth month kyohō 1 (1716), in TSK-1. Also seen in TSHRK, pp. 16–17 and YSDK, pp. 407–408.

[7]WKKB, pp. 137–138.

5.4 Sinking Junks Incidents in the 1720s

In the crackdown on smuggling junks, there was a difficult issue to handle: identifying whether the junk was a smuggler or a ship drifting after a maritime accident. By this time, there existed a manual for rescuing wrecked junks: after hearing the voice of air cannons as a signal for help from the junk, coastguards would sail nearby; then a Confucian official would be dispatched to the site and deliver questions written in Chinese to confirm what had happened to them; they might to be sent to Nagasaki or sail back if the junk was still able to move, as they chose (Nakamura 1990; Kuroki 2000, 2001). In the process of expelling junks, the leading officials of the relevant domains extensively debated whether to continue obeying this manual.

In the meeting of domains' representatives held in 1718, the suggestion was raised that repelling junks with *shinpai* anchored by rough weather would be immoral and cause people to circulate rumors about Japan being cruel. On the other hand, the opponents to this argued that the smuggler might sometimes hold *shinpai* in order to pretend to be a legal trader. This discussion did not reached a resolution on the issue.[8] Things changed after an accident took place in the same month: a junk appeared in the sea near Karatsu (唐津) domain, northeast of Kyushu (between Nagasaki and northern Kyushu); the area's coastguards received threats of force when they approached the junk and questioned the crew why they came there.[9] This shows that communicating with junks in writing was difficult to execute and it encouraged the officers in charge to take a firmer position regarding approaches by junks.

The magistrate of Nagasaki and the superintendent Wadanabe also suffered from this problem. After receiving the opinion of the city elders (*machitoshiyori* 町年寄) of Nagasaki, they entered into an agreement: in the case of a damaged vessel the junk should be sent to Nagasaki under escort (Matsuo 2010, Chap. 9). However, it is not clear whether the relevant domains received this instruction as the policy of the Nagasaki magistrate.

Even while keeping this matter pending, the shogunate continued to tighten the anti-smuggling operation in the following years in order to resolve the smuggling problem completely. After experiencing violent attacks in the spring of 1718, the smugglers clearly decreased in number, and some of them avoided approaching the coast and preferred to wait for their Japanese transaction partners in the sea a certain distance off the coast. This made it difficult to find and attack them. The shogunate demanded that domains expand attacks on smuggling junks, but representatives of those domains in charge of expelling junks insisted that there seemed no effective ways to expand attacks short of instructing them to freely attack junks. The shogunate seemed to understand those complaints but maintained a relatively

[8]The records are dated the eighth month kyohō 3 (1718), TSK-1.

[9]Ibid. the records are dated the Ninth month kyohō 3 (1718).

restrained attitude, not giving them permission to freely attack any junks that were suspected of smuggling.[10]

For junks appearing far out to sea, the shogunate launched a special decoy operation in 1720 with the assistance of Kokura domain and three former Japanese smugglers, including a famous figure called Kin'emon (金右衛門). These three men pretended to conduct trade with Chinese merchants and sneaked onto the junk, then persuaded the merchants in the junk to approach the coast. When the junks did approach, the soldiers of Kokura conducted a sudden ambush and successfully arrested three executive members of the junk (Yamamoto 2005; Matsuo 2010, Chap. 9).

Meanwhile, there was a junk accident in Fukuoka domain. When Kokura had completed its decoy operation, a fleet from Fukuoka, which stood by to support the operation by Kokura, received information that an approaching junk was affiliated with Fukuoka domain. They made the decision to start attacking. They first damaged the junk by firing, then boarded the ship and killed the crew, and finally sank it by setting it on fire (Ya'o 2002).

Based on the official documents of the Fukuoka domain and the records of the leader of the operation, the Fukuoka clan argued that before the action, they had received directions from the shogunate to attack the approaching junk.[11] However, this seems questionable because the other two domains, Kokura and Hagi, received the same direction and both of them left a copy. According to the records of these two domains and the manuscript copies of the instruction, it is clear that there was a meeting in Edo led by Inoue Masamine (井上正岑), one of the shogunate elders (*rōjū* 老中) and the representatives of the three domains on May 19, 1720; Inoue conveyed the instructions of the shogunate to these domains' representatives. There is no mention of sinking junks.[12]

After the fleet of the Fukuoka domain sank a junk in 1720, the shogunate began to recognize that this sort of aggressive junk attack would not be in its interest. Nevertheless, it appears that the shogunate wished to maintain the anti-smuggler operations and thereby continued to enforce the principle that any junk approaching the northern Kyushu maritime area should be expelled immediately.[13]

In September 1726, there was another incident in which a junk was attacked. This time, the enforcer was Hagi domain. After this, the domain reported the process of the incident in detail to the shogunate and stated that the junk was clearly

---

[10]The records are dated the second month and the eighth month kyohō 4 (1719), TSK-1, TSHR-K pp. 113–114 and pp. 120–124.

[11]See TSUH. A similar opinion is also seen in the *Shintei-Kuroda-Kafu* 新訂黒田家譜 (a new revision of the chronicle of the Kurota clan). It was officially edited by the Fukuoka clan and was published in 1982 by Bunken Shuban.

[12]The record dated kyohō 3 (1720), TSK-2 and TSHRK, p. 142.

[13]This attitude can be seen in the letter from the shogunate to the related domains. Ishigawa, the magistrate of Nagasaki, delivered it to the officials of those domains. It seemed they transcribed the letter in turn. The Hagi clan kept the transcription in its official document, TSK-2, and the Kokura clan kept its in TSHRK.

a pirate ship and even when being warned and expelled it did not move and otherwise tried to resist, and that in response to this the soldiers had to escalate their attack until the boat was sunk.[14] As Yoshitsumi revealed based on analysis of local sources, however, the truth was that the junk had arrived as a wreck and was seeking rescue; the soldiers of Hagi treated it primarily as a wrecked junk, but conducted a sudden attack and sank it (Yoshitsumi 1987). The reason they suddenly changed their treatment is not yet clear.

While conducting investigations, the shogunate revealed its concern that when the expelled junk was damaged too seriously to be able to escape, it was very likely to be sunk. Therefore, in November of that year, the shogunate issued an edict to 15 domains of the Kyushu and Chugoku districts. After appealing for the junk expulsion policies of recent years and the necessity of maintaining the policy in principle, the edict added some new items: in case the junk did not move even when it was being expelled by force, the attack had to stop for two or three days, and, if necessary, sailors had to approach the junk and determine whether its sailing apparatus was damaged and had lost its function; if so, the junk should be sent to Nagasaki; in the event that the junk fled after being attacked, ships should pursue it but only for a short amount of time.[15]

Shortly after the issuance of the edict, Miyake Yasutaka (三宅康敬), the magistrate of Nagasaki at the time, arrived in Kokura City on his way to Nagasaki from Edo for alternate service. He gathered the relevant officials of the three domains, and explained the items newly added to the shogunate's junk expulsion policies. There was certainly a possibility that junks not related to smuggling might drift for having strayed off course; it would be terrible to clash with them immediately, no matter what happened in practice, because rumors might spread to other countries.[16] It is clear that the shogunate had begun to comprehend that violent attacks on drifting junks would cause the relationship with the Qing empire to deteriorate and hence issued the edict to limit these actions to some extent.

5.5 The Penalties on Lawbreaking Chinese in Nagasaki

As a result of the abolition of the Maritime Prohibitions in 1685, 73 junks arrived in Nagasaki the following year, triple the average of the past ten years. Among them, two officials of the Fujian provincial administration of the Qing Empire also visited Nagasaki with 13 junks from that province. One of the two, Jiang Junkai (江君開), had been to Nagasaki many times as a merchant. They explained that the purpose of this visit was firstly to supervise the accounting of these 13 ships and secondly to

[14]See TSK-4.

[15]*Ofuregaki Kanpo Shūsei* 御触書寛保集成 (a collection of the laws and regulations issued in the Kanpo era). Tokyo: Iwanami Shoten, 1934.

[16]The transcription for this is in TSK-3.

regulate the crew and prevent them from violating Japanese laws. This information was sent to Edo immediately by the offices of Nagasaki, and the response of the shogunate was to permit these junks to trade while noting that Japan would not welcome the Qing officials' visit again.[17] There is still no evidence to indicate how the shogunate officials deliberated before making this determination. In any case, the result was that they refused to accept the means by which the officials of the Qing empire intended to discipline the visiting Chinese.

As mentioned above, the shogunate initiated restrictions on the annual amount of junks' trade in this year and the annual number of trading junks several years later and, moreover, built the Chinese Residence to isolate visiting Chinese from the local society of Nagasaki. Under these restrictions and regulations, the Tokugawa regime would have regarded as illicit activities Chinese seeking to carry out transactions directly and freely with ordinary Japanese. The dispute between the Japanese officials in charge of supervision and the Chinese seeking free trade became violent. In order to counter those illegitimate activities, the shogunate tried to strengthen controls and restrictions. However, it appears that the stricter the regulations were, the more severe the resistance became. The shogunate's leaders were constantly vexed as to how to deal with the illegitimate activities of the Chinese.

A violent incident took place in 1708 originating from a dispute over a transaction between a Chinese sailor and a Japanese petty dealer. A number of Chinese were involved in the incident and in response the magistrate of Nagasaki ordered 20 junks to sail back immediately. In his instruction, the magistrate said "the Chinese willfully robbed and destroyed the merchandise from the peddler, violating the regulation not to go outside the main gate [of the Chinese Residence]," emphasizing that such deeds severely violated Japanese Laws, and warned the Chinese that "in the case of killing or injuring innocent Japanese, they should be sentenced to death."[18] To the extent that it can be currently confirmed, this was the first time the shogunate declared that the death penalty would apply to law-breaking Chinese.

In 1709, Tokugawa Ienobu (徳川家宣, ruling from 1709 to 1712) became the shogun and his servant Manabe Akifusa (間部詮房) was appointed as the chief elder of the shogunate. Manabe's friend, Arai Hakuseki (新井白石), a famous Confucian scholar, began to participate in politics as a brain of the new administration and initiated political reforms including limiting the outflow of silver and copper and restoring the trading order. Regarding these items, as Matsuo pointed out, Hakuseki exchanged ideas frequently with the magistrates of Nagasaki (there were three magistrates in this period), and as one of their most essential issues, they extensively discussed ways to treat Chinese who violated Japanese laws (Matsuo 2010, Chap. 7). In his collected essays *Oritaku-Shiba-no-Ki* (折たく柴の木

[17]Hayashi Shunshō (林春勝) and Hayashi Nobuatsu (林信篤), eds., *Kai'i Hentai* (華夷変態, barbarianization of China). Tokyo: Toyo Bunko, 1958. Vol. 1, pp. 492–501.

[18]*Tōtsūji Kaisho Nichiruku* 唐通事会所日録 (diaries of the Chinese interpreters, TTJKS). Tokyo: University of Tokyo Press, 1963. Vol. 4, pp. 341–342.

Told Round a Brushwood Fire), Hakuseki expressed his ideas in this way: "Our country is superior to other counties and has an old tradition of respecting the martial spirit. However, now we have been humiliated by these trading ships. From the view of the national polity, we absolutely cannot tolerate it."[19]

Against this backdrop, in the summer of 1713, the magistrates of Nagasaki directed the Chinese interpreters (*tōtsūji* 唐通事), who served as officials of the Nagasaki administration, to communicate the following to the Chinese in Nagasaki: from now on, those who attempt to gamble or organize a group to cause trouble will be arrested and deposed by the officials of the Chinese Residence, and may be sentenced to death depending upon the conclusion of the investigation; those who help the criminals will receive similar punishment; all Chinese should submit a letter of consent, and anyone who refuses to submit one will be forbidden to go ashore and enter the Chinese Residence. However, the Chinese merchants insisted that they had no authority to make such a promise without the permission of Qing authorities and declined to submit a letter promising to accept the application of the death penalty. Finally, the magistrates shelved the demand.[20]

Two years later, the restrictions of 1715 were issued, one of them was translated into Chinese and Chinese merchants were informed of it as a covenant. Interestingly, the shogunate avoided defining the covenant as an official one and tentatively treated it as a private paper based on a promise between Chinese interpreters and the Chinese merchants.[21] The covenant consisted of nine clauses, and the final one was related to the treatment of "illegal Chinese behavior." It was written that "a man who kills the people of our country will be sentenced to death; in the case of [inflicting a] wound, the man will pay a fine in accordance with the degree [of the injury]."

5.6 Attempt to Apply "Japanese Penalties"

The year after the issuance of the restriction of 1715, Shogun Ietsugu (家継, ruling from 1713 to 1716) died, and Yoshimune (吉宗, ruling from 1716 to 1745), a lord of Ki'i (紀伊) domain and the great-grandson of Tokugawa Ieyasu, succeeded Ietsugu as shogun. Yoshimune is well known as a capable politician and during his shogunate he carried out various political reforms including the development of legal systems. In order to enact a systematic criminal law, his administration referred to Chinese laws and decided to introduce new physical punishments, such as tattooing (*iretsumi* 入れ墨) and beating (*tataki* 敲), which were suitable for light

[19]Arai Hakuseki, *Oritaku Shiba no Ki,* Tokyo: Iwanami Shoten, 1999, p. 397.

[20]TTJKS Vol. 6 (1965), Ibid., p. 231.

[21]There is the draft (*tsūjitomo tōjin no yakujo sōan* 通事共唐人の約条草案, as its primary Chinese translation was *yisi yu tangshang kuanyue* 訳司與唐商款約) in the Nagasaki Museum of History and Culture.

robbery and second offenses (Takashio 2004, pp. 148–149). It seems that the shogunate decided to adapt the tattoo to "Chinese crimes", in view of an edict issued in 1753.

> It had been announced that in the case of a man who was sentenced to "No Re-entry" and who came to [Japan] again, the captain of the junk (that carried the man to Nagasaki) would be sentenced to withholding a certain amount of copper as punishment, and the man himself would be sentenced to tattooing and "No Re-entry." Henceforth, [in that case] for the man himself, he would be exempted from the punishment of tattooing, but the captain who carried that man [to Nagasaki] was assigned responsibility for oversight and hence he would be fined 1000 *kin* copper.[22]

This edict shows that at certain points in the middle of the eighteenth century the Chinese "criminal" might be sentenced to tattooing, in accordance with the Tokugawa penalty regulation; in 1753, however, that regulation was lifted for uncertain reasons, and the punishments were merely that of "No Re-entry" for the criminal himself and a fine in copper for the captain of the junk to which the criminal belonged.

Subsequently, however, the problem of Chinese "crimes" showed no sign of changing for the better, and smuggling within the city seemed to become more serious. One of the possible reasons for this was that the shogunate permitted the crews of junks to conduct individual trade in 1785 (Matsuura 2002). Hence, many sailors also carried their own cargo into Nagasaki, and many of them tried to carry goods into the Chinese Residence and sell them secretly. This certainly adversely affected the maintenance of the trading order in Nagasaki port.

It was reported in 1810 that no more checks on cargo were being carried out because too many Chinese wanted to leave the Residence and walk into the downtown (Kita 1987). Against this backdrop, in July 1812, Tōyama Kagekuni (遠山景晋), the magistrate of Nagasaki, who was staying in Edo at the time, and other three commissioners of finance (*kanjō bugyō* 勘定奉行), who all had experience serving as magistrates of Nagasaki, submitted a proposal to Makino Tadakiyo (牧野忠精), an elder of the shogunate.[23] The main contents of this proposal are as follows: the illicit transactions of the junks crews were increasing and these captains neglected their responsibility to control their crew; Chinese crimes had become so serious that it damaged the authority of Japanese law (*nihon no kokuho* 日本の国法); however, there had been hardly any punishment for the Chinese up to this point apart from the "No Re-entry" orders up, so it was necessary to impose tattooing or beating on them, and in the worst case to impose the death penalty on them as well. If applying these punishments to Chinese criminals was approved, notice of the decision would be sent to the Chinese and the magistrate of Nagasaki would demand that they communicate this information to their

---

[22]*Nihon Zaisei Keizai Shiryō* 日本財政経済史料 (Historical Document on Japanese Fiscal Affairs and Economy). Tokyo: Zaisei Keizai Gakkai, 1922, p. 702.

[23]Yanai Kenji, ed., *Tsūkō Ichiran Zokushū* 通航一覧続輯 (a subsequent collection of the sources on foreign exchanges, TKIR-Z), Osaka: Seibundo, 1968, Vol. 1, pp. 180–181.

bosses, the chief merchants of the two merchants' groups in China (*zaito ninushi* 在唐荷主), and to tell them to submit a letter of consent.

The shogunate adopted this proposal, and a month and a half later, Tōyama departed from Edo, arriving in Nagasaki in October. Some days later, after consulting with his counterpart in Nagasaki, they informed the Chinese in Nagasaki that Chinese criminals might be subject to Japanese penalties (*nihon no keibatsu* 日本之刑罰) such as tattooing or beating, and furthermore might be sentenced to death; in the case of crackdowns, Japanese officials were permitted to kill anyone who tried to resist.[24]

In November, they received the reply from the Chinese merchants. In this letter, the chief merchants of the two Chinese merchants' groups mentioned that the Chinese in Nagasaki should unfailingly obey the Japanese regulations; they requested that the Japanese administration firstly imprison those who caused problems and then extradite them to the captains to which they belonged; after coming back to China, these violators would be sent to the court of justice and be punished in accordance with Chinese laws.[25] Even though they used many terms of respect and polite expressions in the letter, it clearly expressed their negative attitude towards the application of Japanese penalties. It seems that the Nagasaki administration did not further enforce this, and for a while tabled the issue.

More than two decades later, in the 1830s, the problem of illicit trafficking once again grabbed the attention of the shogunate. In September 1835, Kuze Hiromasa (久世広正), the magistrate of Nagasaki at the time, received an instruction to strengthen the regulation from Ōkubo Tadazane (大久保忠真), the elder of the shogunate. Ōkubo mentioned that the disorder of the Nagasaki trade had become so serious that the authority of the shogunate was at risk of decline. This was despite the fact that if the Chinese merchants refused to sign and submit the letter of consent as before, the administration would strongly enforce Japanese penalties; in the case that the Chinese merchants attempted to protest, they would not hesitate to stop trading with them.[26]

Three months later, Kuze reached Nagasaki and delivered a notification to the Chinese via the Chinese interpreters. In the notification, he emphasized that they would carry out Japanese penalties such as tattooing and beating the Chinese criminals. Facing the shogunate obdurate attitude, the Chinese merchants in Nagasaki at that time conceded and agreed to submit the letter, mentioning that all the Chinese, not only the merchants but also other crew members, had acknowledged the regulations of the shogunate and they should respect them; in the case that one of them violated the laws, they would have not a single word of objection to their treatment by the Japanese administration.

---

[24]Kanei Toshiyuki ed. *Zōho Nagasaki Ryakushi* 增補長崎略史 (an enlarged and revised edition of the brief Nagasaki history). Tokyo: Harashobo, 1973, pp. 133–134.

[25]Ibid, p. 134. The title of the letter was "Reply of the merchants of *Guanju* and *Gongju*, Wang Yongzeng (汪永增) and Yang Lanzhou (楊蘭洲), on the noticed issues."

[26]TKIR-Z, Ibid., p. 187.

However, just one month later, in January 1836, a large disturbance occurred in Nagasaki. A junk merchant called Sun Yucun (孫漁村) died of a disease and a number of Chinese were allowed to temporarily leave the Residence and enter downtown for his funeral parade. Some sailors took this as an opportunity to conduct transactions downtown. When the Japanese guards in charge of supervision came to stop them, some sailors were reluctant to stop and, furthermore, tried to resist by force. One of them was injured in the strife. After receiving this information, a large number of Chinese ran out of the Residence and collided with the Japanese officials and guards, escalating the fracas. At this time, the soldiers of Fukuoka domain drove these Chinese back into the Residence and surrounded it.[27] The next morning, they entered the Chinese Residence and arrested 180 men involved in the disorder. This was the largest of the riots written about in the history of Nagasaki trade (Kita 1987). After an investigation, 18 men were imprisoned as the main culprits.

In May, captains of five junks submitted an application to the magistrate and to a city elder for the extradition of these prisoners, since they were planning to sail back to China. They begged the magistrate of Nagasaki to show them mercy, promising to send the criminals to the administration in China, and assured the magistrate that the criminals would be severely punished in China.[28] The magistrate, however, did not allow this at first. The 18 sailors maintained in prison for around a year. At that point, the chief merchants of the two Chinese merchants' groups sent a letter to the magistrate asking for their pardon.[29]

One year later the 18 sailors were finally extradited to the captains of the junks, and then two months later, the chief merchants of the Chinese merchants' groups sent a letter to the magistrate thanking them again for their generous treatment. In the related document, there is no word of any physical punishment such as tattooing or beating imposed on the 18 sailors; there was only mention of the one-year imprisonment.[30] Moreover, Hu Shuzhi (胡述之), the magistrate of Pinghu District (平湖県), an administrative district within Jiaxing Prefecture (嘉興府) of Zhejiang province in which there was a departure port that most junks bound for Japan used in this period, sent a letter to the magistrate of Nagasaki as well. He praised and expressed his thanks for the Nagasaki administration's treatment of the case, emphasizing that Chinese in Nagasaki should obey the Japanese laws, while on the other hand insisting that the sentence and punishment of the Chinese should be implemented in China in accordance with the laws of the Qing empire.[31]

[27]The two domains of Fukuoka and Saga sent soldiers to Nagasaki for the security of the port under the direction of the shogunate since the mid-seventeenth century, and they undertook this task every other year by rotation.

[28]TKIR-2, Ibid, p. 468.

[29]Ibid, pp. 491–496.

[30]Ibid., p. 509.

[31]Ibid., p. 507.

There was a pair of contrasting expressions in the letter: "the mercy of your state" and "the laws of our court," which clearly demonstrated his stance and assertion.

5.7 Towards a Comprehensive Account of How the Tokugawa Anti-Smuggling Policies Were Perceived

As in other cases, smuggling was the shadow side of the junk trade in Edo Japan. It can be classified roughly into two types: the ship unit and the individual unit. As discussed above, the former generally occurred in coastal regions other than Nagasaki city; the latter, on the other hand, occurred inside the city. Both began to be problematic in 1685, after which the shogunate began to fix the annual trade volume. However, as clarified in Chap. 3, the *shinpai* policy, established in 1715, rationalized the existing trading control system by making sure the junk merchants' transactions would be permitted in Nagasaki before their departure for Japan. At the same time, the shogunate also applied pressure on the domains in areas with frequent smuggling to expel the smuggling junks by force, causing heavy damages to those smugglers.

Individual smuggling inside Nagasaki city, however, could not be controlled effectively and became more and more serious throughout the Edo period. One of the reasons for this may be the shogunate's punishment policy towards lawbreaking Chinese. As examined above, many shogunate officials, including the magistrate of Nagasaki and the elders, had discussed how to strengthen the punishment of the Chinese who violated Japanese laws, and even issued notifications to the Chinese in Nagasaki regarding the application of Japanese penalties on Chinese violators. Nevertheless, it seemed that no Chinese had been sentenced to any physical penalty under the shogunate and the basic means of punishment were still merely financial penalties such as withholding a certain amount of copper as punishment and prohibition of re-entry.

It is likely that the shogunate was concerned that severe punishments might cause a backlash from the Chinese traders and the Qing authorities, making trade relations unsteady and, in the worst case, interrupting them. Despite the fact that taking such a relatively restrained attitude seemed to be an imperfect political choice from the stance of the shogunate, because it might be interpreted as a sign of weakness and accordingly damage its prestige as ruler of the state, it without a doubt benefited the stabilization of the junk trade in Nagasaki and the trade relations with Qing China. Because there was no diplomatic negotiation between the Qing authorities and the Tokugawa shogunate for resolving trade frictions, including how to treat smugglers, the shogunate had to deal with those sensitive issues with maximum discretion.

Chapter 6
Copper Trading by Qing China's Official Merchants and Affiliated Trading Group

6.1 Academic Studies of Qing China's Official Copper Merchants

As mentioned in the previous chapters, Dutch and the Chinese merchants became the main trade partners of Tokugawa Japan from the middle of the seventeenth century. The Dutch East India Company (VOC) controlled Dutch trade with Japan. On the Chinese merchants' side, there was a shift from dispersed management to unified management. As a result, two monopolistic trading groups in close cooperation with each other appeared in the middle of the eighteenth century.

The two trading groups were generally called *tongju* (銅局) or *liangju* (両局) in official Qing documents. *Tongju* referred in this case to the group of merchants supplying copper for the administration, and *liangju* is an abbreviated expression to describe the two groups. There was a clear difference between the two in their relations with Qing authorities in the late eighteenth century: one was called the Official Bureau (*guanju* 官局), which literally meant "the group led by an official merchant" (*guanshang* 官商), formed largely for repaying debts to the empire; the other was named the "Twelve Families" (十二家 or *minju* 民局 or *gongju* 公局), since it was made up of several private merchants (*minshang* 民商) engaging in the copper trade with the approval of the Qing authorities who mainly used their own capital.

The historical background behind the establishment of both groups was similar: the reform of the Qing authorities' copper-import system around 1737. However, the two groups had distinct managerial structures. This chapter will focus on how and why the Official Bureau formed, and the next chapter will examine the Twelve Families from a similar point of view.

Scholarly attention to the Official Bureau began no later than the study of Yano Jin'ichi in the 1920s on trade with Nagasaki (Yano 1967, first published in 1938 and related papers first published in 1926). Yano introduced related articles in the *Qianbi Kao* (錢幣考 Investigation into the Coin Currency) in *Huangchao Wenxian*

H. Peng, *Trade Relations between Qing China and Tokugawa Japan*,
Studies in Economic History, https://doi.org/10.1007/978-981-13-7685-6_6

Tongkao (皇朝文獻通考), an administrative history book compiled at imperial command in the middle and late eighteenth century (an abbreviated title, *Tongkao*, will be used in the following text), and pointed out that the Qing authorities appointed an official merchant called Fan Yubin (范毓馪) to participate in trade with Nagasaki to import copper into China. He also examined the relationship between Fan and the Qing Empire and the copper-import trade among Fan and his families.

After Yano's pioneering study, Uchida Naosaku (1949) re-examined the genealogy of the representative merchants of the Official Bureau and Twelve Families and argued that the formation of the two groups should be seen as a part of the Qing's system of restricting foreign trade. Later, several other scholars, including Yamawaki Teijirō (1960, Chap. 3, first published in 1958; and 1964, Chap. 2), Matsuura (2002, Chap. 2.1, first published in 1979, and Chaps. 2.2, 2.3), Liu (1986), and Hua (2011), gradually advanced the study of this topic, by analyzing several new sources such as the records of drifting junks, local records, genealogies, tombstones, official documents, and other relevant materials.

The official merchant Fan Yubin and members of his family have also attracted scholarly attention as representatives of the imperial merchants, Shanxi (a province in northwest China) merchants, and salt merchants. A study by Wei Qingyuan and Wu Qiyuan has presented much essential information concerning Fan and his families' official loans (Wei and Wu 1981); and Wang Jingli's dissertation (2007), which aimed to reveal a comprehensive picture of Fan's commercial activities, examined how Fan used the profit from the sale of salt as capital to import Japanese copper. Both studies are based on documents of the Imperial Household Department (*neiwufu* 内務府).

In spite of the accumulation of academic literature, many unclear or controversial issues remain, such as when and why Fan Yubin participated in the copper import business and what attitude the Qing authorities took towards Fan's copper trade. Considering that Fan became the first managerial representative of the Official Bureau and that his group included many individual merchants trading with Japan, it is important to clarify these issues and thereby discuss the ways in which the consolidation of the management of the Chinese merchants started.

6.2 Commercial Activities of Fan and His Families

Fan Yubin is usually considered one of the most famous merchants of Shanxi province, and the ancestors of his clan had been engaged in trade with the Mongolians since the early years of the Ming dynasty. Fan Yongdou (范永斗), Fan Yubin's grandfather, traded with and delivered military supplies to the Manchus. In appreciation for his cooperation, the Qing court granted him a homestead at Zhangjiakou (張家口), northwest of the capital Beijing, and designated a special status for him as the merchant belonging to the Imperial Household Department. His successor, Fan Sanba (范三拔), Fan Yubin's father, expanded his commercial activities from border and frontier trade to the import of copper and

Table 6.1 Commercial activities of Fan Yubin and his families during the mid-18th century

Commence Fields	Representative	Period	Source
Foods transportation for the troops in Mongolia area	Yubin	1724–1736	(1) (3) (5)
Foods transportation for the troops in Shichuan area	Qingzhu	1748–N/A	
Salt business	Yubin	1726–1745	(8) (10)
	Qingzhu	1745–1762	(13) (17)
	Qinghong	1763	(18) (20)
	Qingji	1764–1783	(22) (23)
Food supply	Yubin	1738	(2)
Imported glass purchase	Qingzhu	1759	(4)
Management of lead mine	Yubin	1710–1723	(7)
Lead supply	Yubin	1718–1735	(6) (10)
Copper supply	Qingzhu	1739–1763	(11) (19)
	Qinghong	1763	(19) (21)
	Qingji	1764–1783	(22) (23)
Ginseng collection	Yubin	1740–1743	(12)
Lime supply	Yubin	around 1744	(12)
Wood supply	Yubin	1736–N/A	(9)
		1744	(12)
	Qingzhu	1751–N/A	(14)
Fur purchase from Kyakhta	Qingzhu	1756–1761	(15) (16)

Source: (1) Record in the 2nd month Yongzheng 2 (February or March, 1724) in *Qing Shizong Shilu* (清世宗實錄, Veritable Records of Emperor Yongzheng). (2) Record in the 9th month Qianlong 3 (October or November, 1738) in *Qing Gaozong Shilu* (清高宗實錄,Veritable Records of Emperor Qianlong, QGZS). (3) Record in the 12th month Qianlong 13 (January. or February, 1749) in QGZS. (4) Record in the 9th month Qianlong 24 (October or November, 1759) in QGZS. (5) Record in the 3rd month Qianlong 1 (April or May, 1736) in *Pingding Zhunge'er Fanglue* (see Note 1). (6) Financial Department's Report on the 18th day of the 2nd month Yongzheng 1 (March 24, 1723), FHAC: 04-01-35-1226-003. (7) Yun Xiang's Report on the 23th day of the 12th month Yongzheng 1 (January 18, 1724), FHAC: 04-01-35-0707-006. (8) Maka's Report on the 18th day of the 8th month, Yongzheng 3 (September 24, 1725), NPM: 402019173; (9) Haiwang's Report on the 16th day of the 8th month Qianlong 1 (September 20, 1736), FHAC: 04-01-05-0007-005. (10) Financial Department's Report on the 6th day of the 8th month Qianlong 3 (September 19, 1738), MQD: A84-82. (11) Nasutu's Report on the 17th day of the 3rd month Qianlong 4 (April 24, 1739), FHAC: 02-01-04-13202-013. (12) Financial Department's Report on the 29th day of the 1st month Qianlong 9 (March 12, 1744), FHAC: 04-01-35-1234-007. (13) Fan Yuqi's Report on the 22th day of the 6th month Qianlong 10 (July 21, 1745), FHAC.04-01-16-0023-011; (14) Fu Heng's Report on the 18th day of the 12th month Qianlong 15 (January 15, 1751), FHAC: 05-111-7. (15) Fu Heng's Report on the 15th day of the 6th month Qianlong 22 (July 30, 1757), FHAC: 05-155-39. (16) Report of Imperial Household Department, on the 4th day of the 6th month Qianlong 26 (July 5, 1761), *Qinggong Neiwufu Zouxiao-Dang* (Archives of Qing Imperial Household Department, 清宮內務府奏銷檔). Beijing: Palace Museum. Vol. 257, p. 278. (17) Report of Imperial Household Department, on the 14th day the Leap 5th month Qianlong 27 (July 5, 1762), FHAC: 05-0199-016. (18) Li Zhiying's Report on the 1st day of the 4th month Qianlong 29 (May 1, 1764), NPM: 403017434/403017435. (19) Fude's Report on the 9th day of the 5th month Qianlong 29 (June 8, 1764), NPM: 403017740. (20) Li Zhiying's Report on the 11th day of the 6th month Qianlong 29 (July 9, 1764), NPM: 403018049. (21) Financial Department's Report on the 23th day of the 4th month Qianlong 31 (May 31, 1766), FHAC: 04-01-05-0234-035. (22) Zheng Rui's Report on the 12th day of the 1st month Qianlong 48 (February 13, 1783), NPM: 403043789; (23) Zheng Rui's Report on the 16th day of the 2nd month Qianlong 48 (March 18, 1783), NPM: 403044080

selling salt in the domestic market (Matsuura 2002, Chap. 2.2). When Fan Yubin became the head of the family, the businesses of his clan entered a golden age.

Table 6.1, based on official reports to the emperor and veritable Qing records, shows the diversity of Fan's businesses in the mid-eighteenth century. Fan Yubin was in charge of transporting food for the Qing's troops, who fought a war with the Zunghars (a westernmost group of the Mongols) in Mongolia 1724–1736, and Qing authorities granted him an honorary official title, *Taipusiqing* (太僕寺卿, the chief minister of the Court of the Imperial Stud), as a reward for his assistance in the war (Liu 1986). In later years, Qingzhu (清注), his second-eldest son, undertook the same kind of task for the troops subduing the Tibetan revolts at Sichuan, southwest of Qing China.

Selling salt was the most profitable of all Fan's businesses in this period. It is well known that Qing authorities created a salt monopoly and granted the privileges of selling salt in certain areas to designated imperial merchants such as Fan Yubin. In common with sale of salt, the collecting and selling ginseng was also an activity in which no one in principle could participate without the permission of the Qing authorities. As an imperial merchant, Fan Yubin gained the privilege of collecting and selling ginseng from certain mountain areas under the control of the Qing court.

Furthermore, Fan Yubin and his sons undertook the task of purchasing special commodities for the court such as copper, lead, lime, wood, furs, and glass. In order to obtain some of them, Fan's commercial activities extended to foreign trade and developing the mine. For instance, he developed the lead mine and imported copper from Japan and furs from Russia.

Regarding the copper trade, as Liu pointed out, Fan Yubin became involved in this business in the later Kangxi era, the early years of the eighteenth century (Liu 1986). Unfortunately, however, there are few sources to show more details. It is a common view among scholars focusing on this topic that Fan Yubin restarted the copper trade in the 1730s or 1740s. However, both the timing and reasons for the start of Fan Yubin's copper trade are not clear. The next section will discuss this point in detail by analyzing new-found sources.

6.3 The Restarting of Fan's Copper Trade After 1738

As discussed in Chap. 4, owing to a decrease in the output of Japanese copper in the early eighteenth century, it became difficult for the contracted merchants to fulfil the quotas promised to the Qing authorities. Because they had accepted funds from the Qing authorities in advance, they were required to repay the loss. As this debt problem became more and more serious, the Qing authorities had to reform the quota system (see Sect. 8.3). In 1737, they issued orders switching the source of the copper used for the central coinage services from Japan to Yunnan and permitting private merchants to import copper with their own funds.

When and why Fan Yubin started the Japanese copper import in this period are important questions which previous scholars have not clearly explained. Several official documents introduced in the following text will be helpful in understanding this issue.

As mentioned above, Fan Yubin had for several years been in charge of transporting provisions to the Qing armies fighting the Zunghars. In return for undertaking this responsibility, the Qing court prepaid his transportation costs in silver according to the haulage distance. However, the transportation distance was shortened to half of the previously determined amount because the destination shifted from Kobdo (present-day Khovd, in the northwest of Mongolia, written as 科卜多 in the related document) to Orkhon (in the north of Mongolia, 鄂爾昆) along with the change in the military situation. As a result, transportation expenses had to be cut accordingly. Fan was ordered to refund the money corresponding to the reduced amount. The amount to be refunded was calculated to be approximately 2,500,000 taels (*liang* 両) in silver currency, and Fan had paid more than 800,000 taels by 1736. In that year, the officials in charge of imperial finance deliberated Fan's debt problem and ordered him to repay the outstanding debt (approximately 1,600,000 taels) within five years.[1]

Generally speaking, at that time, the year after the decision date was regarded as the first year of implementation. The annual amount of repayment may be estimated at approximately 330,000 taels.[2] The exact figure was 337,722.9 taels, based on the report to the emperor in 1738 from Nasutu, a governor-general of Liangjiang district (Jiangxi, Anhui, and Jiangsu provinces).[3] According to this report, the amount of Fan's outstanding debt was approximately 1,350,000 taels of silver currency. It is highly possible that Fan Yubin had paid almost 330,000 taels to the Qing authorities. The report also notes the following two points: Fan Yubin entrusted his son, Qingzhu, with purchasing Japanese copper in Jiangsu and Zhejiang at the assigned time. Secondly, Fan Yubin preferred to pay the imported Japanese copper to the Qing authorities every year in an amount equal in value to the silver currency he was to pay instead of paying silver currency directly, and he promised to complete payment of his debt in this way within the next four years.

Given Fan's previous activity of importing Japanese copper, it is obvious that he had guessed the advantage of paying with copper instead of with silver currency based on his past experience. Meanwhile, the Qing authorities still had a great demand for Japanese copper and preferred Fan, the familiar and trusted imperial merchant, to undertake this essential task. Therefore, Fan's proposal was adopted by the central authorities, and, from 1738 onwards, Fan again started to import copper from Japan and supply a great part of it to the central authorities as his debt refund.

---

[1] *Pingding Zhunger Fanglue* 平定準格爾方略 (strategy for the pacification of the Dzungars). The Palace Museum (ed.) (2000) Haikou: Hainan Publishing House, pp. 214–215.

[2] Ibid.

[3] "Nasutu's report (*tiben* 題本) on the 17th day of the third month Qinlong 4 (April 24, 1739)", First Historical Archives of China (FHAC): 02-01-04-13202-013.

6.4 Fan's Copper Trade and the New Official Debt Problem

Fan Yubin embarked on this plan in 1737. As examined in Chap. 4, in 1738 Fan Yubin dispatched his son Qingzhu to Suzhou, the city in Jiangsu province, which was not only the economic center of Qing China but also the city in which most of the merchants who engaged in trade with Nagasaki usually lived. In order to sail to Japan and import copper, Qingzhu borrowed *shinpai* (trading pass/permit), from the financial office of Jiangsu province and dispatched some junks to Nagasaki (see Sect. 4.7). These junks arrived at Nagasaki, completed the trade, and shipped the copper back to China. The *shinpai* were easily renewed at Nagasaki, and after the junks arrived home, Qingzhu returned the passes to the financial office of Jiangsu province.

However, the copper-import trade seemed not to run as smoothly as expected, and problems emerged in other commerce sectors as well. In the spring of 1744, the Ministry of Revenue reported the official debt problem to the emperor.[4] The largest amount was still the refund regarding food transportation for the army, which then amounted to 675,445.8 taels. The second-largest amount came from collecting and selling ginseng. As explained above, Fan Yubin participated in the sale as a ginseng agent. For this procedure, he was to receive licences (*shenpiao* 参票) for collecting ginseng in the mountain areas under the control of the central authorities and then pay the fixed amount of ginseng or the silver currency with the same value to the Qing authorities. There was, of course, a deadline for the payment.[5] This debt problem meant that he could not complete the payment by the deadline, and the unpaid amount was calculated as 511,425 taels.

The third-largest amount was related to the salt business. It seemed that Fan gained the privileges of the monopolistic salt sale in Linying (臨潁) and Yuzhou (禹州) districts of Henan province from a salt merchant named Li Tianfu (李天馥). In return, he was to pay off the official debt under the name of Li. It seemed that Li had engaged in the copper trade in the same period as Fan. The amount of this debt was 3,390 taels.

It was not merely Fan's debts to the empire that the report pointed out. Fan seemed to undertake the task of transporting wood and lime for the Qing authorities and was, therefore, to be paid the transportation expenses. The amount was 79,010.509 taels. The total amount of Fan's official debts was counted as 1,141,250.291 taels.

[4]"The report of the Ministry of Revenue on the 29th of the first month Qianong 9 (March 12, 1744)", FHAC: 04-01-35-1234-007, and Zhang Weiren (ed.) (1986–1995) *Ming Qing dang'an* (*Archives of the Ming and Qing Dynasties*, 明清檔案, *MQD*) 324 vols., Taipei: Institute of History and Philology, Academia Sinica), A129-35.

[5]For the institutions of the ginseng and "shenpiao" management, see Sun 2014.

6.5 The Debt-Repayment and Copper-Import Plan in 1744

The official report mentioned above cited Emperor Qianlong's instruction as well. The key points can be summed up as follows: direct Fan to continually pay back the debt in copper and supply the fixed amount of copper to some provinces to cast copper coins; if there was a surplus, permit him to sell it freely without tax payment.

The officials of the Ministry of Revenue consulted with Fan concerning some undetermined issues, such as how much he could pay each year and the price at which the imported copper should be set. The opinion of Fan Yubin was that after elaborate calculations, the annual amount of copper import would be, at most, 1,300,000 *jin*; approximately 300,000 *jin* could be transported to Shaanxi province and Zhili province respectively by land and its reasonable price including transport cost would be 14 taels of silver for every 100 *jin* in copper; by water, 250,000 *jin* could be transported to Jiangxi province, 250,000 *jin* to Hubei province and 200,000 *jin* to Jiangsu province, and its reasonable price would be 13 taels in silver currency for every 100 *jin* in copper.

According to Liu's calculations based on the dates in several related documents, the purchase price was 14.5 taels in silver currency for every 100 *jin* in copper, and the transport expenses to Beijing were 3 taels before the reformation in 1737 (Liu 1986). It seems that the price including transport expenses (14 taels by water and 13 taels by land) was set slightly lower. Several scholars noticed the 1744 plan as well (Yamawaki 1960, Chap. 3; Matsuura 2002, Chap. 2.1; Liu 1986), based on the account in the *Tongkao*. However, they could not know that the plan related to the transportation and price setting was Fan's own idea, because there is no description in the *Tongkao*. This is significant for understanding why Fan got involved in the copper trade and the timing of the Official Bureau's formation. Participating in the copper trade was Fan's own choice and not a reaction to the Qing authorities' direction, because for him the trade was so profitable he presumed it could help him repay his official debts.

The Ministry of Revenue summarized the repayment plan as follows: to repay the debts (1,141,250 taels in silver currency), Fan Yubin was to pay 8,451,787.12 *jin* in copper based on the price Fan himself proposed. Considering this amount so huge that it seemed impossible for him to complete payment within four years as promised, the authorities prolonged the payment period. Fan was to import copper and pay approximately 1,300,000 *jin* of it to the Qing authorities every year, transporting 300,000 *jin* each to Shaanxi and Zhili provinces, 250,000 *jin* to Jiangxi and Hubei provinces respectively, and 200,000 *jin* to Jiangsu province. In this way, the amount of copper paid would total up to 7,800,000 *jin* in six years (1745–1750), and the balance (651,787 *jin*) was to be paid completely in 1751. The prices including transport expenses would officially be 14 taels for every 100 *jin* in land and 13 taels in water.

According to Fan Yuqi's official report in 1746, analyzed in the next section, this proposal was finally adopted by the central authorities.

6.6 Extension of the Payment Period

Even if Fan had an optimistic outlook regarding the copper trade, the trade seemed not to progress as smoothly as he forecasted in 1744. In the second year after his proposal was approved, Fan Yuqi (范毓奇), his younger brother, who served as chief commander of the troops based in Zhengding, Zhili province (直隸正定總兵), reported to the emperor on the state of copper importation and appealed on behalf of Fan Yubin to extend the payment period. The following text will mainly examine two points from this report: whether Fan Yuqi's statement in his report properly reflected the actual condition of Fan Yubin's copper import business and the ways in which the plan adopted in 1744 changed.[6]

Fan Yuqi described the trading conditions in the following way. Fan Yubin dispatched Qingzhu, his second-eldest son, to prepare to import copper soon after receiving the instruction from the court. Fan sent 22 junks to Nagasaki between the sixth month of 1744 and the last month of 1745 (Chinese calendar), and expected to import approximately 2,800,000 *jin* in copper in two years. However, only one junk returned.

Why could these junks not return? According to Yuqi's explanation, the annual production of copper in Japan was a little more than 2,000,000 *jin*, Japan exported approximately 1,000,000 *jin* each to Chinese merchants and Dutch merchants every year and more than 40 Chinese junks entered Nagasaki port during 1744 and 1745.

Did this explanation reflect the facts? The *Nagasaki Jitsuroku Taisei* (長崎実録大成 compilation of the documents on Nagasaki) is one of the most significant sources for studying the history of maritime trade in Nagasaki in the early-modern period. This book recorded 20 Chinese junks arriving at Nagasaki both in 1744 and 1745.[7] Hence, the sum was 40, which accorded with the dates in Yuqi's report.

According to Kimura's study on the Tokugawa copper-export policies, the shogunate decreased the annual export amount by half, which meant the amount of junk copper trade would drop from 3,000,000 *kin* (*kin* = *jin*) to 1,500,000 *kin*. However, Kimura also mentioned that the reduction plan could not be implemented as scheduled (Kimura 2009 Chap. II-3). Even though it went into operation, the restricted amount that junks could export would be 1,500,000 *jin*, and not 1,000,000 *jin*, as Fan Yuqi had mentioned.

Considering all the issues discussed above, it is clear that Fan Yuqi's report underestimated the available amount of copper imported, although his report reflected to some extent the actual condition of trade with Nagasaki, such as the number of trading junks. He tried to persuade the emperor and the Qing authorities that the failure to reach the quota for importing copper was mainly due to the decreasing amount of copper that could be exported from the Japanese side and not the fault of his brother, Fan Yubin.

[6]"Fan Yuqi's report on the 15th day of the second month Qianlong 11 (March 6, 1746)", FHAC: 04-01-35-1237-002.

[7]*Nagasaki Jitsuroku Taisei* (Chap. 5, Note 2) p. 272.

In the final part of Fan Yuqi's report, he pleaded to the emperor to prolong the payment period and presented the following new payment plan: the copper shipped back by the Nagasaki junks would be transported to the provinces according to the formal plan; the annual amount to be paid would be revised from 1,300,000 *jin* to 800,000 *jin*, and the payment deadline from 1751 to 1754. In other words, the revised plan was to pay 2,600,000 *jin* in the first two years, pay 800,000 *jin* each year over the following seven years, and complete the balance in the last year (1,300,000 × 2 + 800,000 × 7 + 251,787 = 8,451,787).

After viewing the report, Emperor Qianlong wrote these brief comments as follows: "Approve his proposal and inform the related office [Ministry of Revenue]." It is clear that the revised payment plan was successful adopted, and the term for repayment was thereby extended.

6.7 The Re-Extension of Fan's Copper Payment

In 1745, Fan Yubin died of an illness. Although the date of his death is not certain,[8] it is highly likely that he died after Fan Yuqi's report was presented on July 21, in which Yuqi reported to the emperor that Fan Yubin had fallen into a critical condition.[9] After Fan Yubin's death, his second-eldest son, Qingzhu, assumed the duty of repaying the debts under the name of Fan Yubin and continued to import copper .

As mentioned above, Qingzhu was already the person in charge of the copper-import trade and had been based in Suzhou since 1739. Fan Yuqi valued Qingzhu for his ability and remarked in his report that Qingzhu was an appropriate person to inherit his father's business. Once he received this authorization, Qingzhu became the legitimate successor of all the businesses of Fan's family.

The *Tongkao* indicates that in 1750 permission was given to decrease the annual amount of copper paid to 500,000 *jin*. Unfortunately, there is no detailed original document regarding these deliberations. Based on the account of the provincial governor (*xunfu* 巡撫) of Fujian province in 1783, the quotas of those provinces to which Fan was to supply copper were as follows: 250,000 *jin* for Zhili; 50,000 *jin* each for Shaanxi, Hubei, Jiangxi, and Zhejiang; and the surplus 55,906 *jin* for Jiangsu.[10] The sum was more than 500,000 *jin*. These dates can be confirmed in

[8]Matsuura and Liu assume the year of death was between 1745 and 1747 (Chinese calendar), based on the fact that the name Fan Yubin was deleted in the related sources. See Matsuura 2002 and Liu 1986. Hua Li argued that it should be the 15th day of the second month, Qianlong 10 (March 17, 1745), based on the Fan Yuqi's report. See Hua 2011.

[9]"Fan Yuqi's report on the 22nd day of the sixth month Qianlong 10 (July 21 1745)", FHAC: 04-01-16-0023-011.

[10]"Fusong's report on the 22nd day of the fifth month Qianlong 48 (June 21, 1783)", Gongzhongdang Qianlongchao Zouzhe 宮中檔乾隆朝奏摺 (Secret Palace Memorials of the Qianlong Period, GZDQL), Taipei: National Palace Museum, 1982–1988, Vol. 56, pp. 252–253.

other documents.[11] This means that the *Tongkao* merely stipulated the approximate figure. As Liu mentioned, the yearly amount of 505,906 *jin* did not change again for a long time, at least until the period of the next emperor, Jiaqing (1796–1821) (Liu 1986). The price also, which was equal to the exchange rate between silver currency and the imported copper, remained stable until 1787 (for further details, see the next section).

The question remains whether the copper payment was processed smoothly in this period. Based on Wei and Wu's analysis of the documents related to the Imperial Household Agency, Fan had paid approximately 2,896,000 taels in total by 1755; the unpaid amount was still huge, approximately 475,000 taels, while Qingzhu's commercial operation was very difficult (Wei and Wu 1981). In order to sustain his family's businesses, Qingzhu and his successor frequently had to borrow silver currency from the Imperial Household Agency. On the first occasion, Qingzhu borrowed 200,000 taels and promised to repay the amount within ten years with 12% annual interest. As early as the second year, he became unable to repay and had to appeal for an extension. After this was approved, he borrowed silver currency once again in the name of injecting funds into the copper import business.

Fan Qingzhu died of an illness in 1762, and it became difficult to sustain the family businesses. Fan Qinghong (范清洪), who was Qingzhu's older brother and had previously served a local official, succeeded to the businesses and the debt payments. He borrowed money from the Imperial Household Agency as well, and a greater amount than his brother's loan. Unfortunately, the management did not take a turn for the better. In 1764, Qing authorities retired Fan Qinghong as the general manager of the main businesses of the Fan family and chose Fan Qingji (范清濟), the nephew of Fan Yubin and regarded as the person with the most extensive commercial experience in the clan, to run the main businesses including the sale of salt and the import of copper. It would be difficult for the Qing authorities to recover the loan, if the Fan's commercial management worsened. Therefore, the Qing authorities agreed to make another interest-free loan to Fan Qingji. Qingji sustained the copper-import trade until 1783 by using the profits from selling salt and the loan capital. The decrease of the annual payment amount meant postponement of the payment deadline as well. The repeated extensions resulted in the formation of the copper-import agency by the families of Fan's clan as official merchants.

Fan Qingji ran the family business for almost 20 years. In this period, he extracted nearly 80,000 taels of silver currency every year from the profits of selling salt to subsidize copper imports, as he mentioned himself in 1766.[12] According to the "official price" (14 taels in silver for every 100 *jin* in copper by land and 13 taels by water), and the quotas of related provinces determined in 1764

[11]"Min'eyuan's report on the 21st day of the third month Qianlong 48 (April 22, 1783)" Ibid. Vol. 55, pp. 447–450; "Wang Zhiyin's report on the 18th day of the fifth month Jiaqing 11 (July 4, 1806)", FHAC: 04-01-35-1353-041.

[12]"Zhengrui's report on the 12th day in the first month Qianlong 48 (February 13, 1783)", GZDQL, Vol. 54, p. 699.

(250,000 *jin* for Zhili; 50,000 *jin* each for Shaanxi, Hubei, Jiangxi, and Zhejiang; and the surplus 55,906 *jin* for Jiangsu), the 500,000 *jin* in copper was valued at nearly 69,000 taels in silver currency. Given this, it was still necessary for Fan Qingji to inject approximately 80,000 taels every year into the copper trade. At least at this time, paying copper might not have been as beneficial as paying silver currency itself. Even though paying copper had become a large financial burden, it seems that Fan Qingji was not permitted to change the method of payment any further.

6.8 The Management of the Official Bureau in the Post-Fan Period

According to the reports of the related provinces, Fan Qingji's delivery of copper was often delayed. Nevertheless, he maintained the copper trade and payments until 1781. In that year he had to borrow money again from the Imperial Household Agency. An official in charge of supervising salt sales submitted an investigative report to the emperor which stated that Fan Qingji appealed to be allowed to withdraw from the sale of salt and copper trade. According to Qingji's explanation in the report, he lacked capital, had utilized half of the loan in the management of selling salt, and had invested another half in copper imports as capital. Unfortunately, three junks dispatched to Nagasaki were wrecked, for which the loss reached nearly 60,000 taels in silver currency; the sale of salt incurred a huge loss valued at nearly 30,000 taels since much raw salt was swept away by the destructive storm.[13] The damage to Fan Qingji's businesses was too serious to last any longer; therefore, Fan Qingji decided to retire and wished to sell the assets along with the privilege of selling salt.

Fan Qingji declared the assets and debts under his name as follows: the debts were estimated at more than 770,000 taels in silver currency, and the total would be no more than 800,000 taels, even adding the interest of the loan; the right to sell salt monopolistically in 20 districts was worth approximately 1,000,000 taels at the then market price, and the assets in the sale of salt and the copper import business were also worth more than 500,000 taels. The officials checked the declaration, with the following results: although the sum of Fan Qingji's assets including the privilege of selling salt was not as much as he declared, it was undoubtedly more than 1,000,000 taels and enough to pay off all the Fan's officials debt.[14]

After a further investigation, the Qing authorities concluded that it would permit the retirement of Fan Qingji; entrust ten salt merchants to manage the salt sale business in those 20 districts on behalf of Fan; entrust one of the ten, named Wang

[13]"Zhengrui's report on the 6th day of the eleventh month Qianlong 47 (December 10, 1782)", GZDQL, Vol. 53, pp. 684–686.

[14]Ibid.

Shirong (王世榮), with undertaking the copper trade; order him to extract 80,000 taels as subsidy for the copper import business every year from the profit of selling salt; and complete the copper payment within the formally determined deadline.[15] As a result, Wang became the new official merchant engaged in importing copper from Japan for the Qing authorities.

However, Wang's management was merely maintained for merely four years. The districts in which Wang inherited from Fan the right to sell salt monopolistically were mainly in Henan province, and salt could not sell well there during the drought in 1785.[16] Due to the huge deficit in the salt of sale, Wang lost the financial ability to raise funds for copper imports. Consequently, several years later authorities requested his replacement as the official merchant in charge of copper imports.

During these four years, Wang Shirong himself mainly concentrated on the salt sale and, as to copper imports, entrusted them to his commercial associate, at first Wang Yuanzhang (王元章) and then Qian Mingcui (錢鳴萃) after Wang Yuanzhang's retirement due to illness. In 1787, when Wang Shirong had to withdraw from the copper import business, Qian Mingcui was appointed the official merchant in charge of copper imports and supplied them for the Qing authorities.[17]

As Matsuura pointed out, Qian's domicile by birth was Huzhou (湖州) in Zhejiang province, and he had even been the prefectural magistrate Pingdu (平度) in Shandong province in 1767–1770 (Matsuura 2002, Chap. 2.1). It seems that he had participated in the copper trade before being appointed a local official because there is a historical document to demonstrate that a junk owned by him traded at Nagasaki and drifted down to the coastal waters of Fujian.[18] In other words, he might have engaged in trade with Nagasaki as a private merchant for nearly 30 years before being appointed as an official merchant. Qian Mingcui appealed to the provincial authorities to find that the chief merchant of the Twelve Families underreported the amount of copper they had imported in 1772.[19] According to the empire's investigation of the case, Qian Mingtai (錢鳴泰), Qian Mingcui's older brother, had participated in trade with Nagasaki as a merchant belonging to the Twelve Families, and when he decided to retire there occurred a dispute over the disposition of his trade-related assets between him and the chief merchant of the Twelve Families, Yang Hongfu (楊宏孚). Considering all this related information, it is obvious that Qian Mingcui and some of his family members had been involved

---

[15]"Zhengrui's report on 21st day of the twelfth month Qianlong 47 (January 23, 1782)", GZDQL, Vol. 54, pp. 517–519. "Zhengrui's report on the 16th day of the second month Qianlong 48 (March 18, 1783)", GZDQL, Vol. 55, pp. 164–167.

[16]"Mutengge's report on the 12th day of the fifth month Qianlong 52 (Jun. 26, 1787)", GZDQL, Vol. 64, pp. 357–359.

[17]"Mutengge's report without an unclear date", GZDQL, Vol. 64, pp. 561–562.

[18]"Kaerjishan's report on the 15th day of the fourth month Qianlong 17 (May 28, 1752), GZDQL, Vol. 2, pp. 688–689. The owner of the wrecked ship was recorded as "Qian Mingcui, a merchant from Zhejiang Gui'an".

[19]"Gaojin's report on the 7th day in the sixth month Qianlong 37 (July 7, 1772)", FHAC: 04-01-35-1284-018.

in trade with Nagasaki for a long time before he entered the Official Bureau as an official merchant.

Once he became an official merchant, Qian Mingcui continued as before to use the nearly 80,000 taels in funds from the profits of selling salt in the monopoly districts under the name Fan. However, the price of copper payment was raised to 15.8 taels for every 100 *jin*.[20] This helped Qian Mingcui to manage the copper trade smoothly. In 1795 or 1796, Qian Mingcui died of an illness and his son Qian Jishan (錢繼善) thereby succeeded him.[21] In 1796, the 14th year after Fan Qingji's retirement, the copper payment reached the set amount and eventually repaid all the debt.

Afterwards, as the previous study revealed, a private merchant affiliated with the Twelve Families was appointed the chief merchant (zongshang 總商) of the Official Bureau; the Qing authorities would not involve themselves in the funding problem any longer; the managers of the Official Bureau had to collect all the capital for the copper trade by themselves (Matsuura 2002, Chap. 2.1). Although the Qing authorities called this organization the Official Bureau just as before, this group became no different to the Twelve Families at least with regards to the managerial construction and in the relationship with the Qing authorities.

6.9 The Institutionalization of the Official Bureau

According to the close analysis above of many firsthand historical documents, it is obvious that the formation of the Official Bureau was closely related to Fan's official debt problem. The institutionalization of the organization took a long time and was associated with repeated extensions of the debt repayment periods.

In order to resolve his debt problem, Fan Yubin appealed to the Qing authorities to allow him to import copper from Japan and pay back the debt in copper. The Qing authorities accepted his request and set a term for payment. However, Fan was unable to supply sufficient copper on time, and so his term for repayment was extended.

After Fan Yubin's death, his sons Fan Qingzhu and Fan Qinghong, his nephew Fan Qingji, a salt merchant named Wang Shirong, a copper merchant named Qian Mingcui, and his son Qian Jishan each served as official merchants one after another. The fixed purchase prices of the imported copper including transport expenses were so low that they had to convert the money from the profits of the salt sale to financially support the copper imports. Therefore, the managerial conditions

[20]"Suringga's report on the 27th day in the first month Jiaqing 2 (February 23, 1797)", FHAC: 04-01-03-1853-019.

[21]Previous studies have pointed out that, Qian Jishan had been engaged in the Nagasaki trade as an official merchant, based on the date written in a trading pass issued by the Maritime Custom House of Zhejiang province (Matsuura 2002 and Liu 1986). "Suringga's report" also shows that Qian Mingcui had died by this time (February 23, 1797). According to all of these sources, we can conclude that Mingcui died in 1795, or fell into a critical condition in 1795 and died the next year.

of selling salt to a large degree affected the copper-import trade. Moreover, there is a high possibility that the decrease of Japanese copper output and the Tokugawa's limitation of copper exports led to the hardship the Official Bureau faced in importing sufficient Japanese copper.

Another significant conclusion of the investigations reported in this chapter overturns the prevailing orthodoxy: viewing the formation of the two groups—the Official Bureau and the Twelve Families—as a part of the Qing's restrictive system of foreign trade. The next chapter will discuss the Twelve Families in detail. For the Official Bureau, this orthodox point of view was based on a misunderstanding: the Qing authorities compelled Fan Yubin to undertake the import of copper. However, the official documents demonstrate that Fan himself devised the plan first and of his own accord, importing Japanese copper and using it to pay off official debt instead of using silver currency. Fan seemed to consider that paying in copper was more advantageous than paying silver currency, based on his previous experience of importing copper from Japan.

There is no evidence to demonstrate that the Qing authorities attempted to recommend that Fan import Japanese copper before Fan presented the copper-trade plan himself. Nevertheless, this proposal was certainly favorable for the Qing authorities too: receiving copper from Fan was not only a way to resolve Fan's debt problem, it also supported the supply of copper for the official coinage services. This accidental harmony in the speculation of both sides, Fan and the Qing authorities, contributed to the start of Fan's copper trade and consequently the formation of the Official Bureau.

Chapter 7
The Consolidation of Private Chinese Merchants into the Twelve Families Association

7.1 Key Points in the Study of the Twelve Families Association

As mentioned in the previous chapter, from the middle of the eighteenth century, two merchant groups, the Official Bureau and the Twelve Families Association, engaged in and monopolized the junk trade with Japan for nearly a century. Chapter 6 focused on one of the two, the Official Bureau, and examined the process of its formation and development. This chapter will shift the focus of the discussion to the Twelve Families.

The official name of the Twelve Families Association in Chinese is *minju* (民局) or *gongju* (公局). The term *min* generally means "private" or "nonofficial." It is clear that the Qing authorities wished to use this title to distinguish it from the Official Bureau (*guanju* 官局) in official documents, literally the official group. The term *ju*, in this case, can be thought of as a commercial guild with the approval of the Qing authorities. In the case of *gongju*, the word *gong* means "public". It directly expressed the group's nature and character: a commercial organization that consisted of several authorized merchants. As noted in the following sections, this group primarily consisted of 12 merchants. Therefore, the original term referring to the Twelve Families is *shierjia* (十二家, *Jūnike* in Japanese), which is often seen in many Chinese or Japanese sources in Nagasaki.

The primary aims of this chapter are to re-examine how the Twelve Families formed and to analyze the reasons why the Qing authorities granted it the privileges of monopolizing Chinese merchant trade with Japan, while cooperating with the Official Bureau.

Several previous studies have aimed to clarify these subjects (Yano 1967; Uchida 1949; Yamawaki 1960; Matsuura 2002, Chap. 2.1; Liu 1986; Hua 2011). However, most of them used secondary sources, especially the article in the *Tongkao* (see Chap. 6), and drew the shared conclusion that the Qing authorities promoted the formation of the two groups in order to firmly control and regulate the

H. Peng, *Trade Relations between Qing China and Tokugawa Japan*,
Studies in Economic History, https://doi.org/10.1007/978-981-13-7685-6_7

foreign trade. This chapter will challenge this common view by analyzing several primary-source official documents and focus on the role of the private merchants in the organization and consolidation process.

7.2 The New Framework for Copper Imports After the Reform of 1737

Chapter 4 introduced the reform of the copper administration in 1737. In the early reform plan, the Maritime Customs Houses would purchase Japanese copper from private merchants, when Yunnan copper could not meet the demands of the central coinage services in Beijing.[1] As a response to the plan, some related departments of the Qing authorities drew the following conclusion: when copper production in Yunnan could not meet the demand of the central coinage services, the Qing authorities would recruit merchants who desired to import copper from Japan; order the Maritime Customs Houses of the two provinces, Jiangsu and Zhejiang, to register the merchants' information; purchase the copper they imported according to demand; and then allow them to sell the surplus freely in the market.[2]

However, at that time they had not discussed how much copper the Qing authorities should purchase every year. Several months later, Ji Zengyun (嵇曾筠), the governor-general of Zhejiang province, reported to the emperor that the private merchants in Zhejiang hesitated to sail to Japan to import copper. The reason was thought to be that Japanese copper on the market could be sold for more than 20 taels in silver currency for every 100 *kin*, but the existing official price was merely 14 taels. The merchants strongly wished to sell as much copper as possible on the market and were reluctant to deliver it to the Qing authorities. Ji's proposition was to purchase half of the imported copper from these merchants at the official price and permit them to sell the other half on the market.[3] Following Emperor Qianlong's comments on the report, Ji's proposal was adopted immediately.

Afterwards, Li Wei (李衛), the governor-general of Zhili province, described the situation of coinage services in several provinces in his report to the emperor and proposed that the local administrations of the two provinces, Jiangsu and Zhejiang, should buy imported copper from the private merchants, use it to mint currency within their ministries, and thereby increase the amount of copper coins in circulation and suppress its soaring prices.[4] As a response, the Ministry of Revenue

---

[1]"Yin Jishan's report on the 27th day of the fifth month Qianlong 2 (June 24, 1737)", First Historical Archives of China (FHAC): 04-01-35-1227-011.

[2]"The report of Yunlu and other officials on the 10th day of the seventh month Qianlong 2 (August 5, 1737)", FHAC: 04-01-35-1227-013.

[3]"Ji Zengyun's report on the 15th day of the eleventh month Qianlong 2 (February 3, 1737)", FHAC: 04-01-35-1227-019.

[4]"Li Wei's report on the 16th day of the second month Qianlong 3 (April 4, 1738)", FHAC: 04-01-35-1227-027.

agreed that it was necessary to order the two provinces to purchase the copper in the hands of private merchants at an appropriate price, as Li had said, and emphasized that the imported copper should be sent to Beijing in case Yunnan copper was insufficient.[5] Unfortunately, there is no evidence of how this deliberation concluded among the Qing authorities, whether more and more merchants in Jiangsu and Zhejiang started to engage thereafter in importing copper from Japan, or whether their imported copper was purchased by the provincial administrations.

Around the turn of the year of Qianlong 4 (1739) and early into the following year, the official purchase price of copper once again became a crucial topic since Qing authorities received reports which revealed surging demand for copper coins and a soaring market price in Jiangsu and Zhejiang.[6] Against this background, Zhang Qu (張渠), the provincial governor of Jiangsu, mentioned in his report that the official purchase price of the imported copper was merely 14.5 taels of silver for every 100 *kin*; in contrast, the market price had increased to 19.8 taels. It was necessary to raise the official price to 17.5 taels in order to stimulate the private merchants to import copper from Japan.[7] However, the Ministry of Revenue expressed a dissenting view: raising the purchase price would increase the cost of minting copper coins.[8] Under the emperor's direction, the discussion continued among certain departments and provinces. Finally, the plan from Jiangsu province was adopted, in which the purchase price was to be set at 17.5 taels and Zhejiang province was also to purchase imported copper from private merchants at the same price.[9]

In 1744, Jiangxi province also started to cast copper coins. The provincial officials consulted with copper merchants and agreed that their copper would be sole at the same price as Jiangsu and Zhejiang. This plan soon received the emperor's approval.[10]

Henceforth, the authorities ordered that 60% of copper imported by private merchants was to be delivered for the three specified provinces (25% for Jiangsu, 25% for Zhejiang, 10% for Jiangxi) at a regulated price of 17.5 taels, and merchants themselves were permitted to deal freely with the surplus. This system was sustained for a long time thereafter. It is notable, however, that this system exclusively

---

[5] "The report of Hai Wang and other officials of the Ministry of Revenue on the 25th day of the second month Qianlong 3 (April 13, 1738)", FHAC: 04-01-35-1228-001.

[6] "Lu Zhuo's report on the 13th day of the twelfth month Qianlong 4 (January 11, 1740)", FHAC: 04-01-35-1230-007; "Zhang Qu's report on the 21st day of the third month Qianlong 5 (April 17, 1740)", FHAC: 04-01-35-1230-016.

[7] "Zhang Qu's report", Ibid.

[8] "The report of Na Qin and some other officials of the Ministry of Revenue on the 16th day of the fourth month Qianlong 5 (May 11, 1740)", FHAC: 04-01-35-1231-001.

[9] "The report to the emperor of E'rtai and some other officials on the 24th day of the fourth month Qianlong 5 (May 19, 1740)", FHAC: 04-01-35-1231-003; "Lu Zhuo's report on the 9th day of the intercalary sixth month Qianlong 5 (August 1, 1740)", FHAC: 02-169-13257-11.

[10] "Ce Lengge's report on the 21st day of the first month Qianlong 9 (March 4, 1744)", FHAC: 04-01-35-1234-005.

related to the private merchants' copper trade. The price and delivery destination of copper imported by the Official Bureau was considerably different, as mentioned in Chap. 6.

7.3 Debts of Retired Merchants and the Repayment Plan

As mentioned above, previous studies on the copper trade by the Twelve Families based their discussions on the abstract of the report of Zhuang Yougong (荘有恭), governor of Jiangsu province, from second day of the second month of Qianlong 19 (February 23, 1754). The abstract in the *Tongkao* is merely a secondary source. The original report is in the Taipei National Palace Museum.[11] Compared with the original source, the abstract in the *Tongkao* cut out many crucial points, and these points will show us clearly what caused the consolidation of private merchants.

This report was very long and cited another report to Zhang himself from Peng Jiaping (彭家屏), the provincial administration commissioner (*buzhengshi* 布政使). Peng's report first delivers basic information regarding the debt problem of some "retired merchants" (*jiushang* 舊商) as follows.

In the spring of 1754, the Qing authorities made a firm resolution to resolve the debt problem of retired copper merchants within one year and ordered Jiangsu provincial officials to give an investigatory report on the unresolved debts to the Ministry of Revenue. Based on the investigation of Jiangsu province, the Qing authorities began to deal with the debt problems from 1737 onwards, but it remained unresolved even 18 years later; the total sum of all the unpaid debts was 127,820.02 taels, and more than half of the debtors had died. Jiangsu province favored canceling all the unpaid debts, but this was not approved by the central authorities, especially the Ministry of Revenue. Facing pressure from the authorities, the indebted merchants had to find a practical way to resolve their official debt problem and eventually submitted a repayment plan to the local administration of Jiangsu province. Peng Jiaping, the provincial administration commissioner, cited the plan in his report as follows.

> They (the retired indebted merchants) in the past began the overseas trade and copper import trade. The Japanese established the *wozhao* (Japanese trading pass, *shinpai*) system with the excuse of having too many ships of a wide variety to check, and demanded a price [of a *shinpai*] worth 8,000 or 9,000 taels (silver currency). Yang Yuhe (楊裕和) and some other "current merchants" (*xianshang* 現商) are enjoying the privileges free of cost and using their (the retired merchants') *wozhao* to go abroad. The Japanese permitted the ships [into the harbor] after checking the passes and have not learned yet that the trade is managed by these private merchants (the merchants managed the trade with their own capital). According to the investigation, [in the case of salt sales] the merchant should purchase the *yanyin* (鹽引, the official license for salt sales) before conducting salt sales.

---

[11]"Zhuang Yougong's report on the 2nd day of the twelfth month Qianlong 19 (Feb. 23, 1754)", *Gongzhongdang Qianlongchao Zouzhe* (GZDQL, Chap. 6, Note 10) Vol. 10, p. 200-201.

> The trade with Japan which they launched is similar to the salt sales with *yanyin*. Now they have lost the ability to repay the debts and hence have to expect that the "successor merchants" (*xinshang* 新商) will help them pay their debts in return for inheriting the trade. They have received the consent of the "successor merchants" and are begging for the permission [of the court] via a consultation.

As discussed in Chap. 4 and mentioned just above, *wozhao* (倭照, in Chinese) was the trading pass/permit called *shinpai* (信牌) in Japanese. It refers to the commercial qualification for trading in Japan. In fact, there were various certificates or licenses in Qing China's economy which demonstrated the same commercial qualification as the *shinpai*. The *yanyin* issued by the Qing authorities, was the most famous one among them, and no one could engage in the salt trade without it. When someone fell into debt, he could transfer the *yanyin* to someone else with the permission of the Qing authorities, and in return he could demand that the successor who accepted the certificate have an obligation to pay his official debt. This seemed to be a common practice at the time. Therefore, the retired copper merchants used this principle to support their idea that the copper merchants engaging in the copper trade as their successors had the responsibility to pay their debts.

Chapter 4 has clarified that the provincial administration office of Jiangsu confiscated the fortunes of debtor merchants including the trading passes, *shinpai*, and then lent them to newcomer merchants in order to sustain the copper trade. In the view of the merchants who had withdrawn from the copper trade due to debts, the "current merchants" utilized their trading passes to continually import copper from Japan, and it was certainly reasonable to demand that the "current copper merchants" pay the debts.

7.4 Motives of the Merchants Paying Debt by Proxy

Why did the current merchants agree to pay the retired merchants' debts? Did they recognize the reasons claimed by the retired merchants? Their motives come to the surface in the latter half of the report.

> Yang Yuhe and some other current merchants preferred to help their colleagues out of a sense of duty and yearning to serve the country. After deliberating, they drew up a plan and submitted it to the government. That is, [the court] entrusted the twelve merchants engaging in the copper trade currently as regular members to prevent the delay [in the copper supply] and the arbitrary emergence [of newcomer merchants]. In return for inheriting commercial privileges, they are willing to pay [the debts of retired merchants] accumulated over the past several years.

Entrusting the current merchants as regular members clearly authorized them to have a monopoly on trade with Japan. It is clear that the real motive of those merchants was to gain exclusive commercial privileges, not the idealistic ideas of showing sympathy to former colleagues or serving the country.

It seems that the local officials of Jiangsu province stood up for those merchants. They stated that Japan limited the annual number of Chinese ships with trade qualification to 15 in 1749, and except for the ships belonging to the Official Bureau, the number of ships of private merchants could not surpass 12. Based on this observation, they expressed their opinion that the authorities should "entrust the current 12 men as regular members and dispatch 12 ships every year and make them finish the [debt] payment within six years." Regarding the possibility of a monopoly by the 12 merchants, they added, "if some other merchants wish to participate in the trade, they should be ordered to join the 12 regular merchants and repay the old debts together. Entering [the trade] without the permission [of the court] should be forbidden." They avoided revealing a clear stance on whether or not the Qing authorities should grant the 12 merchants a monopolistic privilege, and the issue that they focused on was how to have the debts repaid as soon as possible.

The officials of Jiangsu province also advised that, because some ships were sailing back to the harbors in Zhejiang province, it seemed better to notify the officials in Zhejiang to transfer the surplus copper to Suzhou (the central city in Jiangsu) after taking a fixed sum, which was used to mint copper coins in the local coinage services. Furthermore, they also noted the possibility that the merchants in Fujian and Guangdong province traded in Japan, and mentioned that it was necessary to notify the officials of these two provinces to forbid the local merchants in their domains to sail to Japan.

Notably, the repayment term was considered to be six years. In the proposal by Jiangsu officials, the Qing court was to tacitly approve the exclusive privilege of trade with Japan in order to collect the official debts of those merchants as soon as possible. The payment term, however, was set at six years as well. There is no other definite evidence to show whether the Qing authorities would allow a de facto monopoly run by the 12 "representative merchants" (*e'shang* 額商) in case the debt problem was resolved within six years. Therefore, granting commercial privileges to the 12 merchants can merely be seen as a provisional measure.

After reading the report of Jiangsu province, the Emperor Qianlong instructed the Ministry of Revenue to deliberate this plan. Even though the original report of the conclusion of this deliberation has not been found, the information can be learned from its official duplicate—such official documents were called *fuzhe* (副摺) or *lufu* (錄副) in Qing China—in the official documents collection *Mingqing Dang'an* (MQD).

According to this source, the Ministry of Revenue approved, for the most part, the plan Jiangsu officials had submitted and added that the provincial administration should register not only the names of the representative merchants but also those of "subordinate merchants" (*fushang* 附商). However, regarding whether to forbid merchants in Fujian and Guangdong provinces from trading with Japan, the Ministry of Revenue did not express a definite opinion. This occurred at a later time, related to a dispute among provincial administrations.

7.5 Junks from Fujian Province in Nagasaki

On the Japanese side, the Tokugawa shogun did not grant any privileges to the two trading groups, the Official Bureau and the Twelve Families, and did not regard them as uniquely monopolizing trade in Nagasaki as the representatives of the Chinese merchants. However, as mentioned above, most Chinese merchants engaging in trade in Nagasaki lived in Suzhou. The Twelve Families gained the approval of the local administration of Jiangsu province, which meant Jiangsu officials would forbid any other merchants in this area from taking part in the trade, except as members of the group. Among the sources related to trade with Nagasaki, there is almost no record of any junks unrelated to the two groups appearing in Nagasaki after their formation in the middle of the eighteenth century.

However, there was no specific restriction limiting the merchants of other provinces such as Fujian province (which is well known as the hometown of some Chinese maritime merchants, especially the merchants engaging in trade with Southeast Asian areas), from importing copper from Japan. In fact, Fujian province established a coinage service as did Jiangsu and Zhejiang provinces, and started to cast copper coins from 1740.[12] Under the directions of the Qing authorities, the coinage service of Fujian mainly used the copper of Yunnan province (the main copper production area in China). It should be seen as exceptional that the provincial administration was permitted by the Qing authorities to purchase copper from the junks drifting down its coastline (Liu 1999).

In the summer of 1768, however, the provincial administration of Yunnan reported to the Qing authorities that the output of the copper mines in Yunnan had decreased and that it was therefore unable to supply sufficient copper to the coinage services in accordance with the established quota set by the authorities.[13] After receiving this report, the Qing authorities directed provinces such as Jiangsu to stop dispatching officials to purchase copper from Yunnan as they did before, once every 3 years; at the same time, they consulted some provinces on the southeast coast, such as Fujian, on whether they could import copper from Japan.[14] In reaction, the officials of Fujian consulted the provincial merchants on whether they wished to import copper from Japan, but these merchants responded negatively to this suggestion, as they claimed that Japan was far from Fujian and they were unfamiliar with the route.[15] Nevertheless, it appears that the officials continued to encourage local merchants to import copper from Japan. According to another report from the

[12]The report of De Pei and Wang Shiren on the 13th day in the second month Qianlong 5 (March 10, 1740), FAHC: 04-01-35-1230-011.

[13]"Yunnan Provincial Governor Ming De's Report on the 15th day of the sixth month Qianlong 33 (July 28, 1768)", GZDQL Vol. 31, pp. 35–36.

[14]"Liangjiang Governor-General Gaojin's Report on the 11th day of the tenth month Qianlong 34 (November 8, 1769)", FHAC: 04-01-35-1272-031.

[15]"Minzhe Governor-General Cui Yingjie's Report on the 19th day of the twelfth month Qianlong 34 (January 15, 1770)", FHAC: 04-01-35-1273-021.

Fujian side, two local merchants, You Zhongyi (游中一) and Ye Rizhang 葉日章), expressed their willingness to engage in the trade. After receiving their applications, the provincial administration immediately issued them the trading certificates called *sizhao* (司照).[16]

Matsuura Akira has outlined the voyages and trading activities of those merchants unconnected with the two groups based on a set of documents called the "True Records" (*shilu* 實錄), compiled in the reign of the Emperor Qianlong (Matsuura 2002, Chap. 3.2). As he pointed out, the merchants of the Official Bureau and the Twelve Families asserted that these two groups were the only ones with permission from the Qing authorities to trade with Japan, and, therefore, anyone outside the two groups should be regarded as smugglers and should not be permitted to trade at Nagasaki. However, the magistrate of Nagasaki took a strong position, not only permitting trade with the unaffiliated merchants, but also demanding that merchants with contrary ideas sail back to China if they maintained their obstructionist stance. In the end, those merchants of the two groups had to yield to the decision of the magistrate.

7.6 Trade of Junks not Affiliated with the Two Groups

From some seldom-used firsthand Chinese sources, such as official reports to the emperor from Jiangsu and Fujian provinces, the events of the trading dispute can be ascertained clearly and in detail.[17]

As seen in Table 7.1, properly speaking, four junks were involved in the incident. The earliest one to arrive was a drifting ship, at least so it appeared. The captain (*chuanzhu* 船主) was Li Daohuai (黎道懐), who was not the real owner but merely a managing agent. The cargo's owner was Zheng Kongyang (鄭孔陽), the younger brother of Zheng Kongdian (鄭孔典), who was known as a famous merchant in the Nagasaki trade prior to this period. Captain Li stated that the junk

[16] "Minzhe Governor-General Cui Yingjie's Report on the 26th day of the sixth month Qianlong 35 (August 16, 1770)", FHAC: 04-01-35-1276-009.

[17] "Minzhe Governor-General Zhongyin and some other officials' Reports on the 1st day of the tenth month Qianlong 36 (November 7, 1771)", FHAC: 04-01-35-1281-019. "Interim Deputy Jiangsu Provincial Governor Sazai's Report on the 19th day of the eleventh month Qianlong 36 (December 24, 1771)", FHAC: 04-01-35-1281-036. "Minzhe Governor-General Zhongyin's Report on the 25th day of the third month Qianlong 37 (April 27, 1772)", FHAC. 04-01-35-1283-016. "Minzhe Governor-General Zhongyin and some other Officials' Report on the 15th day of the fourth month Qianlong 37 (May 17, 1772)", FHAC: 04-01-35-1283-023. "Jiangsu Provisional Provincial Governor Sazai's Report on the 28th day of the eleventh month Qianlong 37 (December 22, 1772)," FHAC: 04-01-35-1286-030. "Jiangsu Provincial Governor Sazai's Report on the 24th day of the sixth month Qianlong 38 (August 12, 1773)", FHAC: 04-01-35-1289-019.

Table 7.1 Voyages of Chinese merchants in or outside the two groups, 1769–1770

Arrival year and ship number	Departure port	Cargo owner	Captain (managing agent)	Ship owner
No. 10 in 1769 (drifting ship)	Zhapu	Zheng Kongyang	Li Daohuai	Wang Antai
No. 11 in 1770	Annam	Lin Chenghe	Xu Xiufeng	Lin Tailai
No. 12 in 1770	Amoy	Ye Rizhang	Ye Wenxiu	Unknown
(Did not reach Nagasaki)	Amoy (N/A)	You Zhongyi	You Chaojin or Wei Honghui	Liu Faxiang

was primarily aimed for the Sulu (蘇祿, islands in the Sulu Archipelago) and had drifted along the coastal area of Guangdong province first due to an adverse wind, then drifted once again midway, and finally arrived at Nagasaki. Its cargo was permitted to be offloaded in Japan. However, on the return voyage, the junk met with an accident again and drifted along the Fujian coastline, and the copper imported from Japan was purchased from the provincial administration. Considering how fortuitous these events were, it is highly possible that Captain Li had not been truthful in saying that he had met with maritime accidents, because in fact he had traded with Japan without the permission of the Qing authorities.

In the following year, 1770, a junk led by Captain Xu arrived at Nagasaki and was registered as the 11th trading ship of the year. There is no definite information related to this junk. The merchants of the two groups heard from the Chinese interpreters in Nagasaki that the junk came from Annam (安南), and the cargo's owner was called Lin Chenghe (林承和).

The junk registered as the 12th trading ship of the year 1770 departed from Amoy (*Xiamen* 厦門), Fujian. The cargo owner was Ye Rizhang, the merchant mentioned above, who applied for the copper trade at Fujian. The junk's voyage and trade seemingly went well. It imported copper from Japan and sold it to the local offices in Fujian province as the owner had expected.

In contrast, another person, You Zhongyi, seemed not to have been so lucky. His partner was expected to serve as the captain of the junk, but this had to be changed due to illness. There is no certain information regarding the departure port. Considering the similarity with Ye's case, the departure may have been from Amoy, the same as Ye's. In any case, his junk ultimately did not arrive in Nagasaki.

7.7 The Logic Behind Monopoly by the Two Groups

After the merchants of the two groups sailed back to Suzhou from Nagasaki, the representative merchants reported their interactions with unaffiliated merchants and the Nagasaki Magistrate's Office to the officials of Jiangsu province. They also requested that the Qing authorities confirm their monopolistic position and forbid other coastal provinces from dispatching merchants to Nagasaki.

They attempted to persuade the Qing authorities with the following logic: it was true that if there was no limitation on copper exports in Japan, more ships could be sent to Japan, and more copper could be imported to China. In this case, the two groups (the Official Bureau and the Twelve Families) would simply dispatch more ships than they had done up to that point (merely 13 ships a year) and would not interfere in any other merchants' trade with Japan. However, the annual number of trading ships allowed had indeed been fixed at 13 by the Japanese authorities, and the two groups had to obey this restriction. This being the case, the entry of other merchants would cause a decrease in copper import by the two groups, and accordingly the two groups would thereby be unable to fulfil the quota that Qing authorities had fixed.

It seems that this logic had the expected effect. The Qing authorities soon issued an edict to Fujian province to suspend the dispatch of local merchants to Japan. From that point onwards, the records show hardly any merchants unaffiliated with the two groups voyaging to Nagasaki and conducting trade there. In other words, the two groups successfully excluded their trade competitors and confirmed their position as the only privileged merchant organizations allowed by the Qing authorities to engage in this trade.

7.8 Re-Evaluation of the Authorities' Attitude towards the Merchants' Consolidation

The process by which the merchants were consolidated can be abstracted as follows. In 1754, many merchants who had withdrawn from trade with Nagasaki because of their failure to fulfill the quotas while having to repay their debts to the Qing authorities had to discuss their debt problem with the 12 "current merchants" engaged in the trade. They argued that the current merchants had a duty to repay their debts because these "current merchants" were utilizing the *shinpai*, which the previous merchants had received from Japan, and their trade would not have been permitted there without the *shinpai*. Eventually, the "current merchants" agreed to pay the debts of these retired copper traders to the Qing authorities. However, the reason they agreed to this was not the same as that given by the merchants who had withdrawn, and their real motive was to monopolize the trade with Japan with the approval of the Qing authorities.

Considering the result of the consolidation, it appears that the Qing authorities granted these "current merchants" the privilege of monopolizing the trade from the beginning. However, things were not so simple. The provincial administration of Jiangsu indeed expressed its clear approval, and the Qing authorities basically allowed the debt repayment plan as well. However, the final instruction of the Qing authorities merely emphasized that the 12 merchants had the responsibility to repay the debts and that other newcomer merchants should contribute to the repayment as well as those 12, and did not mention the monopoly of trade at all. Behind this opaque deliberation, it can be seen that the focus of the Qing authorities had been mainly on debt collection and the copper supply. Such financial and economic issues induced the policy makers to tacitly approve the monopoly trade by the Twelve Families and the Official Bureau. Finally, the Qing authorities began to publicly approve the monopoly trade by the two groups, after disputes which occurred nearly 15 years later persuaded them that the monopoly system was advantageous to the copper imports of Qing China.

The two groups succeeded in monopolizing the trade with Japan by obtaining the approval of the Qing authorities. This is clearly reflected in the number of junks that actually arrived in those years, as seen in Fig. 7.1. During the following almost two decades, the annual number of junks was maintained at 13, which was the same as the number fixed by the shogunate. The two trading groups negotiated with each other to decide how many ships each side should dispatch. This was certainly helpful for the stabilization of the trading relationship.

Again the background of a fluctuating and declining trend in the last years of the eighteenth century, which can be seen in Fig. 7.1., it can be concluded that the shogunate adjusted the fixed number of ships from 13 to 10 and conducted several subsequent rearrangements in 1790, as part of the political reforms generally called the Kansei Reformation (*kansei* 寛政 was the Japanese era name, 1789–1801).

On the Japanese side, the output of copper had decreased gradually since the last years of the seventeenth century. Meanwhile, the shogunate became more and more conscious of the value of copper, and so it had begun to limit the quantity of exported copper in 1715. Furthermore, in order to prevent a sudden rise in smuggling due to this restriction, the shogunate introduced a trading control system based on *shinpai* into the Chinese junk trade. As noted earlier, the *shinpai* can be

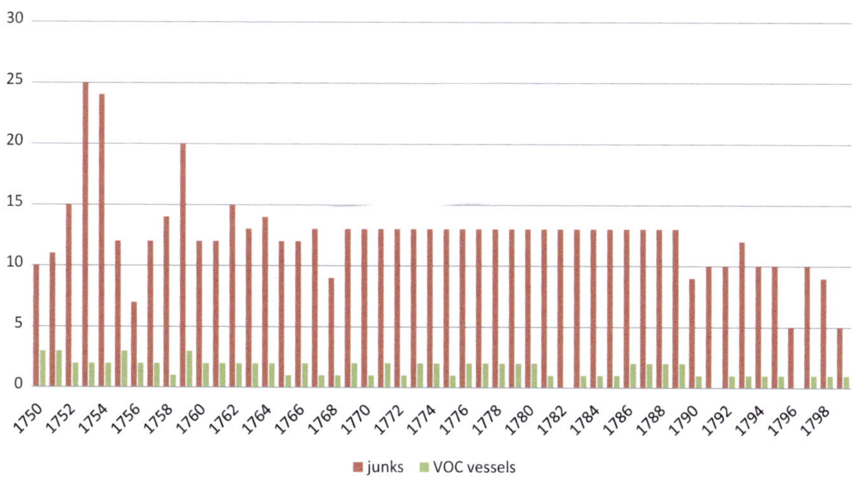

Fig. 7.1 Number of junks and VOC vessels arriving at Nagasaki 1750–1799. *Source* See those in Fig. 1.2. *Note* The years in the figure are those used in the old Japanese calendar

seen as a type of certificate used to check the qualification of the junks to trade. Subsequently, the competition for *shinpai* became relatively intense among Chinese merchants, and it became necessary for the merchants to cooperate with each other in the utilization of the *shinpai*. The management consolidation among the traders can be considered a result of this kind of competition and cooperation.

Chapter 8
Internal Organization of Chinese Trading Groups in Relation to the Qing Authorities

8.1 Management of the Junk Trade

The two preceding chapters re-examined the consolidation of the Chinese merchants under the two groups, the Official Bureau and the Twelve Families Association. In this chapter, the focus will be turned on the management framework of the merchants engaging in trade with Nagasaki, especially during the period in which the two groups formed.

Regarding studies of the management framework of the junks traders, Matsuura Akira's work is most representative (Matsuura 2002, Chap. 1-1, first published in 1972). Matsuura has carefully investigated the roles of the merchants and other crew in the junks, especially the three main members in the management of the junk trade, *caidong* (財東, called *ninushi* 荷主 in Japanese, "the cargo owner"), *xingshang* (行商,[1] also called *chuanzhu* 船主 in Chinese and *funegashira* 船頭 in Japanese, in the case that they served as captains of junks), *chuanhu* (船戸, called *funanushi* 船主 in Japanese, "the ship owner"), and analyzed the management relationships among the three. There are many other studies on the two trading groups, introduced in Sect. 6.1, which are helpful in better understanding the junks' management as well as elucidating fundamental issues related to it.

Nevertheless, merely based on previous studies and references, scholarship is still far from reconstructing the overall the management structure of the junks' Japanese trade. As emphasized previously, more and more original Qing official documents are being made available in archives and institutions in Beijing or Taipei, and many of them are related to management issues of the junk trade with Japan. Utilizing these sources fully will be helpful in deepening our understanding of this issue.

[1]The Chinese term 行商 is also seen in the sources on Guangzhou trade in Qing China, referring to the merchants permitted by the Qing authorities to do business with foreign traders in Guangzhou. In this case, the pronunciation is *Hangshang*. This differs from the pronunciation *Xingshang*, even though the same Chinese characters are used.

H. Peng, *Trade Relations between Qing China and Tokugawa Japan*,
Studies in Economic History, https://doi.org/10.1007/978-981-13-7685-6_8

This chapter attempts to clarify the merchants' composition, the flow of capital, and the commercial conditions, based on seldom-used primary sources. Meanwhile, a further aim is to outline the management frameworks in different periods by referring to the results of other related studies mentioned above.

8.2 Officials and Privileged Merchants in the Copper Trade, 1684–1715

This section will explain the management of junks and cooperation among Chinese merchants before the formation of the Official Bureau and the Twelve Families. Based on studies of Qing China's copper trade (Hall 1949; Kōsaka 1981; Sun 2010), Qing authorities first entrusted *guanchai* (関差, officials in charge of customs houses) or *yanchai* (鹽差, officials in charge of salt sales) with purchasing Japanese copper from the merchants and later entrusted the merchants belonging to the Imperial Household Agency (*neiwufu* 内務府) with importing copper from Japan. However, the commercial relationship between these officials or privileged merchants and the traders who sailed to Nagasaki themselves has not yet been clarified. Here, we introduce two seldom-used official documents called *tiben* (題本, the report to the emperor via the Grand Secretariat, *neige* 内閣) among Qing documents, in order to elucidate this issue.

Both were reports submitted by the provincial governor of Jiangsu in the early years of Emperor Qianlong's reign and discuss the official debts of Liu Shitai (劉世泰), a merchant belonging to the Imperial Household Agency.[2]

Liu had been one of the individuals who promised to supply Japanese copper to the Qing authorities and received money (silver currency) from the authorities to fund the trade. However, his management did not proceed smoothly and he could not attain the copper-importation volume he had promised to the authorities. Therefore, the Qing authorities ordered him to repay the silver currency, and thus emerged his official debt problem. The two reports indicate that brokers called *shangya* (商牙) were involved in the case. It can be assumed that the *shangya* were the merchants or commercial agencies of so-called *yahang* (牙行) in Chinese commercial history. More than six of these brokers had not paid the copper to Liu as promised, which caused the delay of Liu's payment to the Qing authorities. In other words, Liu played the role of a general manager who did not sail to Japan himself and generally charged other brokers with the task of importing copper.

These brokers might then purchase the copper from or contract with overseas merchants who directly imported copper from Japan. There was certainly the

[2]"Chen Dashou's report without an unclear date" First Historical Archives of China (FHAC): 02-01-04-14541-001; "Chen Dashou's report on the 29th day in the eleventh month Qianlong 8 (January 13, 1744)", FHAC: 02-01-04-13591-005. The two seemed to be parts of one report, respectively the first half and the second half. "An Ning's report on the 18th day of the eighth month Qianlong 12 (September 22, 1747)": FHAC 02-01-04-14123-009.

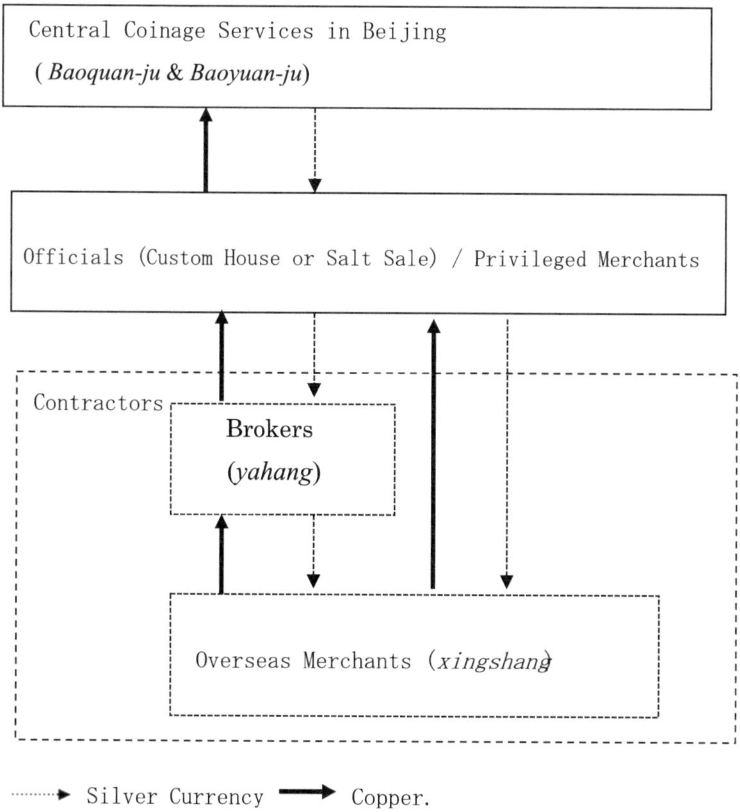

Fig. 8.1 Management framework of Chinese copper merchants, 1684–1715

possibility that a general manager like Liu charged the copper supply not only to the brokers but also directly to the overseas merchants (Fig. 8.1).

8.3 The Provincial Quota System, 1716–1737

In order to facilitate the importation of copper, the Qing authorities introduced a provincial quota system in 1716. To be more precise, the Qing authorities would set the total quantity of copper to be imported annually and distribute this quota among certain provinces. The provincial administrations would appoint local officials to take charge of the imports for a fixed period of time.

These officials in charge of purchasing copper for their provinces were generally called *ban-tong-guan* (弁銅官, the *ban-tong* referred to undertaking tasks related to copper, and *guan* was the Chinese word for "official") in official Qing documents. *Ban-tong-guan* were classified into two types according to their tasks: those in

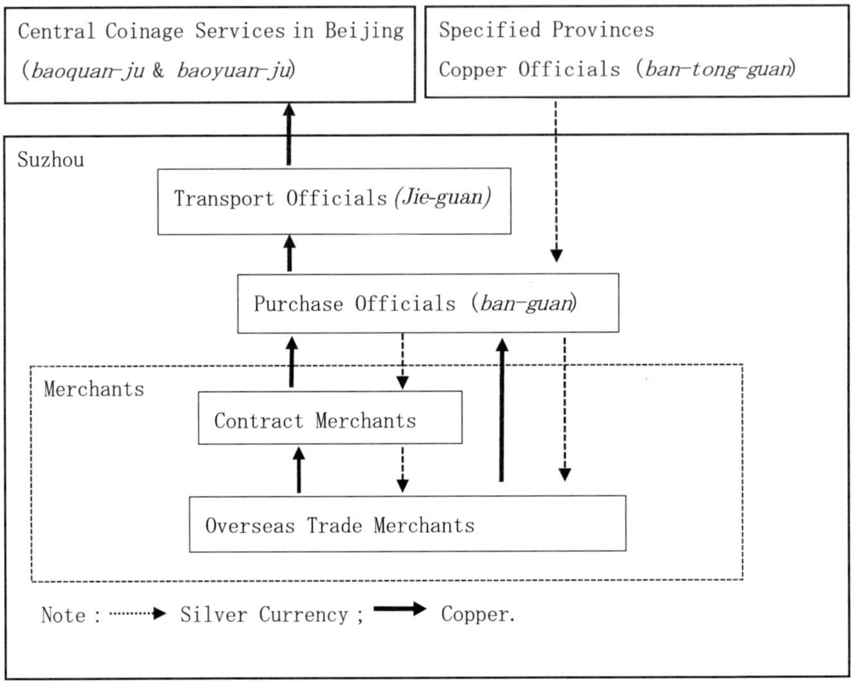

Fig. 8.2 Management framework of Chinese copper merchants, 1716–1736

charge of purchasing copper from merchants (*ban-yuan* 弁員) and those in charge of delivery to Beijing (*jie-yuan* 解員).

After a local official was entrusted with purchasing copper—the *ban-yuan*—he would withdraw silver currency from the coffers of his province and carry it (perhaps not the cash but a draft for money) to Suzhou. There, he consulted and then contracted with copper merchants. After the contract was drawn up, he loaned them silver currency to fund the copper imports.

Regarding this point, a report from 1736 submitted by an official belonging to the Grand Secretariat includes more detail.[3] When a contract merchant accepted money from an official in charge of purchasing copper, he would present a letter of acceptance (*lingzhuang* 領狀, showing how much silver currency he had accepted); a consent letter (*ganjie* 甘結, promising how much copper he should pay and what the payment deadline was); and a guarantee letter (*baojie* 保結) by five warrantors to the official. After the merchant returned from Japan and fulfilled the payment of copper, the official would transfer the copper to another official—the *jie-yuan*—dispatched by the same province, who was in charge of carrying copper, while receiving from him a letter of acceptance with his seal. Then this official would

[3]"Wang Shi's report in the eighth month Qianlong 1 (September or October, 1736)", FHAC: 04-01-35-1227-002.

convey the copper to Beijing and deliver it to the central coinage services (*bao-quanju* 寶泉局 of the Ministry of Revenue, and *baoyuanju* 寶源局 of the Ministry of Works) (Fig. 8.2).

8.4 Tasks and Activities of the Copper Officials

This section focuses on the copper officials. It is difficult to ascertain when they were active, for lack of any direct source such as a list of their names. Table 8.1 can be seen as the first attempt to abstract such information from more than 10 official reports relating to the official debt problem in the copper trade. Incidentally, it is notable that the names in the table were merely some of those who had served copper officials, and the real number was much higher.

Table 8.1 Basic information related to the copper officials

Province	Name	Official position	Term
Jiangsu	Zhao Guangmo 趙光謨	Vice prefectural magistrate of Suzhou	1722–1723
	Cai Yongqing 蔡永清	Prefectural magistrate of Suzhou	1725
	Wen Erxun 溫而遜	Prefectural magistrate of Suzhou	1726
	Huang Tingquan 黃廷銓	Sub-Prefectural magistrate of Taichang	1733 (1st)
Zhejiang	Li Fu 李馥	Provincial governor	1724
	Wu YongFang 吳永芳	Prefectural magistrate of Jiaxing	1722–1723
	Yang Jingzhen 楊景震	Prefectural magistrate of Quzhou	1734 (1st)
Fujian	Zhang Binglin 張秉綸	Prefectural magistrate of Funing	1731 (2nd)
	Zhu Shuquan 朱叔權	Circuit Intendant of Xingquan	1732 (1st)
	Wang He 王輅	Prefectural magistrate of Yanping	1732 (2nd)
	Su Benjie 蘇本潔	Prefectural magistrate of Xinghua	1733 (1st)
	Zhuang Lingyi 莊令翼	Circuit Intendant of Yanjianzhao	1733 (2nd)
	Ren Huan 任煥	Prefectural magistrate of Yanwu (N/A)	1734 (1st)
	Jiang Chaojun 姜朝俊	Prefectural magistrate of Jianning (N/A)	1734 (2nd)
Anhui	Li Fu 李馥	Provincial administration commissioner	N/A
	Li Zhang 李暲	Prefectural magistrate of Taiping	1731 (1st)
	You Bashi 尤拔世	Sub-Prefectural magistrate of Bozhou	1731 (2nd)
Jiangxi	Zhang Daoquan 張道源	Circuit Intendant in charge of transport and salt	1716

Source Most of this information is based on official reports in two collections: GZDYZ and YZCHW. There are also some unpublished official reports: the Report of Baihuang (白潢) dated the 21st day of the fourth month Kangxi 58 (June 8, 1719) (NPM: 401002693); the Report of An'ning (安寧) dated the 18th day of the eighth month Qianlong 12 (September 22, 1747) (FHAC: 04-01-35-1226-031) and the Report submitted by Ji Zengyu 嵇曾筠 and some others dated on the 12th day of the third month Qianlong 1 (April 22, 1736) (FHAC: 002-01-04-14123-009)
Note "1st" = first half of year; "2nd" = second half of year

As is seen in the table, most copper officials were in the position of *zhifu* (知府 prefectural magistrate), *dao* (道 circuit intendants), *zhizhou* (知州 sub-prefecture magistrate), and *tongzhi* (同知 vice prefectural magistrate), except for the special case of Li Fu (李馥), who was in the top class among the local officials and served as the provincial administration commissioner (*buzhengshi* 佈政使) of Anhui and the provincial governor of Zhejiang.

The Qing authorities established two periods in which they would receive copper from the provincial officials. In summary, the copper officials were to finish their task of purchasing copper from merchants and delivering it to Beijing within half a year. Most periods were half a year or one year. To be more specific, there were many cases of one-year periods before 1726 and many cases of half-year periods after 1731. It is highly possible that the Qing authorities determined that the periods for the copper officials to procure copper should generally be fixed at half a year.

There is even less information concerning the contract merchants. The officials of Jiangsu province reported that Zhao Guangmo (趙光謨) had served as the copper official for two years and contracted with 39 copper merchants including Chen Qideng (陳啓登). It is also known in those sources that Li Fu, in his term as provincial administration commissioner in Anhui province, contracted with the famous merchant Guo Yugan (郭裕觀) under another name, Guo Hengtong (郭亨統), to import copper from Japan (see the 4th paragraph of Chap. 4-2).

A merchant named Chen Bowei (陳伯威) is recorded in the sources as well. According to *Tōsen Shinkō Kaitō Roku* (唐船進港回棹録),[4] Chen had been to Nagasaki at least six times between 1719–1727. It can be assumed that Chen imported copper from Japan as the contracted merchant not only of Huang Tingquan (黃廷銓), but also of other copper officials.

8.5 Trading Activities of the Copper Merchants

The records concerning these contracted merchants in the related documents are abbreviated, as in the following text: "39 merchants including Chen Qideng". Only one merchant's name was recorded as the representative, and the other names were omitted. It is difficult to gather the dates related to these contracted merchants. Table 8.2, based on three official reports, is essential for studing the copper traders.

Table 8.2 shows the list of names of merchants who contracted with the copper official of Jiangsu province, either Zhao Guangmo or Cai Yongqing (蔡永青), and other information such as where they came from and when they arrived in Nagasaki. The official reports on the Chinese side provide information about

[4]*Tōsen Shinkō Kaitō Roku* (a book recording much information on the departure and arrival of Chinese junks at Nagasaki port) in Nagasaki Museum of History and Culture (NMHC). The published version is included in Ōba Osamu (ed) (1984) *Tōsen shinkō kaitō Roku, shimabarabon tōjin fūsetsugaki wappu tomechō* (唐船進港回棹錄・島原本唐人風說書・割符留帳：近世日中交涉史料集). Osaka: Kansai University Press.

Table 8.2 Merchants contracted with the copper officials, Zhao Guangmo or Cai Yongqing

Name	Domicile by birth	Arrival year
Chen Qideng 陳啓登	Guangdong (Haiyang, Chaozhou)	1715
Wang Mu'an 王慕菴	Fujian	1721, 1723, 1726
Yu Meiji 兪枚吉	Zhejiang (Wucheng, Huzhou)	1719, 1721, 1722, 1725, 1726, 1729, 1731
Chen Biyong 陳璧雝	Zhejiang (Zhenhai, Ningbo)	1723, 1726, 1730
Shao Youzhang 邵又張	Anhui (Xiuning, Huizhou)	1719, 1721, 1722, 1725, 1727, 1729
Zha Yuanmao 査元茂	Anhui (Xiuning, Huizhou)	N/A
Shao Dongru 邵棟如	Anhui (Xiuning, Huizhou)	1729, 1732
Yi Taoji 伊韜吉	Anhui (Xiuning, Huizhou)	1717, 1718, 1720
Wu Zhishan 呉芝山	Fujian (Changle, Fuzhou)	N/A
Wei Deqing 魏徳卿	Fujian (Min, Fuzhou)	1718, 1720, 1723
Wei Chenyu 魏宸余	Fujian (Fuqing, Fuzhou)	N/A
Li Changtai 李長泰	Anhui (She, Huizhou)	N/A
Wang Shangcheng 汪尚珵	Anhui (She, Huizhou)	N/A
Wang Shangyi 汪尚益	Anhui (She, Huizhou)	N/A
Wang Youxing 汪右興	Anhui (She, Huizhou)	N/A
Wang Junyi 王君貽	N/A	1717, 18, 20, 22

Sources "Report of Chen Dashou without a clear date" (FHAC: 02-01-04-14541-001); "Report from the Ministry of Revenue on the 19th day of the third month Qianlong 9 (May 1, 1744)" (FHAC: 02-01-04-13712-003). An Ning's report on the 18th day of the eighth month Qianlong 12 (September 22, 1747) (FHAC: 02-01-04-14123-009). The records on the arrival year are from *Tōsen Shinkō Kaitō Roku* (Note 4)

"domicile by birth." The records of Japanese officials, *Tōsen Shinkō Kaitō Roku* mentioned above, shows the year of arrival in Nagasaki. This table indicates that at least nine merchants, Chen Qideng, Wang Mu'an (王慕菴), Yu Meiji (兪枚吉), Chen Biyong (陳璧雝), Shao Youzhang (邵又張), Shao Dongru (邵棟如), Yi Taoji (伊韜吉), Wei Deqing (魏徳卿), and Wang Junyi (王君貽) arrived in Nagasaki.

Zhao Guangmo acted as the copper official of Jiangsu province for two years, 1722 and 1723. According to the records on the Japanese side, entitled *Shinpaikata Kiruku* (Chap. 3, Note 6), word arrived in 1724 from Chinese merchants that some merchants could not come as scheduled due to their official debt problems. In the same year, the provincial administration of Jiangsu confiscated the estates of those merchants who had not paid sufficient copper to the government as they had promised to the official Zhao. It can be assumed that between 1724 and 1727 only four of these men, Wang Mu'an, Yu Meiji, Chen Biyong, and Shao Youzhang, received silver currency from the copper official, Zhao, bought goods at the market in China using the silver money, shipped them to Japan, and exchanged them for copper and other Japanese products. For other merchants with their names in Table 8.2, one possibility is that they piggybacked on other merchants' ships, so their names are not seen in the Japanese documents, which merely recorded the captain of each junk; another possibility is that they contracted or employed another merchant or merchants to manage the copper trade as their agents.

8.6 Merchant Cooperation and Networks in the First Half of the Eighteenth Century

There is already a wealth of scholarship on merchant networks in Asian economic history. Among the Chinese merchants engaging in trade at Nagasaki, there were many merchants' networks, and they related with each other in various ways. This section will introduce this aspect of the trade by focusing concretely on the activities of Chen Qideng and his commercial partners.

Chen Qideng is known as a Guangdong merchant, and it seemed that his commercial activities were mainly based in the same city, Suzhou, as some other Japanese copper traders. His name appears frequently in the sources related to trade with Nagasaki.

As seen in Table 8.3, some records indicate that he had been to Nagasaki several times before 1715, and his name seems to be missing from those trade-related

Table 8.3 Merchants in the network centered around Cheng Qideng in the 1710s

Years of departure and return	Ship no.	Departure port	Name of the captain	Relationship with Qideng
1712/ N/A	43	Quang Nam	Chen Qideng 陳啓登	Himself
1713/ N/A	13	Quang Nam	Chen Zuguan 陳祖観	Relative
1715/1716	1	Quang Nam	Chen Qideng	Himself
1715/ N/A	N/A	Nanjing	Yu Meiji 兪枚吉	Partner
1715/1716	4	Quang Nam	Guo Hengtong	Partner
1716/1717	1	Guangdong	Chen Zuguan	Relative
1716/1717	4	Nanjing	Yi Taoji 伊韜吉	Partner
1717/1718	7	Guangdong	Chen Qiying 陳啓瀛	Relative
1717/1718	30	Quang Nam	Guo Hengtong	Partner
1718/1718	10	Nanjing	Yi Hanchen 伊漢臣	Partner
1718/1719	18	Guangdong	Chen Qiying	Relative
1718/1719	31	Nanjing	Yi Taoji	Partner
1719/1720	33	Quang Nam	Guo Henglian 郭亨聯	Partner's relative

(continued)

Table 8.3 (continued)

Years of departure and return	Ship no.	Departure port	Name of the captain	Relationship with Qideng
1719/1720	5	Guangdong	Guo Hengtong	Partner
1719/1720	29	Nanjing	Yu Meiji	Partner
1720/1720	33	Quang Nam	Guo Henglian	Partner's relative
1720/1721	11	Guangdong	Guo Hengtong	Partner
1720/1721	23	Nanjing	Yi Hanchen	Partner
1720/1721	27	Quang Nam	Chen Juguan 陳鋸観	Relative
1721/1721	4	Guangdong	Wang Mu'an 王慕菴	Partner
1722/1722	29	Quang Nam	Chen Qihui 陳啓輝	Relative
1722/1723	17	Guangdong	Guo Hengtong	Partner
1723/1724	9	Ningbo	Chen Liangxuan 陳良選	Relative
1723/1724	11	Ningbo	Wang Mu'an	Partner
1724/1724	28	Guangdong	Guo Hengtong	Partner
1724/1724	29	Quang Nam	Guo Henglian	Partner
1725/1725	16	Guangdong	Guo Hengtong	Partner
1726/1726	24	Guangdong	Guo Yuguan 郭裕観	Partner
1725/ N/A	N/A	Amoy	Chen Zongyuan 陳宗遠	Partner's relative
1726/1726	8	Nanjing	Si Yiting 施翼亭	Partner's partner
1726/1726	15	Guangdong	Guo Hengkai 郭亨愷	Partner's relative
1726/1727	20	Ningbo	Wang Mu'an	Partner
1727/1728	21	Quang Nam	Chen Zhenyu 陳振裕	Partner's partner
1729/1729	2	Siam	Yu Meiji	Partner

Sources Tōsen Shinkō Kaitō Roku (Note 4); *Shinpaikata Kiruku* (Chap. 3, Note 6); *Ka'i Hentai* (Chap. 5, Note 17)

sources on the Japanese side after that year. In 1715, he arrived in Nagasaki as the captain of the first registered junk, and the accountant (*caifu* 財副) of the junk was his commercial partner, Guo Hengtong, a famous merchant as mentioned above and in the former chapter. Since 1715, Guo Hengtong and his family members such as Guo Henglian (郭亨聯) and Guo Hengkai (郭亨愷) came to Nagasaki to conduct trade frequently. In the same period, Chen Zuguan (陳祖觀), a relative of Chen Qideng; Chen Juguan (陳琚觀), and Chen Liangxuan (陳良選), the younger brothers of Zuguan; Chen Qiying (陳啓瀛), the younger brother of Chen Qideng; and Chen Qihui (陳啓輝), who seems to have been a member of Chen Qideng's family as well, engaged in trade at Nagasaki in the decades after 1715.

Furthermore, some records also indicate that his commercial partners, such as Yi Hanchen (伊漢臣) and Yi Taoji, Yi Hanchen's father, had been to Nagasaki as merchants involved in the official debt problem of the copper official Zhao Guangmo. Another merchant, named Wang Mu'an, arrived in Nagasaki at least four times. On the first occasion, he acted as the accountant (*caifu* 財副) of Chen Qideng's junk, and on the second occasion, he led a junk to Nagasaki as the captain and showed the Japanese officials the *shinpai* with the name of Chen Qiying, the younger brother of Chen Qideng, as pointed out above.

It is highly possible that Chen Qideng entrusted the management of his trade in Nagasaki to other merchants, such as his family members or commercial partners, and he merely stayed in Suzhou to preside as a general manager.

8.7 The Official Bureau's Copper Trade under Fan's Direct Management, 1738–1782

This kind of management style based on the networks of the private merchants changed greatly after the formation of the Official Bureau and the Twelve Families. The following two sections will examine the Official Bureau's management.

As clarified in Chap. 6, especially in Table 6.1, Fan Yubin and his family members engaged in various commercial activities. However, the family business began to concentrate on salt sales and the copper trade after his nephew Fan Qingji was appointed as the official merchant. At this time, Fan Qingji normally stayed in his home office in Tianjin, entrusting his third-eldest son, Fan Li (范李), to take charge of the salt sector based in the same city; and appointed his second-eldest son, Fan Du (范杜), to run the copper sector based in Beijing, whose task was mainly to supply copper to the central coinage services.[5]

According to official reports in the 1780s by the official in charge of salt sales, Fan Qingji entrusted the management of the copper-trade office in Suzhou to his nephew Fan Chai (范柴) and his commercial partner Huang Liangdong (黃良棟). In order to smooth the copper trade, the Suzhou office accepted 80,000 taels in silver currency every year from the salt-sale office in Tianjin as the copper-import capital.[6]

These official reports reveals the merchants of copper merchants in Fan's group as follows.

> The Suzhou office is also called *Tianxiju* (天錫局) (*Tianxi* seemed to be the house name of Fan Qingji and his family). They send seven ships to Nagasaki every year. Each ship requires 27,000 taels in silver currency to purchase the shipment. Moreover, wages, taxes

[5]"Rui Zheng's report on the 18th day of the fifth month Qianlong 48 (June 17, 1783)", GZDQL. Vol. 56, p. 187.

[6]"Rui Zheng' report on the 21st day of the twelfth month Qianlong 47 (January 23, 1783)", GZDQL. Vol. 54, p. 519; "E Mingyuan's report on the 21st day of the third month Qianlong 48 (April 22, 1783)", GZDQL. Vol. 55, p. 450.

> and transportation expenses will cost about 3,000 to 4,000 taels. Thus, when the items of the seven ships are combined, the total will be more than 200,000 taels. In accordance with Japanese restrictions, the amount of copper in each ship is set at 100,000 *kin*. In other words, each ship gets 100,000 *kin* of copper as payment for the cargo they shipped here. Then the difference will be paid in goods other than copper. In this way, the amount of the copper shipped by the seven ships back to China adds up to 700,000 *kin*. Most of it, 505,906 *kin*, is transported and supplied to the six provinces which the Qing authorities assigned for repayment of Fan's official debts. The surpluses are permitted to be sold freely and equal more than 30,000 taels. Goods other than copper, imported from Japan, equal about 100,000 taels. Therefore, it is necessary to compensate the capital for the copper trade with 80,000 taels in silver currency every year in order to operate the trade smoothly.

It is easy to imagine that not every merchant affiliated with the Official Bureau sailed to Nagasaki themselves. According to the reports of the Imperial Household Agency in 1783, the Official Bureau only sent three ships to Nagasaki due to lack of funds and entrusted the management of these ships to three merchants, Zhang Yucang (張雨蒼), Fan Ningyuan (范寧遠), and Cui Huanian (崔華年).[7] Each of the three served as the captain of a junk. Their names are also seen in the Japanese records. For instance, Cui Huanian had been to Nagasaki three times, in 1774, 1778, and 1780 (Nakamura 1997).

We can outline the management of the Official Bureau as follows: Fan Qingji acted as an official merchant like the general manager of an enterprise and ran the commercial activities of the group as a whole based in his home office in Tianjin; his family members such as Fan Chai and commercial partners such as Huang Liangxuan were entrusted to be the managers of the copper-trade office in Suzhou; and some merchants were affiliated to or contracted with the copper-trade office, such as the merchants referred to above, Zhang Yucang, Fan Ningyuan, and Cui Huanian.

8.8 The Official Bureau's Copper Trade in Post-Fan Era, 1783–1796

Fan Qingji retired from the copper trade and salt sales in 1783 due to financial difficulties, and this also signified the end of direct management of the Official Bureau by Fan Yubin and his family members. The Qing authorities chose ten merchants to share the salt sales which Fan had directly managed previously and entrusted one of the ten men, Wang Shirong (王世榮), to run the copper-trade sector after accepting the proposal from an official in charge of salt sales. This personnel change at the top level of the Official Bureau seemed to have no great influence on the basic management structure of the group. For instance, Peng Yilai (彭義來), who was known in the Japanese trade-related documents as a merchant in

[7]"The report of the Imperial Household Agency in Qianlong 48 without clear dates", FHAC: 03-0787-041.

Table 8.4 Genealogies of the official merchants, 1738–1796

Name	Term	Birthplace	Official position	Relations
Fan Yubin	1738–1745	Shanxi (Jiexiu)	*Taipusi Zhengqing* 太僕寺正卿	
Fan Qingzhu	1745–1762	Shanxi (Jiexiu)	*Taipusi Shaoqing* 太僕寺少卿 *Hubu Langzhong* 戸部郎中	The third-eldest son of Yubin
Fan Qinghong	1763	Shanxi (Jiexiu)	*Ningshaotai Dao* 寧紹台道 *Hubu Langzhong* 戸部郎中	The second-eldest son of Yubin
Fan Qingji	1764–1782	Shanxi (Jiexiu)	*Houxuan yuanwailang* 候選員外郎	Nephew of Yubin
Wang Shirong	1783–1787	Zhili	*Juanzhi langzhong* 捐職郎中	
Qian Mingcui	1788–1795	Zhejiang (Guian)	*Jiansheng* 監生	
Qian Jishan	1795–1796	Zhejiang (Guian)	N/A	Son of Mingcui

the Official Bureau, made voyages to Nagasaki as the captain of a junk in 1777 and 1778, and came to Nagasaki again in the same role in 1787, a year in which Wang had been the official merchant of the Official Bureau instead of Fan (Nakamura 1997). This indicates that the merchants generally called *xingshang*, who came to Nagasaki to carry out transactions by themselves, seemed to experience no great changes with the change of the top manager (Table 8.4).

For the capital needed to import copper, the official in charge of the salt sales proposed that it was necessary to deliver 80,000 taels in silver currency every year as funds for the Official Bureau's copper import and that the capital source might be the same as before.[8] Emperor Qianlong instructed the related departments of the Qing authorities to deliberate this proposal. Even though no evidence shows the conclusion of this consultation, some later official reports indicate that the Official Bureau continued to get 80,000 taels in silver currency every year from the profit of salt sales in the areas in which Fan's family kept monopolistic sale privileges.

Wang acted as the official merchant for only 4 years. His successor was Qian Mingcui (錢鳴萃). Unlike Wang Shirong, Qian was merely a copper merchant and was not engaged in salt sales at the time. In the years in which Wang led the Official Bureau, he sent his commercial partner Wang Yuanzhang (王元章) to manage the copper office in Suzhou and ran the salt sales himself, as before. After Wang Yuanzhang retired from the copper trade due to illness, Qian, who was Shirong's commercial partner as well, succeeded him in this role. Qian was thought to be suitable as an official merchant mainly because of his long experience as a copper trader. At the same time as he began to run the Official Bureau, the management of the copper sector and the salt-sales sector were separated entirely. However, the

[8]A report without clear date and author, GZDQL, Vol. 64, pp. 561–562.

close relationship of the capital flows between the two remained; the merchants in the salt sector had to collect 80,000 taels in silver currency every year as before from their profits selling salt to support the management of the copper-trade sector, because the managers of both sectors had the same task: repaying the official debts under the name of Fan.

8.9 Management Framework of the Twelve Families

In the case of the Twelve Families, 12 men became the representatives of all the private copper merchants in the eyes of the Qing authorities, after they had promised to pay the official debts in 1755 instead of the retired copper merchants (see Chap. 7). Since that time, any other merchants who wanted to enter the trade were in principle to pay those debts in common with and under the names of representative merchants. The Qing authorities called the 12 merchants *e'shang* (額商) and some other merchants who wanted to enter the trade later, *fushang* (附商). These *e'shang*e were regarded as being fully responsible to the Qing authorities; it is clear that *fu* indicated that they were attached. To make this easier to remember, this study uses the term "representative merchants" to express *e'shang* and "subordinate merchants" to express *fushang*. Later discussion and narration will follow this usage.

The identity of the 12 representative merchants has attracted the interest of many scholars for a long time. Unfortunately, there is no clear answer because of a lack of related sources such as a list of their names. The official reports discussed above merely mentioned the case in the following way: "the twelve merchants such as Yang Yuhe (楊裕和)." In other words, only one name appears in the official documents, generally speaking. The reason might be that the central authorities were not interested in the identity of the 12 men but only cared about how they would—and whether they could—pay the official debts. Upon examining this kind of record keeping, it is easy to believe that Yang was a chief representative of the 12 merchants in the officials' view. In fact, the later related official reports to the emperor himself had the same kind of convention, which was merely to record one name instead of referring to all of them.

There is a report from 1796, delivered by the provincial governor of Jiangsu to the Grand Secretariat of the Qing Empire, which was related to electing an individual as the "chief merchant" (*zongshang* 總商) of the Official Bureau.[9] According to this report, there were only six representative merchants such as Yang Lanzhou (楊蘭洲) and Wang Lyujie (王履階) in the so-called Twelve Families. Yang was the chief merchant of the Twelve Families at this time, so that it was difficult for him to act in the same role of the Official Bureau. Among others, Wang was a

[9] A transcript of the official report submitted by Fei Cun on the 30th day of the eighth month Jiaqing 1 (September 30, 1796), FHAC: 03-1776-060.

merchant with rich capital and estates, and therefore he could be regarded as a suitable person to play this role. As some scholars have revealed based on other sources, Wang then became the chief merchant of the Official Bureau, and the two other merchants, Gu Yuanqi (顧元起) and Liu Yuntai (劉雲台), were registered by the authorities as his assistants (Matsuura 2002, Chap. 2-1).

8.10 The Number of Representative Merchants and the Registration System

The number of regular merchants in the Twelve Families registered by the Qing authorities decreased gradually after its formation. In regard to this point, the official report in 1772 to the Emperor Qianlong by Gao Jin (高晉), a governor-general of the Langjiang area (including Jiangsu, Anhui, and Zhejiang provinces), provides some significant details.[10] The main topic of this report was related to a suit by Qian Mingcui. Qian was a copper trader and later became an official merchant of the Official Bureau in 1788, as mentioned above. There is no obvious evidence to confirm whether he had any direct connection or relationship with the Official Bureau at this time. In his suit, Qian pleaded that Yang Hongfu (楊宏孚), who was the son of Yang Yuhe and had succeeded his father as the chief merchants of the Twelve Families, changed the number of representative merchants in this group without report it to the Qing authorities. In response, Gao stated that they had implemented an investigation and explained that the change in members had been approved and registered by the provincial administration.

This report referred to an important term, *gu* (股). As a commercial term, *gu* or *gufen* is generally translated as "stock". However, in the case of the Twelve Families, the *gu* seemed to be like the term *kabu* (株) in Edo Japan, which denoted membership in an organization or a commercial community with authorized, exclusive privileges in a certain commercial field. When the Twelve Families formed in 1755, there were 12 representative merchants. As time went on, the number changed due to disease, death, or retirement. In order to control the management of this organization, the provincial administration of Jiangsu in 1766 instructed the officials to carry out an investigation, then demanded that all of the representative merchants deliver letters of guarantee, and finally permitted the number of members in the Twelve Families to be reduced.

It was necessary for the Qing authorities to manage an accurate number of representative merchants in the Twelve Families because each of them had the responsibility to pay the official debts of the retired copper traders and moreover to guarantee the supply of copper to the coinage services.

[10]"The report of Gao Jin on the 7th day in the sixth month Qianlong 37 (July 7, 1772)", FAHC: 04-01-35-1284-018.

According to the report in 1796, explained in the previous section, it is known that the number of representative merchants in the Twelve Families decreased to merely six. Nevertheless, the term "Twelve Families" was still in use.

8.11 Management of the Official Bureau After Privatization

Compared to the management of the Twelve Families Association, that of the Official Bureau seemed to be difficult because the official merchants had to fill the import quotas and deliver copper to the Qing authorities at a lower price (much lower than the market price, see Sect. 7.2). As previously noted, the Official Bureau was privatized after the payment of official debts under the name of Fan Yubin was completed in 1797. The Qing authorities selected three merchants from the Twelve Families and appointed one of them as chief merchant and the other two as his assistants.

After the privatization, the name of the trading organization—Official Bureau—and the copper supply system to the designated provinces were both maintained as before. However, the management was shifted in the same way as that for the Twelve Families. The newly selected managers of the Official Bureau were to operate this trade organization with their own funds but were still required to fill the copper supply quota at the same low price as before. Owing to these unfavorable conditions, the privatized Official Bureau was unable to escape its management difficulties.

Previous studies of the two groups have revealed many chief merchants succeeded the first, Wang Lyujie. This study will add new evidence and show the genealogies of the Official Bureau's chief merchant in Table 8.5.

Table 8.5 Genealogies of the chief merchants of the official bureau after 1797

Name (relative relationship)	Term	Reason for change	Subordinate merchant (relative relationship)
Wang Lyujie	1797–1799	Death	Wang Wen'ao 王文鏊 Sun Bangjie 孫邦傑
Wang Rigui 王日桂 (younger brother of Lyujie)	1799–1807	Retirement	
Cheng Hongran 程洪然	1807–1812	N/A	
Wang Yongzeng 汪永增	1813–1816	Lack of capital	
Wang Yu'an 王宇安 (son of Rigui)	1817–1839	Death	Jiang Shanchang 江善長 Wang Bingfu
Wang Bingfu 汪炳符	1839	Death	Wang Yuanzhen (son of Yu'an) Jiang Chengde 江成德 (son of Shanchang)
Wang Yuanzhen 王元珍	1840–N/A	N/A	Wang Chengjin 汪承晉 (son of Bingfu)

8.12 The Management Framework of the Official Bureau and the Twelve Families

This section aims to summarize the results of the above examinations according to the two images of the management of the Official Bureau and the Twelve Families Association.

First we must examine the management of the Official Bureau in the middle and later eighteenth century. The Official Bureau was formed after 1739, in which year Fan Yubin, an official merchant, restarted the copper trade and used the imported copper to pay his official debts. Fan and his successors as official merchants were required to supply imported copper to the five specified provinces at fixed quantities and at a regulated price (see Sect. 6.5). In principle, the Official Bureau could sell the surplus freely at market price once they had exceeded the annual quota. However, the Tokugawa shogunate increasingly reduced the amount of copper exports throughout this period, until it became difficult for Fan to reach the quota, and naturally there was seldom surplus copper to be sold in the market. Therefore, Fan's copper trade deficit increased and, accordingly, it became a large fiscal burden, forcing the managers to redirect large amounts of money from profits in the salt-sale sector to sustain the copper trade. This management of the Official Bureau continued for more than a half-century.

Copper importation by the Official Bureau could not meet all of the Qing's demand for Japanese copper. Some provincial administrations had to purchase copper from private merchants in order to meet the demands of the provincial coinage service. Accepting some officials' opinions, the Qing authorities decided in 1744 to purchase 50% of the copper imported by private merchants at a regulated price, and some years later they raised the purchase rate to 60% (see Sect. 7.2) (Fig. 8.3).

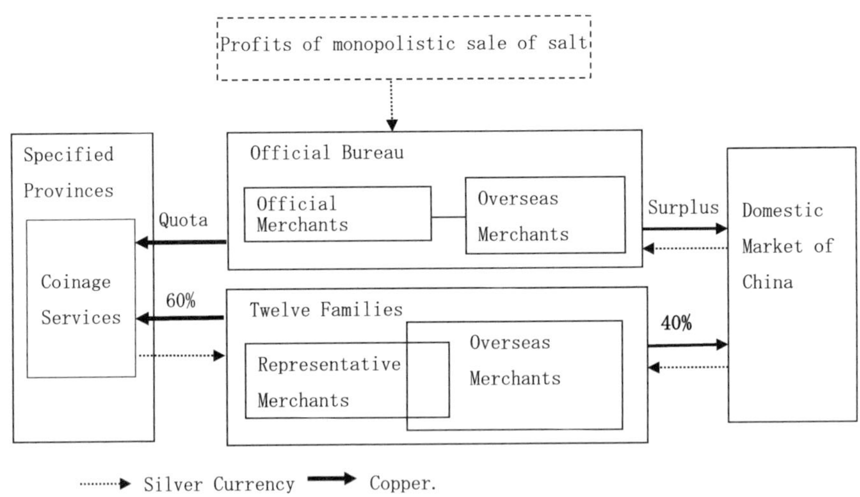

Fig. 8.3 Management framework of the Official Bureau and Twelve Families, 1755–1797

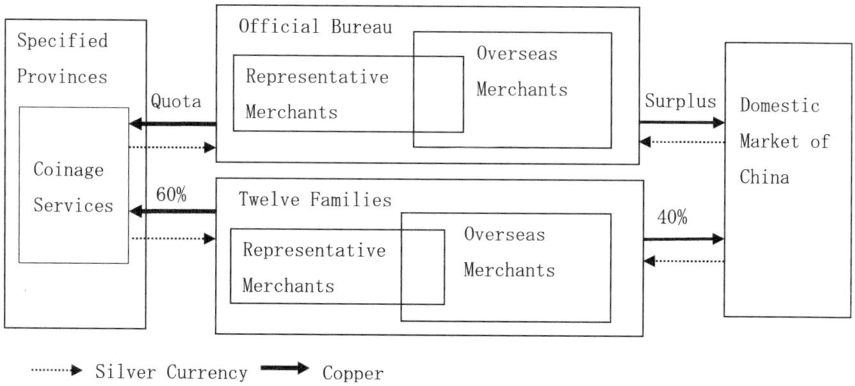

Fig. 8.4 Management framework of the Official Bureau and the Twelve Families, 1797–1859

In 1754, the 12 copper-trade merchants found an opportunity to monopolize the Chinese junk trade with Japan, separate from the trade by Official Bureau. This was the formation of the Twelve Families Association. The representative merchants of this trading group were registered by the Qing authorities, and one of them was appointed as the chief merchant. In principle, other merchants could join the association as subordinate merchants. Of the copper they imported from Japan, 60% was purchased by several specified provinces at a regulated price, while the other 40% was permitted to be sold on the market (Fig. 8.4).

As mentioned above, compared to the management of the Twelve Families, that of the Official Bureau seemed difficult, because the official merchant had to fulfill the import quota and deliver copper to the provinces at a lower price. Management deficits obliged the Qing authorities to propose the corporatization of the Official Bureau in 1797. They selected three private merchants to be representative merchants of the Official Bureau and appointed one of them as the chief merchant of the group and the other two as assistants. These three merchants were to collect capital to run the Official Bureau but were still required to fulfill the import quota at the same low price as before. Owing to these unfavorable factors, the privatized Official Bureau encouraged unavoidable management difficulties.

Chapter 9
Trade Under Pre-Arranged Conditions: A New Commercial Style in the Late Eighteenth Century

9.1 Dutch–Japanese "Contract Trade" in Nagasaki

Before delving into this subject, it is particularly worth noting a similar systemic shift that occurred in Dutch–Japanese trade. In 1752, a trading contract was concluded between the VOC (Dutch East India Company) and the Nagasaki Trading House (*Nagasaki Kaisho* 長崎会所). In content it was merely a confirmation of the existing trading rules. However, its significance can be seen when viewing the style of transaction, because the VOC was demanded to merely obey the trading rules set by the shogunate previously and, at this time, they not only negotiated with the Japanese officials but also received from them a contract as an agreed-upon certificate (Suzuki 2004, pp. 399–406).

A recent study on this topic by analyzing the writings of G.F. Meijlan, the head of the VOC's Dejima Factory in the 1820s, has revealed that the Dutch merchants at that time called this new transaction style "Contract Trade" (*Contract Handle* in Dutch) (Matsukata 2013). As defined by Meijlan, the contract trade was a trading method which mainly applied to importing merchandise into Japan according to the orders of the Nagasaki Trading House, whereby the price would be set by negotiation and would mainly be influenced by the evaluation of the professional imports appraisers (*mekiki* 目利) of the Nagasaki Trading House.[1]

These studies bring up the question of whether there were similar systemic changes in Sino–Japanese trade in the same period, especially in light of the consolidation of the Chinese merchants.

---

[1]Meiljan, Germain (1833), *Geschiedkundig Overzigt van den Handel der Europezen op Japan.* Batavia, pp. 166–168.

H. Peng, *Trade Relations between Qing China and Tokugawa Japan*,
Studies in Economic History, https://doi.org/10.1007/978-981-13-7685-6_9

9.2 The Economy and Foreign Trade of Japan in the Tanuma Era

The overall re-orientation of the shogunate's economic policy in the late eighteenth century should also be considered. The years in question are considered generally to be the beginning of the Tanuma era (in a broad sense, 1767–1786), which is generally characterized by the shogunate adopting a series of mercantilist policies under the initiative of the chief elder, Tanuma Okitsugu (田沼意次, 1719–1788). Scholars argued that during this period there was an increasing concern to ensure economic profits for Japan as a whole, referred to in this context as *kokueki* (国益), and the Tanuma administration adopted many policies to stimulate the economy and increase government revenues.[2]

Certain aspects of Tanuma's economic reforms are broadly known, such as authorizing the commercial privileges of many *Kabu-nakama* (株仲間 merchants guild-like associations) and collecting special commercial taxes from them; granting monopoly patents for numerous goods including brass, iron, ginseng, etc.; launching large projects of drainage and farmland cultivation; and encouraging foreign trade. All these measures aimed to expand the tax revenue of the shogunate.

In such mercantile atmosphere, many "prospectors" emerged at each level of society with the characteristics of so-called *yamashi* (山師). Many shogunate officials who tried to submit plans for increasing financial revenues were promoted to positions of responsibility (Fujita 2012).

In the case of trade at Nagasaki, as many scholars such as Uchida Ginzō and Nakai Nobuhiko have noted, the shogunate began to import silver and gold via trade with Chinese merchants and the VOC, and expanded the production and exportation of marine products (Uchida 1921, Nakai 1971).

The terms *yakujō* (約条) and *hyōbun* (憑文) can be seen in sources regarding the silver- and gold-import trade, but these terms are seldom seen in sources related to the Nagasaki trade before this period. Considering the meanings of the Chinese characters used to record these two terms, *yakujō* seems to have been a type of trading agreement, and *hyōbun* seems to have been a paper certificate. As examined in the following sections, these two imprecisely-defined terms contain clues about a new trading model for the Nagasaki trade.

---

[2]While in this context *kokueki* does refer to the economic profits of Japan as a whole, in other contexts it may very well refer to economic profits of individual domains. See Robers (1998).

9.3 Chinese Silver-Currency Importation by the Twelve Families

The *Nagasaki Jitsuroku Taisei* (長崎実録大成 compilation of the documents on Nagasaki, NGJR, see Chap. 5, Note 2) is one of the most significant sources for studying the history of maritime trade in Nagasaki in the early-modern period. It contains a great deal of information concerning the *yakujō* and *hyōbun*. One of the early cases contained in this source concerns the import of Chinese silver currency by junks in 1763.

On August 15 of that year, a junk arrived at Nagasaki. It was registered as the 9th trading ship of that year and carried 300 *kanme* of *genshi-gin* (元絲銀), a kind of Chinese silver bullion, called *yuansi-yin* in Chinese. The captain of the junk, Wang Lyujie (王履階), who became the chief merchant of the Official Bureau after its privatization in 1797 (see Sect. 8.9), submitted a trading certificate to the Nagasaki officials. The certificate contained a transaction agreement that set the price of 300 *kanme* in Chinese silver at 300,000 *kin* in copper, stipulating that 70% would be paid in copper and 30% in marine products, and fixing the period in which this agreement was in effect at 20 years.[3] The records of the Nagasaki magistrate in 1764 reveal that this agreement was initially drawn up in 1762.[4] Briefly speaking, Wang Lyujie accepted the certificate concerning this transaction agreement in 1762 and returned to Nagasaki again with it the next year.

According to the records in the *Nagasaki Kaisho Gosatsu-Mono* (長崎会所五冊物 five books on the Nagasaki Kaisho) edited by the staff of the Nagasaki Trading House as a reference manual for managing trade with foreign merchants, Wang Lyujie was a merchant affiliated with the Twelve Families, and based on a contractual agreement the taxes and service charges for all transactions involving Chinese silver were to be paid by the Twelve Families.[5] This evidence strongly suggests that the Japanese regarded the contractor on the Chinese merchants' side to not be the individual merchant but the merchants' group as a whole.

Some sources, such as the *Nagasaki Jitsuroku Taisei* and the *Mei'an Chōhōki* (明安調方記 The Investigation Records in Meiwai and An'ei Era, MACHK),[6] make it possible to track who carried Chinese silver to Nagasaki over the next 20 years.[7]

---

[3]NGJR (Chap. 5, Note 2). The published version (1973), p. 278.

[4]Article dated the 20th day of the eighteenth month Meiwa 1 (September 15, 1764). *Meiwa Gannen Okakitsuke no Utsushi* (明和元年御書付之写 Manuscript of the Official Documents in Meiwa 1) in Nagasaki Museum of History and Culture (NMHC).

[5]Nagasaki Kenshi Hensan Iinkai (ed.) *Nagasakiken-shi Shiryō-hen* (The History of Nagasaki Prefecture: Historical Sources) Vol. 4 , Tokyo: Yoshikawa Kobunkan, 1966. The original source is in the possession of NMHC.

[6]The original source is in the possession of NMHC, and the published version is included in *Nagasakiken-shi Shiryō-hen,* Vol. 4, Ibid.

[7]Especially in one of the chapters of the book *Mei'an Chōhōki*, titled "Tōsen Yatomachi Jūn" (唐船宿町順 The Before-and-After Order of the Shipping Servicing Neighborhoods).

Table 9.1 Merchants importing "Chinese silver currency" to Japan

Year	Ship number/captain/affiliation: O. (Official Bureau) or T. (Twelve Families)
1764	No. 4/Song Jingting/T.; No. 13/Wu Guoting/T.
1765	No. 4/Cheng Jiruo/T.; No. 8/You Pu'an/T.; No. 10/Gong Zixing/T.
1766	No. 5/Tang Chonghua/O.
1767	No. 1/You Pu'an/T.; No. 10/Wei Dongting/T.
1768	No. 1/Liu Qingshang/T.; No. 7/Zhang Yunwen/T.
1769	No. 1/Liu Qingshang/T.
1770	No. 1/Cheng Jiruo/T.; No. 2/Cheng Jian'nan/T.; No. 7/Gong Yunrang/T.; No. 13/You Pu'an/T.
1771	No. 9/Cheng Jian'nan/T.
1772	No. 1/Gu Lantang/T.; No. 2/You Pu'an/T.; No. 7/Wang Zhuli/T.; No. 12/You Pu'an/T.
1773	No. 1/Shen Nanlei/T.; No. 12/Cheng Jian'nan/T.
1774	No. 1/Qian Xingyu/(N/A); No. 4/You Pu'an/T.; No. 6/Wang Shengwu/O.; No. 9/Xu Yutang/T.
1775	No. 1/Wang Zhuli/T.; No. 2/Gu Lantang/T.; No. 9/Xu Rongguang/T.*; No. 11/Wang Shengwu/O.*
1776	No. 3/Xu Yutang/T.*; No. 5/Wang Zhuli/T.* (N/A); No. 6/Gu Shuchang/T.*; No. 8/ Huang Yongtai/T.*
1777	No. 3/Qian Paqian/(N/A); No. 10/Cheng Jian'nan/T.
1778	No. 5/Wang Tongfeng/T.
1779	No. 9/Zhou Renlu/T.*
1780	No. 5/Gu Shuchang/T.*
1781	No. 6/Wang Tongfeng/T.
1782	–
1783	No. 7 /(N/A); No. 8 /(N/A); No. 13 /(N/A)

Source: (1) NGJR (Chap. 5, Note 2). (2) MACHK (Note 6). (3) Matsura Tokei, *Nagasaki Kokin Shūran* (*Nagasaki Kokin Shūran* (長崎古今集覧, *comprehensive records of accidents and modern Nagasaki*). There are some transcript books in the Historiographical Institute, The University of Tokyo, and the Nagasaki Museum of History and Culture, and other locations. A version published in 1976 by Nagasaki Bunken Sha. (4) Nakamura Tadashi (1997), "Nihon Raiko Tōsen Ichiran" ((来航唐船一覧 List of the Junks Arriving in Nagasaki) in *Kyushu Bunkanshi Kenkyūsho Kiyō* (Bulletin of the Research Institute of Kyushu Cultural History) 41.
Note Entries such as "T.*" or "O.*" mean the captain's affiliation can be surmised based on other records in the same kinds of sources, despite no clear notification in the directly related items

Table 9.1 accumulates the dates in the period 1764–1783. "Ship Number" indicates what number the junk was registered under by the Japanese officials after arriving at Nagasaki port; "the captain" was generally called *chuanzhu* (船主) in Chinese and refers to the top manager of each junk, as explained several times in this book; regarding "the affiliation", "T." and "O." respectively designate the "Twelve Families" and the "Official Bureau." As seen in the table, it is clear that the absolute majority of the 43 junks' captains belonged to the Twelve Families. Why were there at least two exceptional cases? Considering the close cooperation between the two groups, a reasonable explanation might be that the

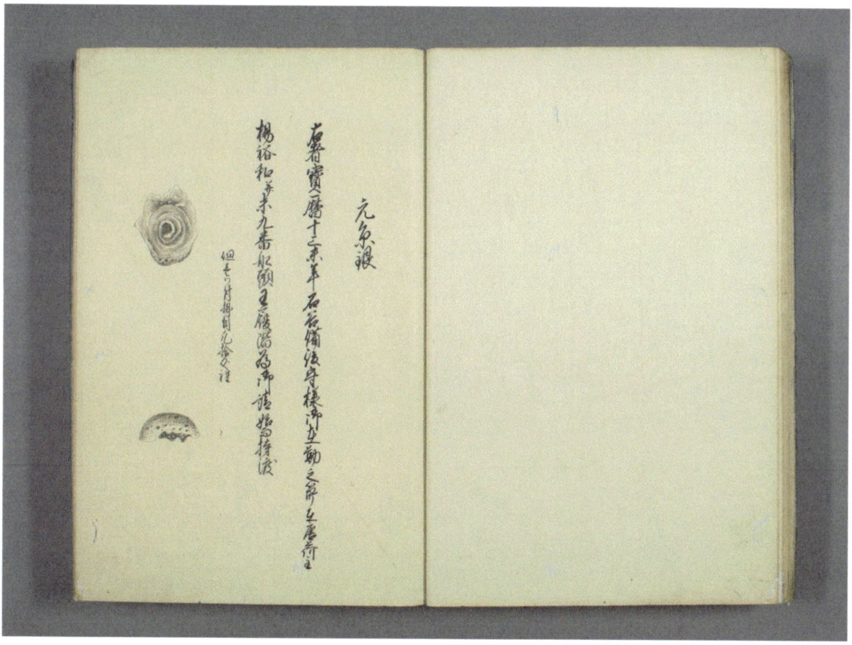

Fig. 9.1 *Genshigin* (元糸銀, a sort of Chinese silver currency imported by Junks to Japan), In: *Tō Oranda Mochiwatari Kinginsen Zukan* (唐阿蘭陀持渡金銀銭図鑑, Illustration of the Gold and Silver Currencies Imported by the Chinese and Dutch). Courtesy of Waseda University Library

Twelve Families would charge the transportation or the transaction of Chinese silver currency to a merchant of the Official Bureau, in case the junk or the merchant of the Twelve Families could not sail to Nagasaki owing to special reasons or emergency conditions (Fig. 9.1).

9.4 Spanish Dollar Importation by the Official Bureau

At the same time as the events mentioned above, the Official Bureau also initiated a new import transaction in the same way, dealing with Spanish dollars. A merchant affiliated with the Official Bureau named Cui Jingshan (崔景山) proposed to the Nagasaki magistrate in 1764 that thereafter 50 *kanme* of Spanish dollars might be imported to Japan from China every year.[8]

With the permission of the Nagasaki magistrate, Cui Huishan (崔辉山), who also belonged to the Official Bureau and was likely a relative of Cui Jingshan, shipped 50 *kanme* of Spanish dollars to Nagasaki in the summer of 1766 and

[8]Ibid. Also see the published version in *Nagasakiken-shi Shiryo-hen*, Vol. 4 (Note. 5), p. 66.

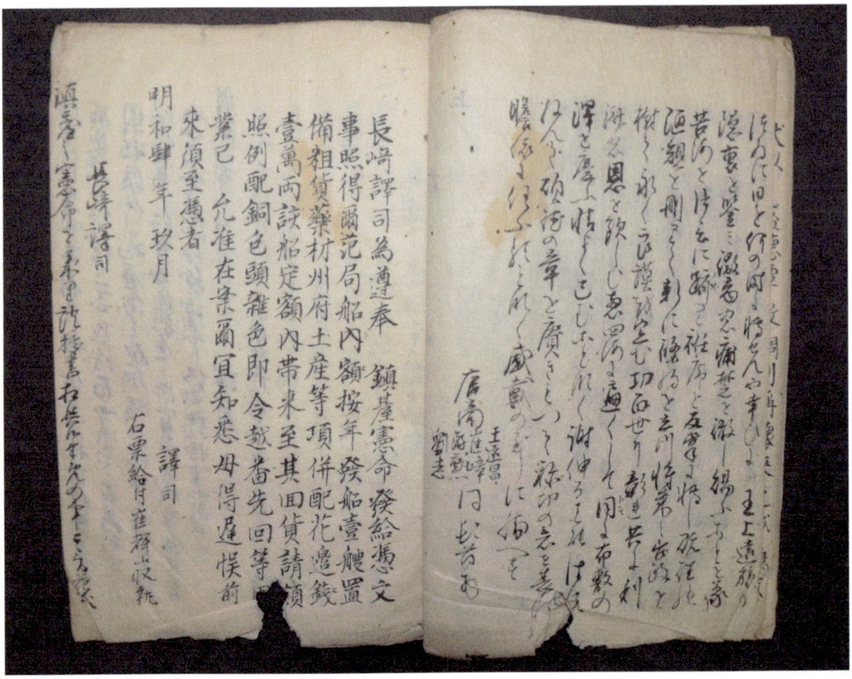
長崎譯司為遵奉　鎮臺憲命發給憑文
事照得爾范局船內額按年發船壹艘置
備粗貨藥材州府土産等項併配花邊銀
壹萬兩該船定額內帯來至其回貨請領
照例配銅色頭雜色即令越番先回等
業已　允准在案爾宜知悉毋得遲悞前
來須至憑者
明和肆年玖月　譯司
長崎譯司

Fig. 9.2 The Manuscript of *Pingwen*. In: *Shibun Narabini Shōbaikata Shomotsu-Shō* (咨文幷商売方書物抄, Copies of Some Official and Transaction Documents). Courtesy of the Nagasaki Siebold Memorial Museum

brought with him a certificate (called *pingwen* 憑文 in Chinese) based on this contract.[9]

A manuscript of this certificate can be found in the Nagayama collection of the Siebold Memorial Museum. As far as can be confirmed, this is the only extant document which shows us the full text of the certificate. It is important to read and analyze the text of the certificate in detail. The Chinese text can be translated as follows (Fig. 9.2).

> The Nagasaki interpreters issue this certificate following the direction of the magistrate. Fan's Trading House (范局, the Official Bureau led by Fan) should dispatch a ship [to Nagasaki] every year within the fixed number of annual ships, and also ship miscellaneous goods, medicines, special inland products, and 100 *kanme* of Huabian-Yin (花邊銀, Spanish dollars). The price of all these cargos can not exceed the total sum [already fixed by the shogunate]. You can be reimbursed for these items in the form of copper, marine products, and other goods as usual. Your ship can also sail back whenever it is ready, no matter the order in which it arrived. These transactions have been approved [by the shogunate]. You should heed these instructions and must not be late. We duly issue this certificate as evidence.

[9]NGJR, Ibid., p. 280.

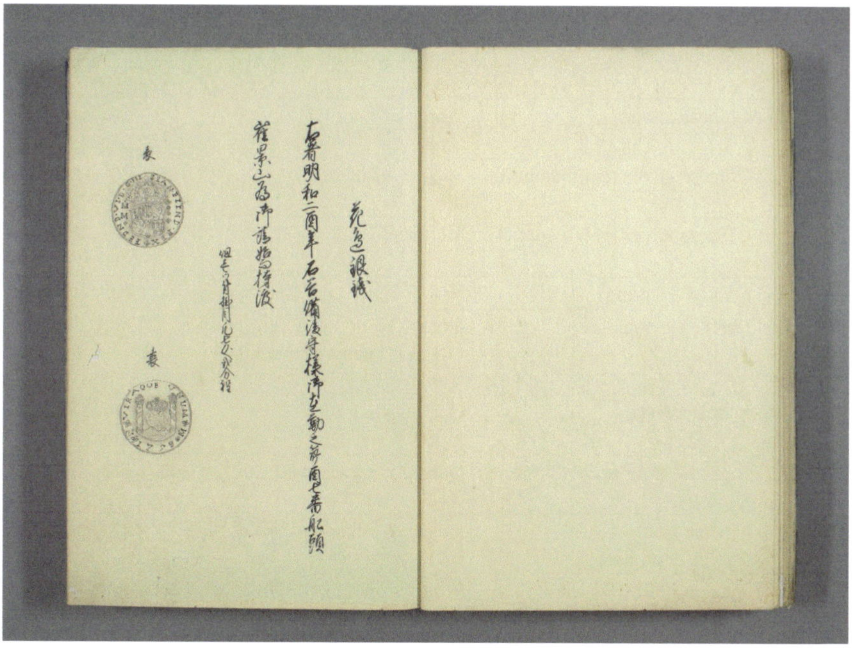

Fig. 9.3 *Kaben Ginsen* (花辺銀銭, Spanish dollars imported by junks to Japan). In: *Tō Oranda Mochiwatari Kinginsen Zukan* (see Fig. 9.1)

In this case, there were mainly two differences between the trade based on pre-arranged transaction conditions and the conventional and regular trading method. Firstly, the junk with the certificate containing the pre-arranged transaction conditions was to be laden with 100 *kanme* of Spanish dollars (see Fig. 9.3) for its voyage to Japan. Secondly, this junk received the privilege of prior transaction. It might sail back after transaction and did not have to wait for junks that arrived earlier to depart first.

9.5 Diversification of the Newly Introduced "Contract Trades"

Besides these two innovations, many other new transaction items that came to be based on this kind of pre-arranged transaction conditions emerged one after another in the late eighteenth century, as listed in Table 9.2.

As seen in Table 9.2, the most imported items during this period were silver and gold currencies, including the same kind of Japanese gold currencies as were exported to China in previous times. The new transaction contracts were mainly concerned with how much and what kind of silver or gold currencies should be

Table 9.2 New-style transactions based on pre-arranged conditions in the late eighteenth century

Year	Item of trade	Presentative/affiliation	Period/year of suspension
1762	(1) Chinese silver	Wang Lyujie (T.)	20 years (since 1763)
1783	(2) Chinese silver (continuation)	Shen Yunzhan (T.)	20 years/ 1784
1785	(3) Chinese silver (new contract)	Merchants of T. & O.	N/A/1790 (halt)
1763	(4) Chinese ginseng	N/A	N/A
1763	(5) Southeast Asian goods	Gong Zixing and Wang Lyujie (T.); Yu Hanxuan and Cheng Yutian (O.)	N/A/1767
1764	(6) Spanish dollars	Cui Jingshan (O.)	N/A/1791 (halt)
1764	(7) Japanese gold (exported to China in past)	Gong Zixing (T.) and Cui Jingshan (O.)	N/A/1766
1772	(8) Tibetan gold	Huang Weihan and Wang Shiji (O.)	15 years/
1780	(9) Tibetan gold (revised contract)	Wang Shiji and Gu Ningyuan (O.)	N/A/1781
1778	(10) Annam gold	Gu Shuchang (T.)	10 years/ 1781
1785	(11) High-quality gold bullion (for expenses during stay in Nagasaki)	N/A (O. & T.)	N/A
1789	(12) Silver (alternative to fabrics)	Cheng Chicheng and Song Jingting (T.)	N/A/1790
1789	(13) Tibetan gold	Feng Shengyuan and Fei Qinghu and Cheng Yongchun (O.)	First term: 3 years Second term: 3 years
1789	(14) Tibetan gold	Song Jingting (T.)	3 years
1790	(15) High-quality gold bullion (alternative to fabrics)	Fei Qinghu (O.)	N/A/1791

Source *Osadamegai Betsudan Shōhō Ryakuruku* (Note 10)
Notes "T." = the Twelve Families; "O." = the Official Bureau

imported to Japan. In the majority of cases, the merchandise to be exchanged for these silver or gold currencies was copper, marine products (*tawaramono*, 俵物), and other minor-export goods (*shoshiki*, 諸色). There were also several special cases. For instance, in the case of the importation of high-quality gold bullion, called *zuchijin* (足赤金) in Chinese, which began in 1785, the imported gold bullion might have been used to offset the expenses of the merchants' stay in Nagasaki instead of merchants being paid in commodities as usual. Some transaction contracts stipulated that silver- or gold-currencies could be imported into Japan as alternatives to fabrics.

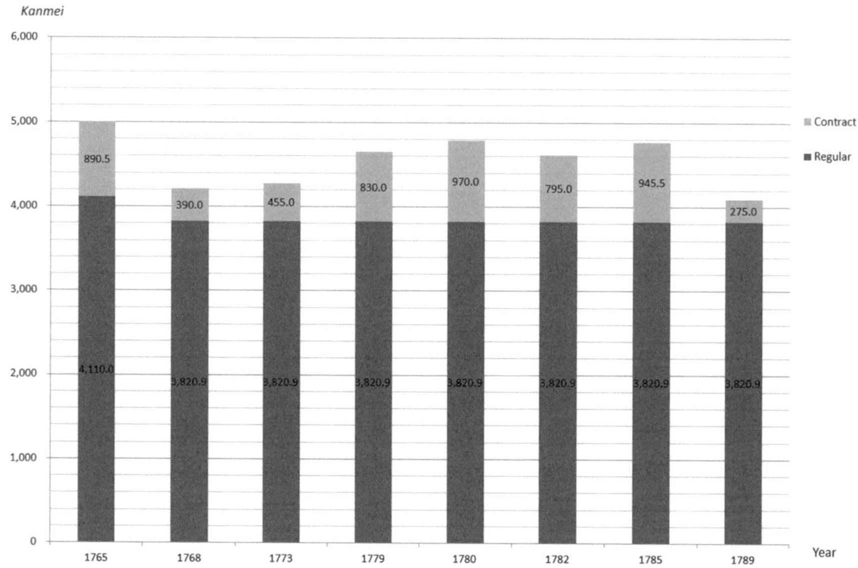

Fig. 9.4 Quantitative outline of trade based on pre-arranged conditions in comparison with regular trade

Apart from metal or metal coins, Chinese medicines such as ginseng and various Southeast Asian goods were very attractive to the Japanese in this period, so much so that the Nagasaki Trading House tried to import them through the "contract trade."

The dates of Table 9.2 are mainly based on the source entitled *Osadamegai Betsudanshōhō Ryakuroku* (御定外別段商法略録, a brief record of the special transactions outside the regular trade).[10] Most of these were the equivalent of "contract trades" in this period. An approximate quantitative image of the contract trade can be seen in Fig. 9.4.

The gross amount of the regular trade was fixed by the shogunate and relatively stable, even though it decreased several times in the eighteenth century. In 1765, it reached 4,110 *kanme*, and it decreased to 3,820.9 *kanme* in 1768. Compared to the regular trade, the gross amount of the contract trade was unstable, sometimes lower than 10% and sometimes over 20% of the regular volume. In the last years of the eighteenth century, the shogunate changed its relatively proactive trading policy of the so-called Tanuma era, and reduced or emerged most of the transactions based on contractual agreement.

[10]The original version of the document is in the possession of NMHC.

9.6 Formation of the "Contract Trade"

As mentioned above, this kind of trade model based on a contractual agreement between each or both of the two Chinese merchants' trading groups and the Nagasaki Trading House was used broadly and frequently in the late eighteenth century. Every junk coming to Nagasaki would hold some kind of contract certificate. An incident which took place in 1788 was an exemplary case. In that year, a junk of the Official Bureau arrived at Nagasaki port without the *shinpai*, and its trade was still permitted by the magistrate of Nagasaki, Sueyoshi Toshitaka (末吉利隆). After this breach was discovered, Sueyoshi suffered serious punishment. The staff of the VOC in Dejima recorded the incident in a letter as follows:

> The Governor (the magistrate of Nagasaki) had received mail from Edo with the information that he had committed a mistake on a Chinese junk. This junk came to [Nagasaki] without the ordinary pass, but only had a book in which there were some kinds of contract projects and orders concerning the cargos they loaded with the Account House (Nagasaki Trading House). After being shown [the book], the governor permitted the junk to continue the trade.[11]

Undoubtedly, the word "pass" (*pas* in the original Dutch letter) indicates the *shinpai*, and the records in Japan can be seen as evidence. It is important to determine what was meant by "some kinds of contract projects and orders" (*een soort van contract proiect en eijsch* in the original article). As seen in Table 9.2, there might be many certificates based on the trading contract (3, 6, 8, 11 in the table were contracts related to transactions with the Official Bureau in this period). The captain of this junk was Peng Yilai (彭義来), who had been to Nagasaki at least three times (1773, 1777, and 1779) before this year, 1788, according to Japanese sources such as *Mei'an Chōhōki*. Based on this fact, it seems reasonable to believe that the merchant Peng Yilai had been familiar to the local officials at Nagasaki for his trading experience. His status was also guaranteed by other merchants of the Official Bureau. Furthermore, he held some contract certificates in his hands. This background made the managers in the Trading House or the magistrates office treat the qualification of this junk flexibly; especially from the point of view of the local society, allowing trade would benefit all the residences of Nagasaki, including the officials themselves.

In the late eighteenth century the two trading groups, the Official Bureau and the Twelve Families Association, succeeded in monopolizing the junk trade at Nagasaki. As a result, it became less important for Japanese officials to judge junks' trade qualifications by checking one after another whether or not they held the *shinpai*, as long as each junk belonged to one of the two groups. The two groups would supervise each merchant in their organization to make sure they obey the trading rules and the deals they promised, in order to confirm their trading qualifications.

[11]Frank Lequin (ed.), *The Private Correspondence of Isaac Titsingh* Volume I (1785–1811). Amsterdam: J. C. Gieben, Publisher, 1990, p. 116.

9.7 The Roles and Significance of the New-Style Transactions

By the mid-eighteenth century, the Nagasaki trade system under the control of the shogunate had become fixed; on the other hand, as discussed in detail above, a new trading style emerged based on the pre-arranged contractual agreement between the Chinese merchants' organization and the Nagasaki Trading House. In the case of the junk trade, the contractual agreement was called *yakujō* in Japanese. Generally speaking, the commonly-held image of a contemporary commercial contract can be described as follows: the representatives of two enterprises reach an agreement via negotiation and stipulate the agreed items on paper; they then prepare two copies of this kind of document and both parties to the agreement sign their names on each document. In contrast, the fact that in this case there was no material contract document itself was a significant difference. The Chinese interpreters of the Nagasaki Trading House conducted negotiations with the representative merchant of the Official Bureau or the Twelve Families. After reaching an agreement and obtaining the permission of the magistrate and city elders, they stipulated the agreed conditions on paper as a transaction certificate (*hyōbun*). Then they prepared a number of such transaction certificates based on the agreement and issued them to the representative of the Chinese merchants. This representative merchant took these certificates back to China and then the trading group with which he was affiliated would use them according to demand. The Chinese merchant who held the certificate could use them to deal with the Nagasaki Trading House trade under the pre-arranged transaction conditions.

As pointed out above, on the VOC's side, there appeared a similar transaction as well in this period. The staff of the VOC called it "contract" in Dutch. The contract was established in September 1752 via negotiation between the VOC and the Nagasaki Trading House. The text came to be included in the treaty collections of the VOC (Matsukata 2013, p. 239 and p. 241). At the end of the text are the signatures of four local Nagasaki officials serving as Dutch interpreters. This was an essential point it had in common with the transaction certificate, *hyōbun,* in the Chinese junk trade.

The formal trading style remained: foreign merchants shipped the goods that were considered to be well-selling items to Nagasaki based on their experience and traded them with the Nagasaki Trading House. In the mid-eighteenth century, the trading groups of foreign merchants tried to first gain consent from the Nagasaki Trading House, such as which goods were welcomed for import to Japan and at which price these goods could be bought. They hoped that all these agreement and promises could be written down on paper like a contract certificate; then they would fulfil the transaction based on the terms of the certificates. This trading style may also have been seen in special cases such as the orders of the shogunate and others. However, the feature of the "contract trades" at that time was that the transaction counterparts were not individual merchants but a trading group, and the contract was not merely related to a one-time transaction but was always connected to a long-term trade relationship.

Another point worth focusing on here is that the new commercial style was aimed at the merchants' consolidation. In the past, shogunate issued the special *shinpai* to individual merchants who wanted to undertake its orders. However, it was possible that the task would not be fulfilled, since the person undertaking it could not guarantee to return due to uncertain factors such as disease or failure in business, and the power of the individual merchant was greatly limited in many aspects. As the commercial partner shifted from the individual merchant to the trading group, most of these kinds of problems could be overcome, and the contract between commercial groups would sustain their cooperation in transactions without such fluctuations and instability.

Chapter 10
Conclusive Discussions and Comprehensive Historical Narratives

10.1 Connecting the Markets with Permanent Trade

As explained in detail in Chap. 1, this study aims to explain why and how Sino-Japanese trade relations were stably maintained in the early modern period by analyzing the formative process and mechanisms of the relevant trading institutions. The majority of discussion points have been examined in detail in previous chapters. When combining these detailed discussions in a comprehensive account, it is necessary to additionally explain the process by which the Sino-Japanese trade developed, and thereby how the markets of the two countries linked with each other. This section will consider this question from a broad historical context.[1]

Based on related historical documents, the formal interaction between the two lands separated by the East China Sea started with the diplomatic visits of Japanese officials to the continent. From the ninth century, due to the commercial activities of Silla merchants from the Korean peninsula, a large trading area emerged to include the Chinese part of the continent, the Korean Peninsula, and the Japanese Archipelago. In association with the expanded bidirectional flow of specialty products, the awareness of the value of imported and exported goods accordingly increased. As the shipping route that crossed the middle of the East China Sea developed, the Chinese merchants living in the Jiangnan area (current day Jiangsu and Zhejiang provinces) became the main players in the trade with Japan, rather than the Silla merchants (E'nomoto 2007, 2010; Tanaka 2011). Through these processes, the markets of the two lands became linked with each other more closely.

In Japan, the imports, especially those from China, were generally called *karamono* (唐物). Among them, the representative items were those processed products made with technological skill, such as silk fabrics and porcelains, and which were prized by the Japanese Imperial family and nobility to the extent that possessing a large number of them was seen as a symbol of wealth and power

[1]Besides the outcomes of this study, the narratives of this section also refer to other recently published studies, especially Arano et al. (2010–2013) and Haneta (2013).

H. Peng, *Trade Relations between Qing China and Tokugawa Japan*,
Studies in Economic History, https://doi.org/10.1007/978-981-13-7685-6_10

(Tanaka 2011).[2] Various Chinese medicines (mainly materia medica) were also frequently brought into Japan, and they gradually became a necessity in the sense that they were thought to be able to cure diseases and prolong human life. For example, a famous classic collection of essays entitled *tsurezuregusa* (徒然草) written and edited in the 1330s states that there would be no inconvenience in force going overseas goods except for medicines.[3] In other words, Chinese medicines were considered to be indispensable to the Japanese, at least by that time. This impression did not change, even into the early modern era. It can be seen also in essays by shogunate politicians such as Arai Hakuseki (新井白石) and Matsudaira Sadanobu (松平定信).[4] In addition to medicines, imports of Chinese books were also broadly regarded as crucial, especially for monks and intellectuals, since Chinese cultural elements including Chinese characters, Buddhism, and Confucianism had already been incorporated into Japanese culture; moreover, due to the improvement of living standards, demands for silk fabrics increased, high-quality silk was used as the raw material for the production of silk textiles and thus became highly valued by the market in association with the development of domestic textile production.[5]

In the early modern period, as domestic production of raw silk, silk textiles, sugar, ginseng, and other items developed steadily, a self-sufficient domestic market gradually formed and developed (Arano 2010). Nevertheless, certain imported goods from China such as medicines that could not be found or produced in Japan and high-quality silk fabrics maintained their high value, and the brand power of Chinese products seemed to be deeply rooted in the society of Edo Japan. As examined in Chap. 5, even though the shogunate severely cracked down on it, the smuggling of the cargos imported by junks was a serious problem throughout the Edo period. Considering this point, it is evident that the Japanese market steadily demanded Chinese goods throughout the Edo period.

---

[2]Recently, many new studies on *karamono* have been published (Seki 2002; Hashimoto 2011; Von Verschuer 2006; Kawazoe and Minagawa 2011; Minagawa 2014; Kawazoe 2014).

[3]Yoshita Kanayoshi, *Tsurezuregusa*. Iwanami Shoten, 1985, p. 202.

[4]Regarding the Nagasaki trade, Ara'i mentioned in this essay *Oritaku-Shiba-no-Ki* (折たく柴の木, Told Round a Brushwood Fire): "Except for the medicines, nothing was needed" (Tokyo: Iwanami Shoten 1999, p. 282); Matsudaira expressed similar sensibilities in his essay *Uge-no-Hitogoto* (宇下人言, Sadanobu's autobiography) "If Chinese junks do not come, we might send ships to China to purchase medicines as in the old times before the *Kanbun* period" (Tokyo: Iwanami Shoten 1996, p. 103).

[5]The Chinese in the Ming dynasty seemed to share this point of view. For instance, Xu Guangqi 徐光啓, Minister of Rites, wrote an article entitled "Haifang Yushuo" (海防迂說, a humble opinion about coastal defense), and states in it that "It is nearly impossible to imagine that there would be no invasion if we refused to trade [with Japan], except that not all Japanese do use silk, silk fabrics, porcelain, medicines, and other Chinese products" (*Huangming Jingshi Wenbian*, 皇明經世文編 vol. 491). In addition, there is a famous resource called *wohao* (倭好 Japanese Favorite Goods) written by the Ming Chinese, which explained the selling of Chinese goods in the Japanese market. For this, Tanaka has a detailed introduction (Tanaka 1997).

Meanwhile, China had been constantly seeking resources in the surrounding areas in response to domestic economic growth and military demands during times of war. It is known that the outstanding products of Japan had been gold, silver, copper, sulfur, and timber. In particular, the fact that Japanese silver was absorbed into the Chinese market alongside silver from the Americas in the sixteenth and the seventeenth century has drawn a great deal of attention as a trend of world integration in recent studies on global economic history (Hamashita and Kawakatsu 1991; Frank 1998). In addition, the demand for Japanese goods was not limited to precious metals and primary products but swords and other Japanese crafts such as lacquerware, fans, and umbrellas gradually became popular items in the Chinese market as well (Kishimoto 1998; Verschuer 2006).

In the mid-seventeenth century, as the Qing stabilized its control over China, the circulation of copper coins gradually expanded and, consequently, the demand for Japanese copper as a casting material grew to become the most promising commodity of the trade with Japan, over that of silver. It has been made evident by recent studies that not only China but also other regions such as Korea and India imported copper from Japan in this period (Shimata 2006, 2010). In response to such demand for overseas markets, specially-refined copper bars became a staple item for export until the end of the Tokugawa period. Since the early eighteenth century, as copper production declined, dried luxury marine products such as abalone, sea cucumber, and shark fin gradually became other important Chinese market-oriented export items in accordance with trends in Chinese consumption. It is also worth noting that some items such as porcelains and ginseng, which had previously been imported, began to be exported to China in this period. In the case of former, the production of porcelains in Arita (有田, now in Saga prefecture) and shipped to Nagasaki from Imari (伊万里) port made a leap in quality due to the relocation of overseas technology in the early half of the seventeenth century. Regarding the latter, the artificial cultivation of Korean ginseng began in the middle years of the eighteenth century and production expanded gradually under the shogunate's encouragement, and in the last years of the same century it began to be exported to China.[6]

10.2 Transformations of the Trade Relationship

As mentioned above, the markets surrounding the East China Sea had been linked with each other since the ninth century. Chinese and Japanese people gradually developed a certain degree of mutual recognition of the merchandise from the other side along with the regular appearance of that merchandise in their own markets,

[6]For detailed dates on imports and exports by Junks, see Nagatsumi 1987.

and thereby merchants were able to estimate the market value of the imports or exports.[7] The long-standing mutual demand for these goods became the driving force behind continuing the trade between the two lands, and trade was maintained in different ways according to changes in the political situation in both these countries and the broader East Asian world.

During the period from the tenth century to the fourteenth century, there were no stable diplomatic relations between the regimes of the two lands. Nevertheless, their economic interactions continued with Chinese merchants frequently sailing to and trading in Japan. In the fifteenth century, the Ming empire, newly established in China, attempted to reconstruct a China-centered world order in eastern Eurasia and thereby demanded the political subordination of neighboring states. Against this backdrop, the Muromachi shogunate, the de facto administration of Japan, dispatched tribute envoys to China and accepted tallies (*kanhe* 勘合) from the Ming dynasty as a certificate of tribute to the country. In principle, the mission came into China through the specific port city, Ningbo 寧波, with a tally; the main members of the mission then traveled to the capital, Beijing, for an audience with the emperor, and exchanged state letters and gifts. After this, the Ming dynasty purchased goods from the mission as part of official trade. On the other hand, private merchants involved with the mission were allowed to conduct transactions with Chinese merchants under the supervision of the officials in the market of Ningbo city. Such tributary trade was profitable and considerably attractive, to the extent that the Muromachi shogunate tried to receive the trading qualifications from Ming empire by which it could strengthen its political authority (Hashimoto 2011). Meanwhile, Ming authorities carried out the Maritime Prohibitions, forbidding the Chinese from traveling abroad and any trade unrelated to the tribute system (Sakuma 1992; Danjō 2013). Consequently, smuggling expanded in the coastal area.

In the sixteenth century, many armed maritime commercial groups active in the East China Sea area began to openly confront the Ming's maritime control and at the same time expanded trade across a wide area, especially the southeast coast of China and islands in the vicinity. This was the so-called warring states era (from the late fifteenth century to the late sixteenth century) in Japanese history, the coast of Kyushu became the theater of operations for such maritime forces, and many Japanese soldiers without masters were also absorbed into them. Since many Japanese became involved in this way, these groups were treated as Japanese pirates (*wokou* 倭寇) by the Ming authorities. However, the composition of the "Japanese pirates" was complex as there were also Korean and Portuguese in those groups. As Murai Shosuke pointed out, it is reasonable to view them as multiethnic communities (Murai 1997).

[7]Prices of the imported goods are in the Japanese market in "Japanese Favorite Goods" mentioned above.

Facing such a problem, some in the Ming empire argued that the Maritime Prohibitions seemed to have no suppressing effect, and on the contrary brought rampant "piracy" activities.[8] What made the situation more complicated was that Western Europeans such as Portuguese, Spanish, English, and Dutch, had emerged in the maritime area. This situation resulted in more and more high official in the Ming regime supporting the removal or relaxation of the Maritime Prohibitions, and in 1567 the Ming finally decided to relax the ban and allow private merchants under its control to engage in overseas trade from a specified port. As discussed in detail in Iwai's studies, this trade model, called *hushi* 互市 in Chinese, was obviously different from the trade model under the tribute system, which had been the only legal form in Ming China for more than a century and a half (Iwai 1996, 2004, 2009).

The seventeenth century was a period of regime change, as the Ming dynasty gave way to the Qing dynasty. Even though the Qing regime was formed in the 1640s and within a few years occupied the majority of Ming territories, many armed groups continued to resist the Qing's domination for a long period of time. In 1683, the Qing finally forced the maritime force led by the Taiwan-based Zheng families to surrender, and stabilized their control over China. The following year, the Qing authorities decided to remove the Maritime Prohibitions aimed at isolating the Zheng's power base, and allowed private merchants to engage in overseas trade again. One result, described in detail in Chap. 5, is that in 1685 two officials of Fujian province called on Nagasaki to supervise 13 trading junks, and even though the trade of these junks was permitted the shogunate notified them that it would not welcome the visit of Chinese officials. Subsequently, no Qing officials visited Japan again until the mid-nineteenth century. During the period 1684–1859, Chinese junks continually sailed to and traded in Nagasaki with the approval of both the Qing empire and Tokugawa regime. Although there were no diplomatic relations or direct negotiations between the two sides, this trade relationship was maintained for more than 170 years.

As outlined above, after trade routes developed which crossed the middle of the East China Sea and connected the continent with the Japanese archipelago, the demand for specialty products from the other side gradually increased and, as a result, trade between the two sides continuously maintained, although different forms emerged according to changing circumstances. The Sino-Japanese trade relations dealt with in this study should also be understood in such a context.

[8]Tu Zhemin (塗澤民) and Xu Fuyuan (徐孚遠), who both served as provincial governor of Fujian, were representatives who argued that the Ming authorities should permit private merchants in coastal regions, especially Fujian, to engage in overseas trade. As Xu pointed out in his report to the government ("Shutong-Haijin-Shu" 疏通海禁疏' in *Jinghetangji* 敬和堂集 vol. 5), people living in coastal regions did not have sufficient money to afford food and clothing without overseas trade. For details on this discussion, see Kobata (1967) and Sakuma (1992).

10.3 The Sino-Japanese Relationship in the Reorganization of the East Asia Regional Order

As discussed above, demand for the other side's products underpinned the maintenance of this trade between Qing China and Tokugawa Japan from the beginning. On the other hand, the political relations between the two sides were also crucial in defining the form of the trade. In this section, we will briefly review the process of reorganizing the East Asian regional order in the early modern period and summarize how political and ideological factors influenced trade relations between the two countries.

Reviewing the East Asian region in the sixteenth century, mainland China under the rule of the Ming empire faced two external threats throughout its reign: one was the so-called Japanese pirates from the southeast; the other was the Mongolian powers from the north. Furthermore, from the late sixteenth century to the early seventeenth century, there came to be two other external threats: the rise of the Jurchen people (the ancestors of the Manchurian people) in the northeast and the approach of the Western powers in the southeast coastal region, which made it difficult to sustain the tribute system of the Ming empire.

By the end of the sixteenth century, a unified administration led by Toyotomi Hideyoshi emerged in the Japanese archipelago and, building upon the momentum of domestic victories, dispatched troops to the Korean peninsula. Even though the expedition failed after meeting resistance from the allied forces of Korea and the Ming, the new administration in Japan demonstrated to the Ming empire its capacity for military mobilization and fighting power. The impact of this was probably not only on the Han Chinese but also on the Jurchen people, whose consolidation was proceeding in areas neighboring the Korean peninsula. Therefore, it is easy to imagine the sense of caution against Japanese power not only at this time but also after the establishment of the Qing empire.

In the seventeenth century Japan entered the Edo era. Soon after its establishment, the Tokugawa shogunate initiated the recovery of diplomatic relations with Korea and the conquest of the Ryūkyūs by the Satsuma domain, while trying to resume trade and diplomacy with the Ming empire. When the attempt at diplomatic negotiations failed, the Tokugawa regime turned to forming a Japan-centered regional political order by adjusting its relationships with Korea and the Ryūkyūs. Meanwhile, on the Chinese side, the Ming gave way to the Qing, and the Qing empire attempted to imitate former Chinese dynasties by constructing a Chinese-centered tribute system and, accordingly, calling for tributes from surrounding countries including Tokugawa Japan.[9] However, the Tokugawa

[9] In the spring of 1637, after an invasion of Korea, Emperor Huang Taiji (皇太極, also written as "Hong Taiji" or "Abahai" in English), an emperor of the Qing empire, allowed Korea to maintain a trade relationship with Japan and demanded that the Korean government send Japan a messenger dispatching tribute to Qing China (Nakamura 1968). Ten years later, the Qing empire also issued

shogunate did not respond to this demand. The Japanese Archipelago had experienced at least two invasions by people on horseback living in an area north of China: first by the Toi (刀伊, a tribute or group of Jurchen people) in 1019 and then by Mongolia in 1274 and 1281 (Ishi'i 2010; Murai 2010). The Tokugawa shogunate was thus cautious about socializing with Manchu regime. Eventually, two politically independent power spheres, distinct in scale and influence, formed on both the eastern and western flanks of the East China Sea region.

Arano Yasunori described the situation as follows: in early modern East Asia, the traditional "China-centered world order" and the "Japan-centered world order" coexisted; they interacted and coordinated relations with each other while also being in conflict and competition with each other (Arano 1992). The so-called "world order" here is a highly abstract concept and might be easier to understand if it is divided into two components: the substantive and the conceptual. Substantively speaking, each of the two "world orders" was merely one sphere of influence within the region, and the geographical ranges over which they had a political influence were limited and, for this very reason the two could coexist. Conceptually, however, the so-called China-centered world order ideologically covered the whole world; there was only one vertex—*hua* (the most civilized place)—it and all other states were arranged hierarchically as *yi* (the barbarians) in accordance with the affinity of their relationship with the *hua*; this idea denies the existence of any equal political constitution. This conception might be helpful for the administration to buttress its political authority within its dominant territories; however, expressing this concept in diplomatic contexts would easily lead to conflicts between the states. This ideological conflict was certainly a negative factor in sustaining a stable trade relationship with other countries.

In the early modern period, Qing China and Tokugawa Japan were politically independent from each other and, in this sense, they were in an equal relationship. As a sphere of influence, both of them exerted to some extent political influence on the Ryūkyūs. On the other hand, however, dealing with the counterpart country in their hierarchical ideology became a crucial issue for both administrations as long as they willingly permitted a trading relationship with each other.

On the Chinese side, the Qing authorities legalized the overseas trade of private merchants after abolishing the Maritime Prohibitions in 1684 and accordingly permitted Chinese junks to trade in Nagasaki, regarding trade relations without diplomacy as so-called *hushi* 互市. As a matter of fact, the *hushi* differed from the tribute relationship since there was no political or ceremonial hierarchical relationship between the Qing empire and other partner countries. However, in order to assert the philosophical "China-centered world order" the Qing authorities had to consider how to deal with not only "tributary states" but also "*hushi* states". Consciousness of the "China-centered world order" is reflected in books compiled as a national project by the Qing. In some official books or volumes, such as the

an edict to the whole country that called on the surrounding states, including Japan, to pay tribute to the Qing empire (Peng 2010).

Daqing Yitongzhi (大清一統志, gazetteer of the Qing empire) and *Huangchao Zhigongtu* (皇朝職貢図, illustration of the tributary states of the imperial family), all the related countries including Japan were treated as tributary states, no regardless of whether diplomatic relations existed in practice.[10] Other books such as the *Daqing Huidian* (大清会典, the collective statutes of the great Qing dynasty), treated the states under the tribute system as *chaogong-guo* 朝貢国, and other states such as Japan, which had trading relations but no diplomatic relations with China, as *hushi-guo* 互市国. It introduces the *hushi-guo* next to the *chaogong-guo* and positions them around the "China-centered world order".[11]

Regarding the "Japan-centered world order" consciousness, according to Ronald Toby's argument, the normative hierarchy constructed by the shogunate can be described as conical in shape: Japan lay at the top; those states keeping diplomatic relations with Japan such as Korea and the Ryūkyūs were beneath it; those states keeping merely trading relations with Japan, such as China and the Netherlands, were further below; and the states without permission to contact Japan were at the bottom (Toby 1986). As other studies have examined in detail, this conceptual formation was expressed in the official documents on the diplomatic relations between the shogunate and other countries: China and the Netherlands were *tsusho-no-kuni* (通商の国, partner states with trading relationships), and Korea and the Ryūkyūs as *tsushin-no-kuni* (通信の国, partner states communicating by official correspondence). However, to a large extent this concept was far removed from the actual situation on the ground—for instance, according to this concept, Korea and the Ryūkyūs were superior to Qing China in their regional political status and political influence— it is difficult to imagine that there were people in Edo Japan who really believed such descriptions. Toby's articulation of a "Japan-centered world order" can be thought of as a normative and extremely idealized model. It seems that many Japanese political thinkers in the Edo period maintained the belief that Tokugawa Japan was superior to other countries in some aspects and some of them may have tried to describe the philosophical composition of a "Japan-centered world order"; however, since there were many inconvenient facts, as mentioned above, they seemed to carefully avoid public arguments over issues such as how to deal with the position of Qing China in this hierarchical world order.

---

[10]*Daqing Yitongzhi* was a geography book compiled continuously by the Qing government from 1686 to 1842. Volumes 421–424 list more than 30 countries as the Qing's "tributary states" and place Japan in 10th position. *Huangqing Zhigongtu* was an illustrated book on the tribute system compiled in 1751–1761, and includes explanations on the related countries and people. Volume 1 introduces the countries Korea, the Ryukyus, and Annam one by one, and places Japan in 12th position.

[11]*Daqing Huidian* is a collective corpus on the political institutions and administrative matters of the Qing dynasty. It was first compiled in 1690 and revised several times afterwards. There is a chapter related to the responsibilities of *zhuke-qingli-si* (主客清吏司), which was a bureau of the Ministry of Rites and was in charge of receiving of foreign envoys. The first three versions listed Korea and the Ryukyus as the "tributary states"; the fourth version, finished in 1818, lists Japan and some other countries as "states with trading relations", next to the "tributary states".

10.4 The Influences of Each Country's Security on the Trade Relationship

The interests of the two regimes with respect to each other went beyond trade and extended to other fields, including security issues. As discussed in previous studies (Yano 1967; Ōba 1984), in order to respond to Shogun Tokugawa Yoshimune's (吉宗, ruling from 1716 to 1745) interests in equestrianism, shooting, and other such activities, in the 1720, the magistrate of Nagasaki issued special *shinpai* (trading passes/permits) to some Chinese merchants, asking them to invite retired military officers from China to Japan as martial artists. In addition to this information, Li Wei (李衛), the governor-general of Zhejiang Province, also heard rumors that the Japanese were building warships. Therefore, he became highly cautious with respect to Japan's intentions and instructed some Chinese merchants to explore the situation there. After receiving Li's confidential reports, Emperor Yongzheng directed the high officials in charge of maritime defense in the southeastern coastal area to secretly collect information on the Japanese and in the meantime to strengthen the area's coastal defenses. Such sensitivity was not irrelevant to the Qing's recognition of Japan place in its world order. In the late sixteenth century and early seventeenth century, after suffering from "Japanese piracy" and war on the Korean peninsula following the Japanese invasion led by Hideyoshi, the Chinese gradually came to hold an image of the Japanese people as savage and merciless. Even after the regime shift from Ming to Qing, this image continued to affect not only the historical memory of the Han Chinese people but also Japan's view of the Manchu rulers (Peng 2010).

Meanwhile, in Tokugawa Japan, as a result of the Ming–Qing regime shift, an attitude emerged which disdained Qing China as a barbarian country; this is demonstrated by the fact that the collection of information about China from junks was entitled *Ka'i Hentai* 華夷変態, meaning a transition from civilized to barbaric.[12] The Tokugawa regime declined to accept requests for support from anti-Qing forces such as the Southern Ming regimes and Zheng's power. However, it has also been confirmed that some vassals of the shogun had developed plans to dispatch troops into China in response to these military requests (Komiya 1990). Regarding the vigilance against the military threat posed by the Qing empire, the idea of invasion by the "barbarians from the North" (*hokuteki* 北狄) by Kumazawa Banshan 熊沢蕃山, a famous Confucian, can be seen as a typical example (Gotō 1971). It is reasonable to assume that some vassals of the shogun shared this wariness. Nevertheless, there is no evidence that the Tokugawa added practical measures to its coastal defense system to prevent a Qing intrusion, a system constructed for possible defense against Portuguese vessels after they were expelled from Japan by the ban on Christianity in the 1630s and 1640s (Yamamoto 1989).

[12]See the introduction of *Ka'i Hentai*. The author was Hayashi Shunshō 林春勝, a Confucian working for the shogunate. Such an opinion on Qing China was common among many shogunate vassals and political thinkers in this period.

In 1714, the shogunate issued an order to strengthen defenses against armed Chinese junks after receiving information that some pirate groups had emerged in the East China Sea and that some crews of junks had landed without permission from the Tokugawa regime (Matsuo 2010). The following year, the shogunate promulgated the regulations of 1715, greatly reducing the number of trading junks. Consequently, as examined in detail in Chap. 5, the number of smuggling junks increased sharply; this immediately became a serious problem that affected not only the commercial order of the Nagasaki trade but also the coastal security of western Japan. In response, the shogunate decided to exert its power against the smuggling junks and instructed the relevant domains to expel those junks by force. As a result, the coastal defense system that was built in the mid-seventeenth century and targeted at Iberian vessels was also applied to a crackdown on smuggling junks. In these anti-smuggling policies, the Tokugawa regime demonstrated a similar public stance to that of the Qing authorities: treating the junks suspected of smuggling as pirate vessels. It can be assumed that adopting this logic in its policy against smuggling junks would be easy for the Qing authorities to comprehend, and this idea was possibly based on the advice of the shogunate's political consultants who were familiar with Chinese politics and history, such as Arai Hakuseki.

Under trade relations without a foundation in diplomacy, the two administrations tried as much as possible to take a calm and flexible response to trade frictions in order to avoid unexpected situations. In Tokugawa Japan, scholars have pointed out the military prestige (*bu'i* 武威) associated with the view of Confucian civilization resulting from Chinese traditional culture and the conception of Japan as the land of gods based on Shintoism as core elements in the Tokugawa regime's dominant ideology (Asa'o 1970). Regarding the punishment of Chinese violating "Japanese laws", as discussed in Chap. 5, even though it was an attempt to apply "Japanese penalties" to the Chinese the shogunate did not turn this into practice since it failed to obtain the cooperation of the representatives of the Chinese merchants' groups and the Qing authorities. Instead, it merely delivered a simple principle in 1715: sentencing to death any man who killed a Japanese person. The punishments for illegal transactions or disturbance were limited to financial penalties, imprisonment, and denial of re-entry, and there was no evidence that any physical penalty was ever imposed on any Chinese in practice. Even though there were in fact some cases in which the Japanese attacked Chinese junks that they suspected of smuggling and suppressed the Chinese disturbances, these were merely temporary measures and daily restrictions on the "illegal conduct" by the Chinese in Nagasaki were moderate. Such flexible responses seemed out of line with so-called military prestige, and as seen in the official documents of Tokugawa Japan were often explained by the Buddhist term "mercy" or the Confucian idea of "being gracious to foreigners" (*rouyuan* 柔遠). In addition, similar terms and ideas can be seen in documents related to the repatriation of drifting ships, including Chinese junks foundering in Japan and Japanese ships that drifted to China.

10.5 Management of Trade Centered on the Nagasaki Trading House

With the exception of the last 15 years of the seventeenth century, there is little doubt that the Tokugawa held an initiative in constructing institutions for the trade with Chinese junks. This was because both the Ming and then the Qing in China enforced the Maritime Prohibitions for so long and regarded Chinese merchants trading in Japan as illegal traders or pirates. Due to the fact that they lacked official support from their home authorities, the Chinese merchants from the ports of China had to obey the rules applied by the Tokugawa Regime. As an exception, a number of junks trading in Japan were affiliated with or under the protection of the Zheng family, and the commercial representatives of the Zheng regime even negotiated with the magistrate of Nagasaki over several trading issues.

In the first decades after its establishment, the Tokugawa regime adopted a relatively welcoming attitude toward the junk trade. Even Chinese merchants who violated the Maritime Prohibitions of the Ming authorities were allowed to trade in Japan and were treated as equals by the shogunate, no matter where they came from, as long as they respected Tokugawa regulations.

The series of edicts promulgated in the Kan'ei era (寛永, 1624–1644) are often described as a turning point in Japanese early modern history, breaking off diplomacy and trade with Portugal and Spain, banning Japanese traveling overseas, and forbidding foreign ships from trading in ports other than Nagasaki. Meanwhile, the shogunate also began to reconsider the management system of the Nagasaki Trade, mainly for Chinese and Dutch merchants.

As the outgoing trade of both Japanese and foreign trading partners had already been limited, the challenge for the Nagasaki trade was how to restrict the rising price of imports while securing the necessary imports from overseas, and preventing the outflow of gold, silver, and copper. For this reason, in 1631 there emerged a transaction method in which a Silk Guild (*itowappu nakama* 糸割符仲間) purchased Chinese silk at an uniform price. This Silk Guild consisted of domestic merchants and initially targeted at Portuguese vessels, but later came to be involved with the Chinese junks and the VOC's ships. In this system, the Silk Guild became the sole purchaser of imported silk and thereby was to a large extent able to control the price.

In the middle of the seventeenth century, soaring prices of imported goods especially of Chinese silk, become a serious problem again and the Silk Guild's bulk purchasing was considered the cause of the problem. As a result, the shogunate decided to abolish the Silk Guild-based trading method. This trading policy adjustment directly resulted in the appearance of a seller's market, which meant that the price of imports rose further and the outflow of silver further increased. As this problem became more and more serious, the shogunate reintroduced the the Silk Guild's mechanism and tried to apply it to all imports. In 1672, under the direction of the Nagasaki magistrate, a new transaction method was initiated. In brief, domestic merchants who wished to participate in the Nagasaki trade would be assigned to five commercial districts respectively based on a large commercial city: Nagasaki, Sakai, Kyoto, Osaka, or Edo. The Nagasaki Agency of these merchants' association (*shihō kaisho* 市法会所), would purchase all the imports in bulk and at an uniform price. This caused a shift from a seller's market to a buyer's market and accordingly the purchase price was heavily suppressed. It was therefore praised and widely welcomed in Japanese society.

In the late 1680s, Chinese junks arriving in Nagasaki sharply increased in number. This was a direct result of the Qing empire's abolishing of its long-term Maritime Prohibitions in 1684, and also was related to the fact that the Qing authorities supported the trade with Japan for importing copper. In this period, for not only the Qing authorities but also private merchants, the greatest appeal of the trade with Japan was the acquisition of copper. Political stability and therefore economic growth increased the need for copper coins, the most often-used currency in Qing China, and at the same time the production of domestic copper mines was limited. In order to meet the high demand for copper, the Qing authorities tried to collect copperware and the copper coins issued during the Ming dynasty to recast them. Nevertheless, it was still unable to meet the demand, so the government relied heavily upon copper imports from Japan.

The sharp increase in the number of trading junks exposed various disadvantages of the existing system of Nagasaki trade therefore its reform became an urgent part of the political agenda of the Japanese administration. In order to prevent the overseas outflow of precious metals, especially silver and copper, the shogunate implemented a series of policy adjustments, restricting the annual trading amount as well as the number of annual trading junks. As a direct result, smuggling became a serious problem and in response the shogunate decided to construct the Chinese Residence in 1688, a means by which they tried to separate the Chinese from the local society of Nagasaki. Then ten years later, in order to strengthen trade control, they set up the Nagasaki Trading House (*Nagasaki kaisho* 長崎会所). It differed from the previous *shihō kaisho*: it was not an agency for an association of domestic merchants and its position in the trade was an intermediary between domestic merchants and foreign traders; the staff of the Trading House came from the local community of Nagasaki and city officials took charge of its management. The Nagasaki Trading House can be seen as a trading management institution under the supervision of the shogunate while, on the other hand, maintaining some degree of independence in its management. The profits from mediating business transactions were, in principle and after submitting a portion of them to the shogunate, distributed among the city residents. The shogunate had established his system, with the Nagasaki Trading House as the trading intermediary, by the end of the seventeenth century after a process of trial and error.

The Tokugawa regime took the initiative in trade, especially in certain aspects such as adjustment of the trade volume or the setting of prices, through intervention in the management of the Nagasaki Trading House. However, for the Chinese merchants, direct transactions with Japanese private merchants were the ideal way to maximize trading profits, and therefore trading via the Trading House was not desirable for them.[13] There were also various restrictions and regulations in Japan, such as the restrictions on trading volumes and activities permitted during the merchants' stay in Nagasaki. Such a strict trading arrangement was rarely seen anywhere in the world at that time. Nevertheless, both the Chinese and Dutch merchants who expected to trade with Japan had to comply with the Tokugawa's trading rules, and even home authorities behind them to a large extent chose to tolerate the Japanese side's leadership in these matters.

10.6 Development of Trading Institutions

The Nagasaki Trading House was established in 1698, which was also the heyday of the Nagasaki trade. Subsequently, the production of copper in Japan fell, in response to which the shogunate began to decrease the quantity of copper exports. Since the demand for Japanese copper in Qing China remained just as high as before, the conflict of interest between the Qing and Tokugawa in the copper trade became clear and serious. As a part of the Regulations of 1715, a new trading policy based on the utilization of *shinpai* was also introduced. The *shinpai* policy has been evaluated by previous studies on the Nagasaki trade as primary purpose of the Restrictions of 1715 (Yamawaki 1964; Nakamura 1988; Ōta 1992).

As examined in detail in Chap. 3, the function of *shinpai* was on the surface a kind of certificate ensuring that the merchant holding it had the qualifications to trade, but what the shogunate expected in practice was for it to effectively control the scale of trading, rather than to check the holder's identity, such as current-day visas. A *shinpai* authorized just one junk and the *shinpai* also stipulate the trading amount of that junk. Therefore, the scale of trade could be controlled by adjusting the number of *shinpai* issued and the amount stipulated in each one. Considering this, what was most significant for the shogunate was not ensuring who would enter Japan but to check whether the traders obeyed the restrictions applied by the Tokugawa regime. Due to this aim, the shogunate permitted the transfer of *shinpai* from one merchant's hand to another's had since the policy was introduced in 1715, and it left open the possibility that the *shinpai* could also be used by the Qing authorities.

Even though there were several inconveniences for the Qing authorities in the Japanese controlling trade via the *shinpai*, such as the description of the Japanese era name and the possibility that the merchants selected by the Japanese would monopolize the trade, the Qing authorities finally conceded to legitimize the

[13]There is a related statement in the official report of Ji Zengyun (嵇曾筠) dated on the 11th day of the seventh month Qianlong 2 (August 6, 1737). Based on this report, in the eyes of Chinese merchants, the trade had been monopolized by six city elders of Nagasaki, which resulted in many inconveniences, such as a fall in the prices of junk's cargos and accordingly, a rise in prices of Japanese copper, as well as the sale of remaining products. The so-called trading monopoly by the city elders clearly referred to the trading management centered on the Nagasaki Trading House.

use of the *shinpai* by the Chinese merchants in order to sustain copper imports. However, this response was not merely a passive acceptance. As one of the most important discoveries of this study, Chap. 4 has presented evidence showing how the Qing authorities positively and proactively used the *shinpai* in possession of Chinese merchants in order to maximize copper imports from Japan. For instance, they confiscated the *shinpai* from merchants with debts to the government and loaned them to other merchants in order to continue the copper trade with Japan. As a trading management method used by both sides, the *shinpai* system contributed significantly to the stable maintenance of the trading relationship.

In the construction of this trading system, it is also worth noting the roles of private merchants. For a long time, Chinese junk merchants individually conducted trade with Japan, and there was no large commercial group such as the VOC that had sufficient negotiating power to affect the transaction rules. This situation changed in the mid-eighteenth century with the emergence of two commercial groups—the Official Bureau and the Twelve Families Association—among Chinese merchants, which gradually realized the monopoly of the junks' trade with Japan. Chapters 6 and 7 reexamined the processes by which the two groups formed and clarified the trends of integration within the merchants' commercial activities through analyzing original documents.

The establishment of the two groups had a major impact on the transaction methods of the Nagasaki trade. As examined in Chap. 9, the shogunate believed that importing gold and silver currencies from overseas would benefit the "national interest" (*kokueki*, 国益) of Japan, and the late eighteenth century saw the import of gold and silver currencies into Japan based on commercial agreements between the Nagasaki Trading House and each or both of the two groups. In particular, the import of Chinese silver currencies based on an agreement contract continued for more than half a century. Based on this new means of conducting trade, trade in goods other than silver also emerged successively in the late eighteenth century.

In addition, when adjusting the size of trade, the magistrate of Nagasaki intended to ask for the opinions of the merchants of the two groups and chose a method that they would easily accept.[14] In particular, in the case of further reducing the amount of trade and volume of the copper export, which would certainly be undesirable from the Chinese side, giving the two groups space to make choices regarding the implementation of concrete methods via negotiations to some extent helped to relieve their dissatisfaction and resistance. Moreover, when adjusting the scale of the trade or discussing the methods of punishment of the Chinese "criminals", the magistrate always requested the chief merchants of the two groups to submit letters promising to comply with Japan's decisions and regulations.[15] Since the two groups

[14]For example, when the magistrate's office gave the Chinese merchants notice of decreases in the volume of copper export, the merchants had two options: to accordingly decrease the number of junks, or to decrease the amount exported by each junk. NGJR (Chap. 5, Note 2), p. 278.

[15]For example, in the spring of 1791 a notification regarding the decrease in the number of junks was sent to the Chinese merchants in Nagasaki under the direction of the magistrate. It demanded the chief merchants of the two groups to promise to comply and submit a letter of acceptance.

were able to monopolize trade with Japan from the late eighteenth century, their consent generally meant that all Chinese merchants would obey the rules of the Japanese side, and the promises were guaranteed by the cohesiveness of the commercial organizations. In this way, even though there were no clear authorizations for the two groups' trading monopoly, the shogunate took it as an established fact and steadily built a cooperative relationship with them, taking their trading relationship in an advantageous direction.

There are several related documents in *Ofuregaki Ōsewatasare Hikae* 御触書被仰渡控 (copies of proclamations and instructions) in the old documents of Moriji's clan 森路家, NMHC, and *Nagasaki Dōkaiwatashi Kiruku* 長崎銅買渡記録 (records on the copper purchase in Nagasaki) in the Historiographical Institute of The University of Tokyo. For the punishments of Chinese criminals, see Chap. 5.

References

An'no M (1967) Sakokugo Nagasaki Tōjin Bōeki Seido ni tsuite (Junk trade policies in the age of National Seclusion). Hōsei Shigaku (Journal of Hōsei Historical Society in Hōsei University) 19

An'no M (1992) Kōshi-ron: Hirado, Nagasaki, Yokoseura (Discussion on the port cities: Hirado, Nagasaki and Yokoseura). Japan Editor School, Tokyo

Arai E (1980) Chūgoku Muke Yushutsu Tawaramono no Mitsubaibai to Nukeni Torishimari (The illegal transactions of the export luxury marine products to China and the anti-smuggling policies). Nihon Rekishi (The Journal of Japanese History) 380

Araki S (ed) (1903) Bakufu Jidai no Nagasaki (Nagasaki in the period of rule by the Tokugawa). Nagasaki Shiyakusho, Nagasaki

Arano Y (1981) Taikun Gaikō Taisei no Kakuritsu (The establishment of the Tycoon's diplomatic system). In: Kato E, Yamada T (eds) Kōza Nihon Kinseishi 2: Sakoku (Lecture on Japanese early-modern history 2: the National Seclusion). Yūhikaku, Tokyo

Arano Y (1985) Jūhachi Seiki no Higashi Ajia to Nihon (East Asia and Japan during the Eighteenth Century). In: Kōza Nihon Rekishi 6: Kinsei 2 (Lecture on Japanese history 6: early modern period 2). The University of Tokyo Press, Tokyo

Arano Y (1988) Sakoku-ron kara Kaikin-ka'i Chitsujō-ron he (Notion change from National Seclusion to Maritime Restrictions and Japanese style civilized/barbarian order). In: Arano Y (ed) Kinsei Nihon to Higashi Ajia (Early-modern Japan and East Asia). The University of Tokyo Press, Tokyo

Arano Y (1992) Jidai Kubun Ron (A discussion on periodization). In: Arano Y, Ishi'i M, Murai S (eds) Ajia no naka no Nihon-shi 1: Ajia to Nihon (New approaches to historical periodization in and comparative studies on East Asia). The University of Tokyo Press, Tokyo

Arano Y (ed) (2003) Edo Bakufu to Higashi Ajia (Tokugawa shogunate and East Asia). Yoshikawa Kōbunkan, Tokyo

Arano Y (2010) Kinseiteki-seikai no Seijūku (The maturity of early-modern society). In: Arano Y, Ishi'i M, Murai S (eds) Kinseiteki-seikai no Seijūku (The maturity of early-modern society). Yoshikawa Kōbunkan, Tokyo

Arano Y, Ishi'i M, Murai S (eds) (2010–2013) Nihon no Taigai kankei (Japanese foreign relations), vol 1–7. Yoshikawa Kōbunkan, Tokyo

Asa'o N (1970) Sakoku-sei no Seiritsu (Formation of the National Seclusion). Kōza Nihon Shi (Lectures on Japanese history). The University of Tokyo Press, Tokyo

H. Peng, *Trade Relations between Qing China and Tokugawa Japan*,
Studies in Economic History, https://doi.org/10.1007/978-981-13-7685-6

Chen, D (1988) Kangyongqian Sandi Dui Riben De Renshi Ji Maoyi Zhengce Bijiao (Comparing the Japanese Views and the Trading Policies of the Three Emperors: Kangxi, Yongzheng and Qianlong). Gugong Bowuyuan Yuankan (Palace Museum Journal) 1988-1.Chin T (2000) Tōjinyashiki to Nagasaki Kakyō (Chinese residence and the Chinese settled in Nagasaki). In: Wata M, Kuroki K (eds) Kakyō Nettowāku to Kyūshū (Overseas Chinese network and Kyushu). Chugoku Shoten, Fukuoka

Danjō H (2013) Mindai Kaikin = Chōkō Shisutemu to Ka'i Chitsujo (The system of Maritime Exclusion = Tribute for the court and huayi order in Ming dynasty). Kyoto University Press, Kyoto

E'nomoto W (2007) Higashi-Ajia Kai'iki to Nitchū Kōryū: 9-14 Seiki (The seas of East Asia and the interexchange between Japan and China from the ninth century to the fourteenth century). Yoshikawa Kōbunkan, Tokyo

E'nomoto W (2010) Higashi-shina-kai no Sō Kaishō (Chinese merchants of Song dynasty in the East Asia sea). In: Arano Y, Ishi'i M, Murai S (eds) Tsūkō, tsūshō-ken no kakudai (Extension of the interexchange and trade block). Yoshikawa Kōbunkan, Tokyo

Fairbank JK (ed) (1968) The Chinese World Order: Traditional China's Foreign Relations. Harvard University Press, Cambridge

Fairbank JK, Teng ST (1941) On the Ch'ing Tributary System. Harvard Journal of Asiatic Studies 6-2

Frank AG (1998) Reorient: Global Economy in the Asia Age. The University of California Press, Berkeley, CA

Fujita S (2005) Kinsei Kōki Seijishi to Taigai Kankei (Political history and foreign relations of the latter half of the Edo period). The University of Tokyo Press, Tokyo

Fujita S (2012) Tanuma Jidai (Tanuma era). Yoshikawa Kōbunkan, Tokyo

Fukase K (2008) Jūkū Seiki ni okeru Higashi-Ajia Kai'iki to Tōjin Sōdō (East Asian maritime region and Chinese riots). Nagasaki Rekishi Bunka Hakubutsukan Kiyō (Bulletin of Nagasaki Museum of History and Culture) 3

Fukuchi G (1902) Nagasaki Sanbyakunen: Gaikō Hensen Jijō (Three hundred years of Nagasaki: the issues of diplomatic transition). Hakubunkan, Tokyo

Fu Y (1956) Ming Qing Shidai Shangren Ji Shangye Ziben (Commerce and commercial capitals in Ming and Qing period). People Publishing House, Beijing

Gotō Y (1971) Kumazawa Banzan no Shōgai to Shisō no Keisei (The life and thoughts formation of Kumazawa Banzan). In: Nihon Shisō Taikei 30: Kumazawa Banzan (A compendium of Japanese thoughts 30: Kumazawa Banzan). Iwanami Shoten, Tokyo

Hall J (1949) Notes on the Early Ch'ing Copper Trade with Japan. Harvard Journal of Asiatic Studies 12

Hamashita T (1990) Kindai Chūgoku no Kokusaiteki Keiki: Chōkō Bōeki Shisutemu to Kindai Ajia (China-centered world order in modern times: tribute trade system and modern Asia). The University of Tokyo Press, Tokyo

Hamashita T (1997) Chōkō Shisutemu to Kindai Ajia (Tribute system and modern Asia). Iwanami Shoten, Tokyo

Hamashita T, Kawakatsu H (eds) (1991) Ajia no Kōeki-ken to Nihon Kōgyō-ka: 1500–1900 (Intra-Asian trade and the industrialization of Japan 1500–1900). Libroport, Tokyo

Haneta M (ed) (2013) Umi kara mita Rekishi (East Asian history viewed from the Sea). The University of Tokyo Press, Tokyo

Harafuji H (1953) Kinsei Nagasaki ni okeru Ikokujin no Keijijō no Chi'i (The criminal status of foreigners in early modern Nagasaki). In: Miyamoto M (ed) Kyūshū Keizaishi Kenkyū (Studies on the economic history of Kyushu). Miwa Shobō, Amagasaki

Hashimoto K (2009) Shōtoku-Shinrei Zengo no Nagasaki ni okeru Nukeni no Shutai Henka to Machi no Tenkai: Hankajin ni yoru Kinsei Nagasaki no Hensei (Change in the main constituent of Nagasaki's smuggling before and after the regulations in 1715 and the city's development: social structure in Nagasaki's smugglers). Shigaku Kenkyū Shūruku (Compilation of historical studies, Kokugakuin University) 34

Hashimoto Y (2010) Taimin Taichosen-Bōeki to Muromachi Bakufu Shugō Taisei (The trade with Ming and Korea and the Muromachi bakufu-shugō politics). In: Murai S, Ishi'i M, Arano Y (eds) Wakō to Nihon Kokuō (Japanese pirates and the King of Japan). Yoshikawa Kōbunkan, Tokyo

Hashimoto Y (2011) Chūka Gensō: Karamono to Gaikō no Muromachi Jidaishi (Adoration to Chinese: the imports and diplomacy in the History of Muromachi period). Bensei Shuban, Tokyo

Hellyer RI (2009) Defining Engagement: Japan and Global Contexts, 1640–1868. Harvard University Press, Cambridge

Hua L (2011a) Shindai Yōdō Kanshō Hanshi Ichizoku no Kiseki (Tracks of the Fan Family, official traders of Japanese copper during the Qing period). Osaka Keizai Hoka Daigaku Runshū (The Review of Osaka University of Economics and Law) 100

Hua L (2011b) Qingdai Yangtong Maoyi zhong de E'shang Jituan (Quota Merchants' group in Qing's Japanese copper-imported trade). Mingqing Luncong (A Collection of Essays on the Ming and Qing Dynasties) 11

Imabori S (1958) Jūruku Seiki Igo ni okeru Gohō (Hegu) no Seikaku to so no Su'i (The nature of he-huo in the sixteenth century and thereafter). Hoseishi Kenkyū (Legal History Review, Japan Legal History Association) 8

Ishihara M (1945) Minmatsu Shinsho Nihon-kishi no Kenkyū (Study on the military support requests to Japan in the late Ming and early Qing period). Fuzanbō, Tokyo

Ishi'i M (2010) Korai to no Kōryū (Relations with Korea). In: Arano Y, Ishi'i M, Murai S (eds) Tsūkō Tsūshō-Ken no Kakudai (Extension of the interexchange and trade block). Yoshikawa Kōbunkan, Tokyo

Itazawa T (1961) Sakoku Jidai ni okeru Mitsubōeki no Jittai (Realities of smuggling in the age of National Seclusion). Hoseidaigaku Bungakubu Kiyō (Bulletin of the Faculty of Letters, Hosei University) 7

Iwai S (1996) Jūroku-Jūnana Seiki no Chūgoku Henkyō Shakai (Marginal society of China in the sixteenth and seventeenth Century). In: Ōno K (ed) Minmatsu Shinsho no Shakai to Bunka (Society and culture in the late Ming and the early Qing period). Kyoto University Press, Kyoto

Iwai S (2004) Jūroku Seiki Chūgoku ni okeru Kōeki Chitsujo no Mosaku: Goshi no Jitsugen to so no Ninshiki (Exploring trade order in the sixteenth-century China: realization and recognition of the administrative trade). In: Iwai S (ed) Chūgoku Kinsei Shakai Chitsujo no Keisei (The order formation of early-modern society in China). Institute for Research in Humanities, Kyoto University, Kyoto

Iwai S (2007) Shindai no Goshi to Chinmoku Gaikō (administrative trade in Qing and the silence diplomacy). In: Fuma S (ed) Chūgoku Higashi Ajia Gaikō Kōryūshi no Kenkyū (Studies on the history of diplomacy and community in China and East Asia). Kyoto University Press, Kyoto

Iwai S (2009) Teikoku to Goshi: Jūroku-Jūhachi Seiki no Tsukō (Empire and administrative trade: order in period from the sixteenth century to the nineteenth century). In: Kagotani N, Wakimura K (eds) Teikoku to Ajia nettowāku: Chōki no Jūkyūseiki (Empires and the Asian networks: the long nineteenth century). Sekai Shisosha, Kyoto

Iwai S (2010a) Chōkō to Goshi (Tribute and administrative trade). In: Wada H (ed) Higashi Ajia Sekai no Kindai: Jūkū-seiki (Modern East Asia: the nineteenth Century). Iwanami Shoten, Tokyo

Iwai S (2010b) Shindai Chūgoku no Kokusai Kōeki to Kaibō: Shinpai Mondai to Nanyō-Kaikin-An kara (International trade and marine defense of Qing China: *shinpai* incident and South China Sea Maritime Prohibitions). In: Inoue T (ed) Kai'iki Kōryū to Seiji Kenryōku no Tai'ō (East Asian coast countries' policies and reactions to maritime exchange). Kyuko Shoin, Tokyo

Iwa'o S (1985) Shinpan Shuinsen Bōeki-shi no Kenkyū (Studies on the history of the red-seal ships, new edition). Yoshikawa kōbunkan, Tokyo

Jin X (2007) Kangxi Neiwufu Shangren he Ribentong (Merchants of Imperial Household Department and the Japanese copper). Shixue Yuekan (Journal of Historical Science) 1

Kamiya N (1990) Bakuhansei Kokka no Ryūkyū Shihai (The Ryukyus under the Japanese Baku-Han System). Azekura Shobō, Tokyo
Kamiya N (1997) Taikun Gaikō to Higashi Ajia (Tycoon diplomacy to East Asia). Yoshikawa Kōbunkan, Tokyo
Kamiya N, Kimura N (eds) (2002) Kaikin to Sakoku (The Maritime Prohibitions and the National Seclusion). Tokyodō Shuppan, Tokyo
Kanei T (ed) (1926) Nagasaki Ryakushi (Essential history of Nagasaki). Nagasaki Shiyakuso, Nagasaki
Kawazoe F (2014) Karamono no Bunka-shi: Hakurai-hin kara mita Nihon (Culture history viewed from *karamono*: the imports in Japan). Iwanami Shoten, Tokyo
Kawazoe F, Minagawa M (eds) (2011) Karamono to Higashi-Ajia: Hakurai-hin o meguru Bunka Kōryū-Shi (The *karamono* and East Asia: cultural exchange history focused on the imports). Bensei Shuppan, Tokyo
Kikuchi Y (1962) Sakoku-ka no Mitsubōeki (Smuggling in the age of National Seclusion). Rekishi Kyoiku (History Education) 10-9/10
Kikuchi Y (1964) Shotoku Shinrei ni okeru Shinpai Seidū no Jittai (The enforcement condition of the trading pass policies of the regulations in 1715). Nihon Rekishi (The Journal of Japanese History) 185
Kimura N (2009) Bakuhan-sei Kokka to Higashi Ajia Sekai (Bakuhan system state in the Edo period and East Asia). Yoshikawa Kōbunkan, Tokyo
Kishimoto M (1998a) Jidai Kubun-ron (A discussion on periodization). In: Kabayama K ect. (eds) Iwanami Kōza Sekai Rekishi 1: Sekaishi he no Appurochi (Iwanami lecture on world history 1: approach to world history). Iwanami Shoten, Tokyo
Kishimoto M (1998b) Higashi Ajia no "Kinsei" (Early modern in East Asia). Yamawaka Shuppansha, Tokyo
Kita M (1987) Bunsei-jū to Tenpō-roku nen ni okeru Nagasaki Tōjin Sōdō: Fukuoka-han Itamike Shiryō o Chūshin ni miru (Chinese riot at Nagasaki in 1827 and 1835: the analysis mainly based on the documents of Itami clan of Fukuoka domain). Fukuoka Daigaku Runshū (Journals of the Graduate School of Fukuoka University) 18-2
Kobata A (1967) Mindai Shōsenjin no Kaigai Tsūshō Haten: toku ni Kaichō no Shōzei-sei to Nichimin Bōeki ni tsuite (Overseas trading activities of the Quanzhou and Zhangzhou people: especially focusing on the tax system of Haicheng and Japan-Ming trade). In: Kobata A (ed) Kingin Bōeki-Shi no Kenkyū (Studies on the history of the gold and silver trade). Hōsei University Press, Tokyo
Koga J (1934) Nagasaki Tōkan ni okeru Seisen oyobi Ginsatsu no Shiyō (The circulation of coins and silver bills in the Nagasaki Chinese Residence). Keizaishi Kenkyū (Study of Economic History) 12-5
Komai Y (1957) Kugen and Kasho (*gongyan* and *guosuo*). Tōyō Gakuhō (The Journal of the Research Department of the Toyo Bunko) 40-2
Komiya K (1990) Minmatsu Shinsho Nihon-Kishi ni taisuru Iemitsu Seiken no Tai'ō" (Iemitsu Administration's responses to the military support requests to Japan in the late Ming and early Qing period). Kyūshū Shigawa (Kyushu History) 97
Kōsaka H (1981) Shindai Zenki no Kansa Bendōsei oyobi Shōnin Bendōsei ni tsuite (A study on the copper supply system by the custom officials and that by the merchants). Tōhoku Gakuin Daigaku Ronshū: Rekishigawa, Chirigaku (The Tohoku Gakuin University Review: History and Geography) 11
Kuroki K (2000) Kinsei Hyūga Hyōchaku Tōsen Jōhō no Dentatsu Kanri Shisutemu (The system for the communication and management of information relating to Chinese ships drifting sshore on the coast of Hyuga in the Edo era). Miyazaki Jōshitanki Daigaku Kiyō (Bulletin of Miyazaki Women's Junior College) 26

Kuroki K (2001) Kinsei Nobeoka Naitohan no Bakufuryō Hososhima Hyōchaku Tōsen Taisho Manyuaru (The manual of the Nobeoka Naito feudal clan for Chinese boats which drifted ashore at Hososhima, one of the territories of the shogunate). Miyazaki Jōshitanki Daigaku Kiyō (Bulletin of Miyazaki Women's Junior College) 27/28

Liu S-F (1986) Shinnichi Bōeki no Yōdōshō ni tsuite: Kenryū-kanbō-ki no Kanshō to Minshō o chūshin ni (Copper traders in Sino-Japanese trade in the Qing dynasty: a focus on official and private merchants in the Qianlong and Xianfeng periods). Kyūshūdaigaku Tōyōshi Ronshū (Kyushu University Essays on Oriental Studies) 15

Liu S-F (1988) Shindai Zenki no Fuken Shōnin to Nagasaki Bōeki (Fujian merchants and Nagasaki trade in the first half of Qing dynasity). Kyūshūdaigaku Tōyōshi Ronshū (Kyushu University Essays on Oriental Studies) 16

Liu S-F (1993) Jūshichi Jūhachi-Seiki no Chūgoku to Higashi Ajia: Shichō no Kaigai Bōeki Seisaku o chūshin ni (China and East Asia in the seventeenth and eighteen centuries: a focus on the external trade policy of the Qing dynasty). In: Hamashita T et. (eds) Ajia kara Kangaeru 2: Chi'iki Shisutemu (The Asian regional system 2: in the Asian perspectives series). The University of Tokyo Press, Tokyo

Liu S-F (1997) Kyōhō Nenkan no Tōsen Bōeki to Nihondō (The Chinese junk trade and Japanese copper in the Kyōhō period). In: Nakamura T (ed) Sakoku to Kokusai Kankei (International trade in the age of National Seclusion). Yoshikawa Kōbunkan, Tokyo

Liu S-F (1999) Qing Kangxi-Qianlong Nianjian Yangtong de Jinkou yu Liutong Wenti (The problem of import and circulation of Japanese copper from the Kangxi to the Qianlong reigns). In: Tang X (ed) Zhongguo Haiyang Fazhanshi Lunwenji (Essays on Chinese maritime history), vol 7. Sun Yat-sen Institute for Social Science and Philosophy, Academia Sinica, Taipei

Mancall M (1968) The Ch'ing Tribute System: an Interpretive Eassy. In: Fairbank JK (ed) The Chinese world Order: Traditional China's Foreign Relations. Harvard University Press, Cambridge

Mancall M (1984) China at the Center: 300 Years of Foreign Policy. Free Press, New York

Matsukata F (2008) Kinsei Kōki Nagasaki-Guchi kara Seiyō Kindai Jōhō Chishiki no Juyō to Honyaku (The receptivity and translation of the information and knowledge about Western modern from Nagasaki in the second half of the early-modern japan). Rekishigaku Kenkyū (The Journal of the Historical Science Society) 846

Matsukata F (2013) "Keiyaku Bōeki' Josetsu: Jūhachi Seiki no Nichiran Motokata Bōeki (A study on the "contract trade': Dutch-Japanse motokata trade in the eighteenth and eighteenth centuries). In: Tokyo Daigaku Nihonshigaku Kenkyūshitsu Kiyō, Bessatsu: Nihon kinseishi Ronsō (Bulletin of the department of Japanese history faculty of letters, The University of Tokyo, Separate volume: studies in the social history of early-modern Japan)

Matsui Y (2013) The Factory and the People of Nagasaki: Otona, Tolk, Compradoor. In: Itinerario, 27-3, issue 3, special issue: Canton and Nagasaki Compared, Leiden

Matsui Y (2015) Dejima to kakawaru Hitobito (The people in relation with the Dejima). In: Matuskata F (ed) Nichiran Kankeishi wo Yomitoku (Introduction to the history of Japanese–Netherlands relations), vol I. Rinsen Shoten, Kyoto

Matsuo S (2010) Edo Bakufu no Taigai Seisaku to Engan Keibi (The foreign policy of the Edo shogunate and coastal defense). Azekura Shobō, Tokyo

Matsuura A (1988) Kōkitei to Shōtoku Shinrei (Emperor Kangxi and the regulations in 1715). In: Yanai K (ed) Sakoku Nihon to Kokusai Kōryū (Japan in the age of National Seclusion and overseas exchange). Yoshikawa Kōbunkan, Tokyo

Matsuura A (2002) Shindai Kaigai Bōekishi no Kenkyū (Studies on the history of overseas trade during the Qing dynasty). Hōyū Shoten, Kyoto

Matsuura A (2007) Edo Jidai Tōsen ni yoru Nitchū Bunka Kōryū (Sino-Japanese cultural interaction by Chinese ships during Edo period). Shibunkaku, Kyoto

Minagawa M (2014) Nihon Kodai Ōken to Karamono Kōeki (Japanese ancient kingship and the import trade). Yoshikawa Kōbunkan, Tokyo

Minoru M (2002) Tōjinyashiki no Setsuritsu to Tōjin no Fuhoko'i (The establishment of the Chinese Residence and Chinese illicit activities). Bunka Ronshū (The Studies in Culture, Kobe College Graduate School) 12

Minoru M (2007) Kinsei Kōki ni okeru Kyōkairyōiki no Tokuchō (The features of the boundary at the late early modern age: the conflicts and troubles at the Chinese Residences in Nagasaki). Keizaishi Kenkyū (Study of Economic History, Osaka University of Economics) 11

Mori K (1948) Nisso-Bōeki no Kenkyū (The study of the trade between Japan and Song). Kokuritsu Sho'in, Tokyo

Morioka Y (1963) Mitsui Echigoya no Nagasaki Bōeki Kei'ei (Trading management of the Mitsui-echigoya) Part I and Part II. Shigaku Zasshi (Journal of Historical Science) 72-6, 72-7

Murai S (1997) Wakō no Taminzokusei o megute (On multiethnicity of the "Japanese Pirates"). In: Ōsumi K, Murai S (eds) Chūsei Kōki ni okeru Higashi Ajia no Kōkusai Kankei (East Asian international relations in the late of medieval times). Yamakawa Shubansha, Tokyo

Murai S (2010) Mōko Shūrai to Ibunka Sesshōku (The mongol invasions and interactions between different cultures). In: Murai S, Ishi'i M, Arano Y (eds) Wakō to "Nihon Kokuō" (Japanese pirates and the "king of Japan"). Yoshikawa Kōbunkan, Tokyo

Nagazumi Y (1987) Tōsen Yushūtsunyu-hin Sūryō Ichiran: 1637–1833 (Chinese junks cargo list: 1637–1833). Sōbunsha, Tokyo

Naka D (2015) Nittō Guhō Junreiki ni Miru Tō no Tsūkō Kyokasho: Kugen no Saikentō (Tang empire's pass in "the record of a pilgrimage to Tang China in search of the Buddhism": reexamination on *gongyan*). In: Sato N (ed) Kentoshi to Nittōsō no Kenkyū (Studies on the embassies and monks visiting Tong China). Koshishoin, Tokyo

Nakai N (1971) Tenkanki Bakuhan-Sei no Kenkyū: Horeki-Tenmeiki no Keizai Seisaku to Shohin Ryutsu (Studies of the bakuhan system in a period of transition: horeki-tenmei period (1751–1788) economic policy and commodity marketing). Hanawa shobō, Tokyo

Nakamura, H (1968) Shintaiso Namhansan-Shōyu ni Mieru Nihon-Kankei no Jōken: Jūnana Seiki ni okeru Higashi Ajia Kokusai Kankei (The Conditions for Maintaining Relations with Japan in the Monte Namhansan from Qing Taizong: Japan and the Change of the East Asia International Order in the seventeenth century). In: Chosen Gakuhō (Journal of the Academic Association of Koreanology in Japan) 47

Nakamura T (1988) Kinsei Nagasaki Bōeki Shi no Kenkyū (Studies on the history of early-modern Nagasaki trade). Yoshikawa Kōbunkan, Tokyo

Nakamura T (1989) Higashi Ajia to Sakoku Nihon: Tōsen Bōeki o Chūshin ni (East Asia and Japan in the age of National Seclusion: focusing on the junk trade). In: Kato E, Kitajima M, Fukaya K (eds) Bakuhan-Sei Kokka to I'iki I'koku (The bakuhan system state and foreign countries and regions). Azekura shobō, Tokyo

Nakamura T (1990) Hyōchaku Tōsen no Nagasaki Kaisō Kitei to Jittai: Hyūga Hyōchakusen no Ba'ai (Policies and practices of sending drifting-ashore Chinese junks to Nagasaki: in the case of drifting ashore in Hyūga). In: Nakamura T (ed) Kinsei Kindai Shi Ronshū (Papers in modern and early-modern history). Yoshikawa Kōbunkan, TokyoNakamura T (1997) Nihon Raikō Tōsen Ichiran: Meiwa-Gannen naishi Bunkyu-Gannen (Table of the Chinese Junks Calling at Nagasaki, 1764-1861). Kyūshū Bunkashi Kenkyūjo Kiyō (The bulletin of Institute of Research in Kyushu Cultural History) 41.

Nagase-Reimer K (2015) There's Method in the Madness: A New Approach to the Early Modern Sino-Japanese Copper Trade. In: Nagase-Reimer K (ed) Copper in the Early Modern Sino-Japanese Trade. Brill Academic Publishers, Leiden and Boston

Nekishi T (1943) Shōji nikansuru Kankō Chōsa Hōkoku: Gōkō no Kenkyū (Investigation report on the commercial practices: studies on *hegu*). Toa Kenkyū Sho, Tokyo

Nishimura K (1973) Edo Bakufu no Nukeni Torishimari o meguru Hō-ishiki no Hensen (Changes in low-consciousness under the Tokugawa regime in the context of smuggle regulations). Nihon Joshi Daigaku Kiyō (Memoirs of the Japan Women's University, Faculty of Literature) 23

Ōba O (1984) Kyōhō Jidai no Raikōtōjin no Kenkyū (A study on the coming Chinese in Kyoho era). In: Ōba O (ed) Edo Jidai ni okeru Chūgoku Bunka Jūyō no Kenkyū (Studies of reception of Chinese culture in Edo period). Dōhosha Publisher, Kyoto

Ōba O (ed) (1986) Kyōhō Jidai no Nitchu Kankei Shiryō (Documents concerning the relations between China and Japan in *Kyōhō* era). Kansai University Press, Osaka

Ogawa K (1973) Edo Bakufu Yushutsu Kaisanbutsu no Kenkyū: Tawaramono no Seisan to Shūka Kikō (Studies on marine products exported by the Edo bakufu: structures of production and collection of dried goods). Yoshikawa Kōbunkan, Tokyo

Ōta K (1992) Sagoku Jidai Nagasaki Bōekishi no Kenkyū (Study on the history of the Nagasaki trade history in the period of National Isolation). Shinbunkaku, Kyoto

Peng H (2010) Shinchō wa Kinsei Nihon no Taigaikankei o dō Mita ka (The knowledges of Qing empire on the foreign relations of Tokugawa Japan). Tokyo Daigaku Nihonshigaku Kenkyūshitsu Kiyō, Bessatsu: Kinsei Seiji-shi Ronsō (Bulletin of the department of Japanese history faculty of letters, the University of Tokyo, separate volume: studies in the political history of early-modern Japan)

Peng H (2016) Tōsen Bōeki no Tōsei to Urikomininn (Tokugawa's restrictions on the junk trade and the Compradors). In: Fujita S (ed) Bakuhansei-kokka no Seijikozō (Political structure of the bakuhan system state). Yoshikawa Kōbunkan, Tokyo

Roberts L (1998) Mercantilism in a Japanese Domain: the Merchant origins of Economic Nationalism in Eighteenth Century Tosa. Cambridge University Press, Cambridge

Sadamune K (1959) Kinsei Chūnichi Bōeki ni okeru Tōtsūji: Mitsubōeki Kenkyū he no Josetsu toshite (Chinese interpreters in early-modern Sino-Japanese trade: an introduction of the study on smuggling). Shigaku Kenkyū (Historical Studies) 72

Saeki T (1958) Kōki Yōsei Jidai ni okeru Nisshin Bōeki (Japanese-Qing trade in the Kangxi and Yongzheng period). Tōyōshi Kenkyū (The Journal of Oriental Researches) 16-4

Saeki T (1986) Shindai Yōsei-chō no Tsūka-mondai (Currency issues in Qing Yongzheng era). In: Toyoshi K (ed) Yōsei Jidai no Kenkyū (Study on Yongzheng era). Dōhōsha Publisher, Kyoto

Sakuma S (1992) Mindai Kōki ni okeru Shōshū no Kaigai Bōeki. In: Sakuma S (ed) Nichi-Min Kankei-Shi no Kenkyū (Studies on the history of the Japanese-Ming relations). Yoshikawa Kōbunkan, Tokyo

Seki S (2002) Karamono no Ryūtsū to Shōhi (Distribution and consumption of the imports). Kokuritsu Rekishi Minzoku Hakubutsukan Kenkyū Hōkoku (Bulletin of the National Museum of Japanese History) 92

Shimata R (2006) The Intra-Asian Trade in Japanese Copper by the Dutch East India Company during the Eighteenth Century. Brill Academic Publishers, Leiden and Boston

Shimata R (2010) Seikai no naka no Nihondō (Japanese copper in the world). In: Arano Y, Ishi'i M, Murai S (eds) Nihon no Taigai kankei (Japanese foreign relations), vol VI. Yoshikawa Kōbunkan, Tokyo

Shimitsu K (1979) Nukeni-kō: Kyōhōki no Nukeni Taisaku o Chūshin ni (A study on the smuggling: focus on anti-smuggling measures in *Kyōhō* period). Chuodaigaku Bungakubu Kiyō (Journal of the Department of Literature of Chuo University) 92

So'eda J (2008a) Kinsei Kōshi Nagasaki no Un'ei to Nukeni (Management of the early-modern port city, Nagasaki, and the smuggling). Nihonshi Kenkyū (Journal of Japanese History) 548

So'eda J (2008b) Jūhachi Seiki Kōki no Nagasaki ni okeru Nukenikan: Tōsen Bōeki o Chūshin ni (Views on smuggling under the Chinese trade in the late-eighteenth-century Nagasaki). Kaikō Toshi Kenkyū (Journal of Port Cities Studies) 3

Sun X (2010) Kōki-chō Naimufu Shōnin to Nihondō (Merchants of the imperial household department and Japanese copper in Kangxi period). Higashiajia Bunka Kanryu (The Culture Circumfluence of East Asia) 3-2

Suzuki Y (2004) Kinsei Nichiran Bōeki-Shi no Kenkyū (A study of the Japan-Netherlands trade by the Dutch East India Company in the seventeenth and eighteenth centuries). Shibunkaku Shuppan, Kyoto

Takashio H (2004) Edo Jidai no Hō to so no Shūen: Yoshimune to Shigekata to Sadanobu to (Law and its marginal problems: Yoshimune and Shigetaka and Sadanobu). Kyuko Shoin, Tokyo

Tanaka F (2011) Taigai Kōryū no Shinten to Kōkusai Kōeki (The development of foreign exchange and international trade). In: Arano Y, Ishi'i M, Murai S (eds) Nihon no Taigai Kankei (Japanese foreign relations), vol 2. Yoshikawa Kōbunkan, Tokyo

Thomaz LFFR (2001) Precedents and Parallels of the Portuguese Cartaz System. In: Malekandathil P, and Mohammed J (eds) The Portuguese, Indian Ocean and European Bridgeheads 1500–1800. Institute for Research in Social Sciences and Humanities, Kerala

Toby RP (1984) State and Diplomacy in Early Modern Japan: Asia in the Development of the Tokugawa Shogunate. Princeton University Press, Princeton

Toby RP (1986) Kinsei ni okeru Nihonkata Ka'i-kan to Higashi-Ajia no Kokusai Kankei (The view of Japan-centered civilized–barbaric world order in early-modern period and the international relations in East Asia). Nihon Rekishi (The Journal of Japanese History) 463

Uchida G (1921) Tokugawa Jidai toku ni so no Chūsei-igo ni okeru Gaikoku Kingin no Yunyū (The importation of overseas gold and silver in Tokugawa era especially after the mid Tokugawa era). In: Uchida G (ed) Nihon Keizai Shi no Kenkyū (Studies on Japanese economic history) Part I. Dobunkan, Tokyo

Uchida N (1949) Nihon Kakyō Shakai no Kenkyū (Study on overseas Chinese community in Japan). Dobunkan Shuppan, Tokyo

Uehara K (1981) Ryūkyū no Shihai (Dominance to the Ryukyus). In: Kato E, Yamata T (eds) Kōza Nihon Kinseishi 2: Sakoku (Lecture on Japanese early-modern history 2: National Seclusion). Yuhikaku, Tokyo

Von Verschuer C (2006) A Cross the Perilous Sea: Japanese Trade with China and Korea from the Seventh to the Sixteenth Centuries. Translated from French by Kristen Lee Hunter. Cornell University Press, Ithaka

Wakamatsu M (1997) Kinsei Chūki ni okeru Bōeki Toshi Nagasaki no Tokushitsu (The specific characters of the trade city Nagasaki in the middle of the early-modern period). Nihonshi Kenkyū (Journal of Japanese History) 415

Wang J (2007) Qing Qianqi Neiwufu Huangshang Fanshi de Shangye Huodong Tanxi (An analysis on the commercial activities of the Imperial Household merchant, the Fan Family). Master's thesis for Graduate School, Minzu University of China

Wei Q, Wu Q (1981) Qingdai Zhuming Huangshang Fanshi de Xingshuai (Rise and decay of the famous Imperial Merchant, the Fan Family). Lishi Yanjiu (Historical Studies) 3

Yamakuchi K (2006) Sakoku to Kaikoku (The closing and opening of Japan). Iwanami Shoten, Tokyo

Yamamoto N (1983) Nagasaki no Tōjinyashiki (The Chinese residence in Nagasaki). Kenkōsha, Tokyo

Yamamoto H (1989) Kan'ei Jidai (Kan'ei era). Yoshikawa Kōbunkan, Tokyo

Yamamoto H (2004) Kyōhō ni okeru Nukeni Torishimari Taisaku no Tenkai: Tōsen-Uchiharai-Metsuke Watanabe Geki Nagatomo o Chūshin ni (Development of the smuggling countermeasures in Kyōhō period: focusing on the activities of Wadanabe Geki Naritomo, a "attacking junk" inspector). Gaiseishi Kenkyu (Studies on Foreign Affairs) 3

Yamamoto H (2005) Tōsen Uchiharai Taisei no Seiritsu to Tenkai: Kyōhō no Nukeni Taisaku o chūshin ni (Formation and deployment of the attacking-junk system: focusing on the smuggling countermeasures in Kyōhō period). In: Mori Y (ed) Chi'iki Shakai no Tenkai to Bakuhan-sei Shihai (Development of local society and the reign under Bakuhan system). Meicho Shuppan, Osaka

Yamawaki T (1960) Kinsei Nitchu Bōeki-Shi no Kenkyū (Studies on the history of the early-modern Japanese-Chinese trade). Yoshikawa Kōbunkan, Tokyo

Yamawaki T (1964) Nagasaki no Tōjin Bōeki (Chinese trade at Nagasaki). Yoshikawa Kōbunkan, Tokyo

Yamawaki T (1965) Nukeni: Sakokujidai no Mitsubōeki (Smuggling in the age of National Seclusion). Nikkei Inc., Tokyo

Yano J (1967) Nagasaki Shishi: Tsūshō Bōeki Hen, Ajia Shokoku Bu (History of Nagasaki city: interaction and trades with Asian counties). Nagasaki Shiyakuso, Nagasaki

Ya'o K (1998) Jūhachi Seiki Kōhan no Nagasaki Bōeki ni okeru Kobore-Mono-Satō no Ryūtsū ni tsuite (On the distribution of spilled sugar in Nagasaki trade, in the latter half of the eighteenth century). Kyushu Shigaku (The Journal of the Kyushu Society of Historical Research) 121

Ya'o K (2002) Sakoku-ka no Fukuoka-han to Kan Higashi Ajia Kai'iki Shakai (The Fukuoka domain in the age of National Seclusion and the East Asian maritime societies). In: Kyōkai NB (ed) Fukuoka-ken-shi, Tsūshi-hen, Fukuoka-han (Fukuoka prefectural history, general history, Fukuoka domain). Nihon Bunka Kyōkai (Western Japan Cultural Association), Fukuoka

Yoshitsumi H (1987) Susa no Tōjinhaka: Tōsen Dajō Jiken Shimatsu (The Chinese tombs at susa: the process of an attacking-junk incident). Yamaguchi-ken Chihōshi Kenkyū (Studies on Local History of Yamakuchi Prefecture) 58

Zhang T (1968) Guanyu Taiwan Zhengshi De Paixiang (On the Zheng's *paixiang* in Taiwan). Taiwan Historica 19-2

Name Index

H. Peng, *Trade Relations between Qing China and Tokugawa Japan*,
Studies in Economic History, https://doi.org/10.1007/978-981-13-7685-6

Z

Subject Index

H. Peng, *Trade Relations between Qing China and Tokugawa Japan*,
Studies in Economic History, https://doi.org/10.1007/978-981-13-7685-6

MIX
Papier aus verantwortungsvollen Quellen
Paper from responsible sources
FSC® C105338

If you have any concerns about our products,
you can contact us on
ProductSafety@springernature.com

In case Publisher is established outside the EU,
the EU authorized representative is:
Springer Nature Customer Service Center GmbH
Europaplatz 3, 69115 Heidelberg, Germany

Printed by Libri Plureos GmbH
in Hamburg, Germany